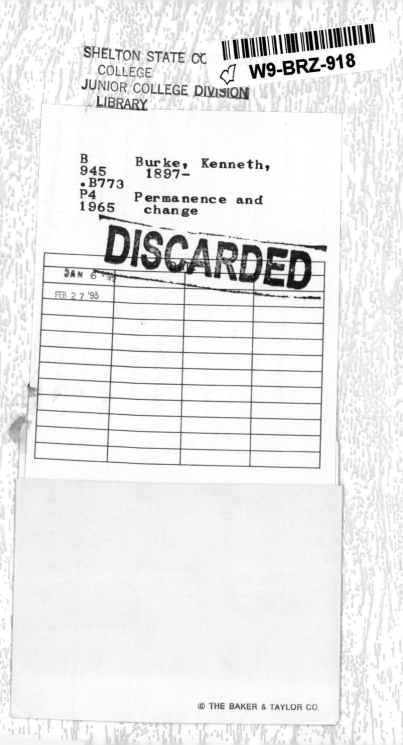

PERMANENCE AND CHANGE

An Anatomy of Purpose

The Library of Liberal Arts

OSKAR PIEST, FOUNDER

PERMANENCE AND CHANGE

An Anatomy of Purpose

KENNETH BURKE

With an Introduction by
HUGH DALZIEL DUNCAN

. . . .

The Library of Liberal Arts

published by

Bobbs-Merrill Educational Publishing
Indianapolis

The Bobbs-Merrill Company, Inc.
4300 West 62nd Street
Indianapolis, Indiana 46268

Second Edition
Fifth Printing—1977

Library of Congress Catalog Card Number: 64–66067
ISBN 0–672–60452–3 (pbk.)

TO MY MOTHER AND FATHER

ACKNOWLEDGMENTS

A somewhat altered version of the section "On Interpretation" was published in *The Plowshare: A Literary Periodical of One-Man Exhibits*, in the issue of February 1934.

For this present work, my debts to the writings of other men are more numerous than I could hope to acknowledge. But in particular I should mention *The Meaning of Meaning*, by C. K. Ogden and I. A. Richards, with its supplements by Crookshank and Malinowski, and its fertile appendices.

I also wish to acknowledge the kindness of several publishers who have permitted me to quote at some length from works published by them. My thanks are due to W. W. Norton and Company, Inc., for permission to quote from I. A. Richards' *Science and Poetry*; to Longmans, Green and Company, for permission to quote from Johan Huizinga's *The Waning of the Middle Ages*; to Covici, Friede, Inc., for permission to quote from John Strachey's *The Coming Struggle for Power*; to Columbia University Press, for permission to reprint part of a letter from Charles Warren Everett's *The Education of Jeremy Bentham*; to Mr. Edwin Seaver, for permission to quote from his novel, *The Company*, published by The Macmillan Company; and to Harcourt, Brace and Company for permission to quote from I. A. Richards' *Mencius on the Mind*, William Marston's *Integrative Psychology*, Karin Stephen's *The Misuse of Mind*, C. K. Ogden's *Bentham's Theory of Fictions*, E. R. Jaensch's *Eidetic Imagery*, and William Loftus Hare's *Mysticism of East and West*.

K. B.

1935

Sharp-cut scientific classifications are essential for scientific method, but they are dangerous for philosophy. Such classification hides the truth that the different modes of natural existence shade off into each other.

ALFRED NORTH WHITEHEAD

TABLE OF CONTENTS

PART II

PERSPECTIVE BY INCONGRUITY

TABLE OF CONTENTS

PART III

THE BASIS OF SIMPLIFICATION

PERMANENCE AND CHANGE

INTRODUCTION

I

IN AN AGE of specialists, Kenneth Burke's writings offend those who are content with a partial view of human motivation. He is offensive to many academicians because he cannot be stuffed into any of the bins whose occupancy brings fame and fortune in the groves of Academe. Yet Burke is nothing if not erudite. While he is the soul of gentility as a critic and, it may be added for the record, as a person, those who tangle intellectually with Burke soon learn to buckle on their heaviest armor for the fray. Many writers on communication use Burke without crediting their source, or they paraphrase without much understanding. Whether this practice is the result of guile or of ignorance it is hard to say, but if there is any modern thinker whose work has been pilfered shamelessly, it is Burke. Fortunately for the vitality of American social thought, however, Burke has attracted followers who are distinguished as much by their productivity as by their reverence.

Burke has been the cause of books by many men, and as writings inspired by Burke increase, we see that he is indeed the seminal figure of our time in the field of symbolic analysis. Not since the days of Charles Sanders Peirce, William James, John Dewey, and George Herbert Mead, in America, or Bronislaw Malinowski, C. K. Ogden, and I. A. Richards, in Britain (to limit ourselves to these countries alone) has there appeared work of such importance. Those of us who believe that the manner in which we communicate determines the manner in which we relate as social beings have gone to school to Burke and will continue to do so. As poets, critics, philosophers, sociologists, anthropologists, psychologists, or linguists, we read Burke to learn something about what happens in our relationships by virtue of the fact that we communicate through symbols, and, at the same time, we invent the symbols used in such communication. More than any other writer, Burke has taught us that the names we give to things, events, and people determine our behavior toward them. And he has done so not by repeating this *is* so, but by showing *how* it is so. For Burke is never content to exhort us to think in a certain way; he is a methodologist seeking always to develop tools for demonstrating the effect of symbols on human motivation.

There is no easy road to an understanding of Burke. He is at once one of the most compact and one of the most "panoramic" writers of our time. He makes his points in highly aphoristic style and, therefore, is highly quotable. But this very compactness creates a density of meaning that exhausts every resource of the reader. This difficulty ends, however, in challenge, not exhaustion or boredom. Burke's capacity to ransack a single discipline or to make sudden and intense forays into many subjects is unsurpassed. His swift sallies into various branches of knowledge make following him an exciting, if arduous, task.

Burke's erudition is staggering enough, and the way in which he stalks an idea through the thickets and jungles of ideas in which modern man dwells is sometimes bewildering. So also is his great capacity for bringing together perspectives that we have become accustomed to hold separate in our thinking. His search for what he calls "proportional" and "synthetic" propositions is one of the great intellectual adventures of our time. No one uses the classics, the "wisdom books" of our culture, so assiduously as Burke, but he also ranges far and wide in contemporary work. It is because of this eclecticism that a reading of Burke is such a rich feast for the mind. It used to be said that if a student could understand

INTRODUCTION

The Education of Henry Adams he was on his way to becoming an educated man. The same may be said about understanding the work of Burke. After a reading of Burke, we comprehend (many of us for the first time) what *problems* have engaged the attention of classical thinkers in various fields, but particularly in the field of communication. He rescues the classics from dogma and returns them to methodology. For some, Burke's use of the classics in the construction of theory and methodology is blasphemous, but it is a great step forward for those who are trying to understand why we behave like human and inhuman beings and who are not convinced that study of caged rats is a helpful approach to studying the behavior of men in society.

If any conviction deepens in the mind of the student of communication, it is the realization that, as Burke says, "experiments with organisms that do not use language cannot tell us anything essential about the distinctive motives of a species that does use language."[1] Words are not merely "signs"; they are names whose "attachment" to events, objects, persons, institutions, status groups, classes, and indeed any great or small collectivity, soon tends to determine what we do in regard to the bearer of the name. War on poverty has recently been declared. Yet no matter how much money is voted for the eradication of poverty, the first battle that must be won is the symbolic battle over how to *name* poverty. Are the poor *lazy, degenerate, shiftless, sick, evil, childlike, cunning, ignorant, proud, humble, victimized,* or *unfortunate?* The name that we give to poverty largely determines how we fight the war against it.

Burke demands that we become masters of *many* perspectives in order that we may understand *one* perspective. He

[1] Kenneth Burke, *Permanence and Change, An Anatomy of Purpose* (Los Altos, California: Hermes Publications, 1954), p. xvii; this edition, p. li.

does not wish us to analyze the conditions of action as they exist in nature or in nature in the laboratories of modern science. He is not against science, even science that tells us that the world must be regarded as a great machine. Rather, he is against the teaching that science based on mathematics and the laboratory is the *only* science. He asks scientists to think about their instruments and methods of inquiry as a language comparable to any other language. The language of science is a symbolic structure that is determined as much by the nature of the symbols employed as by the social milieux in which science is practiced.

If, however, Burke attacks scientists who refuse to think of their instruments and techniques as part of a scientific act that, like any act, depends on the language in which it is expressed, he also attacks symbol analysts who refuse to clarify the way in which they arrive at their conclusions about the meaning of symbols. The danger of confusing science with the methods and techniques of science used in the past cannot be met by refusing to create models that define rigorously both the structure and the function of communicative action in society. If mind as the creator and generator of experience is to be treated as more than an accidental intruder in the realm of matter, then we must demonstrate the way in which the mind functions in communication. If the forms of thought are forms of reality, or what in human studies we think of as forms of action and passion, then what model of such form can we construct? And, further, how can we apply that model to the directly observable phenomena of sociation, namely, the way in which we relate in and through communication?

2

As we read Burke, it is not the weight of the intellectual baggage that strains our capacities. He tells us in the Prologue to this edition of *Permanence and Change*:

INTRODUCTION

Rather than thinking of magic, religion, and science as three distinctively successive *stages* in the world's history, the author would now use a mode of analysis that dealt with all three as aspects of motivation "forever born anew" in the resources of language as such.[2]

But it requires great effort to think about language as an instrument that causes *and* solves our problems. For, as Burke tells us, there is no such thing as perfect communication: "Only angels communicate absolutely."[3] For better or worse, the human condition is a condition of imperfect communication, and we solve our problems in society as best we can through recalcitrant and mystifying symbols that cause the problems we must yet solve if we are to act together at all. Thus, symbols are both blessing and curse—a blessing if we turn our study of their use into a *method* of social control, a curse if we let their power overwhelm us until we accept symbolic mystification as reality.

As Burke points out, the peculiar thing about the interpretations of life reached in communication is that we interpret our interpretations. We may think that the laws of physics are "immutable" (even though physicists do not think so), or we may believe that biological drives "condition" organisms, or that sociopolitical laws of some kind are the "laws of history," or, finally, that cosmic laws exist in the mind of God. But few of us have been taught to argue that communication has unchanging "laws" comparable to these. And even when we argue this point, it becomes difficult to do so because we know so little about the way in which communication really affects us. Yet, as we think about human motives, it becomes increasingly obvious that they depend on the forms of communication available to us as much as they depend on economic, political, social, sexual, or religious "interests."

[2] *Ibid.*, p. xxv (p. lix).
[3] *Ibid.*, p. xv (p. x).

Motives arise and continue to exist in communication, and unless we are willing to assume that communication is some kind of random affair, or simply the wirelike "transmission" of interests and drives that are extra-symbolic, we must say *something* about the relationship between motives and the forms in which they are expressed.

Burke argues that symbolic systems in art, religion, science, philosophy, literature, and, indeed, in all phases of action are answers to questions posed by the situation in which they arose. We cannot act together unless we know how to communicate with each other over the problems we must solve in order to act at all. In the act of communicating, we do not signal each other like semaphores; we *exhort* others, and ourselves, to act in one way and not in another. Before we act, we must "size up" the situation in which we must act. This "sizing up" can be illustrated by our use of proverbs. A proverb "characterizes" a situation and thus creates attitudes necessary to common action. In America, for example, we act together in many situations through the use of money. Americans must be imbued with what Max Weber has called the "Spirit of Capitalism," and a great share of our proverbial lore is devoted to keeping this spirit alive within us.

But proverbs are not simply guides to action, like signposts on a road; they are formed and stylized answers that affect us because the forms used arouse the same expectations of success, failure, or doubt within others as within ourselves. A symbol does not "trigger" us to do something that we were "ready" to do because it was "latent" within us, nor is it the expression of a power that exists beyond the symbol yet can be known and experienced only through the symbol. To say that money "triggers" the market or "releases" social energy is to overlook the fact that money functions as it does in America only because we have certain attitudes and beliefs about the proper ways of earning and spending money.

INTRODUCTION

Money, like all symbols, takes its meaning from action—that is, the manner in which it is *used* in human relationships. This use of symbols may be thought of as strategies in conduct that make it possible for us to "size up situations, name their structure and outstanding ingredients, and name them in a way that contains an attitude toward them."[4] And these symbolic strategies, Burke insists, are observable because the situations in which we must act together are real; " . . . the strategies for handling them have public content; and in so far as situations overlap from individual to individual, or from one historical period to another, the strategies possess universal relevance."[5]

By "public content" Burke means that the forms of expression used in communication exist not solely within our minds but as forms having a public existence. *Huckleberry Finn* is not only a subjective experience of writer and reader; it is also a book that stands on the shelves of thousands of libraries and homes. It has meanings that have been hammered out in many discussions by critics, and it has been accepted by Americans themselves as a characteristic expression of American life. Yet, for reasons that will bemuse future historians of our age, symbolic works like *Huckleberry Finn* are supposed to have far less "reality" than some kind of extra-symbolic reality in space or even the symbolic forms of past history. We teach students that what "really happened" in Mark Twain's time is to be found in history, and usually in the history of economic and political institutions. For, so we have been taught, there are economic "laws," and in history there have been "real" men who did "real" things we can study.

---

[4] This quotation is taken from Burke's discussion, "Situations and Strategies," in *The Philosophy of Literary Form, Studies in Symbolic Action* (New York: Vintage Books, 1957), p. 3.

[5] *Ibid.*, p. 3.

Yet when we reflect for a moment on the reality of history (or memory or any record of the past) we discover that the "facts" of history, and all past experience as we recall it, are symbolic facts. We can only infer what Lincoln did; the only facts we have about him are what someone said he did, or what he said he did, or what others say about what he said. As Burke says:

> People usually think that the non-symbolic realm is the clear one, while the symbolic realm is hazy. But if you agree that the words, or terms, in a book are its "facts," then by the same token you see there is a sense in which we get our view of *deeds* as facts from our sense of *words* as facts, rather than *vice versa*.[6]

The same may be said for purely biological "explanations" of motives in which it is argued that human culture can be explained as a mere "projection" of the body in its purely physiological nature. Experiments with organisms that do not use language cannot tell us anything essential about the distinctive motives of a species that does use language. As Burke said, and as zoologists are now beginning to recognize, even on an empirical basis, data of zoological research, in the process of being applied to the behavior of men need the corrective of a concern *with social motives as such*.

3

The heart of Burke's argument is simple enough, namely, that symbolic forms affect conduct because of the ways in

[6] Burke discusses this point in an essay, written in 1954, entitled "Fact, Inference, and Proof in the Analysis of Literary Symbolism," which was published originally in *Symbols and Values: An Initial Study* (Thirteenth Symposium of the Conference on Science, Philosophy and Religion. New York: Harper & Brothers, 1954), pp. 283-306. The quotation above is from page 284.

which they affect communication, and thus all action. He is saying that motives lie not only in some kind of experience "beyond" symbols, but also *in* symbols. In sum, symbolism is a motive because symbolism is a motivational dimension in its own right. The way in which sex is symbolized largely determines the kinds of emotions we have about sex. This does not mean that somatic sexual "feelings" cannot be studied as we study any kind of somatic experience. But a feeling is not an emotion until the feeling is expressed in some form that "attaches" values to the somatic feeling. The proper study of emotions, therefore, is the study of the forms of their expression in social life. Obviously, it is at this point that many find Burke difficult to follow. The assumption that the way in which we express ourselves greatly determines the way in which we relate in society is a complete inversion of what many of us have been taught to believe about motives. According to this teaching, we "have" sexual "feeling" and then "discharge" it in some way, just as we "have" economic "interests" and then "express" them. It is the "interest" or "content" of the experience, not its form, that is "real."

In this view, as expressed in many contemporary accounts, society is thought of as some kind of machine that "gears" and "meshes" motives. There are symbols in what we call art, language, and communication, but these are something like the music of a merry-go-round, which sounds gaily over the whirr and clank of motors and gears that really make the wooden horses go. The music actually has nothing to do with the motive power of the machine. Music merely makes us "feel good," or, in more elegant discourse, "causes delight." Or, in what are called "scientific" views held by some (but by no means all) students of symbolic action, symbols can be treated as "things" that are independent of the context in which they occur or the forms in which they are expressed, because they possess "traits" or "characteristics" that can be "measured." Such measuring is usually done through techniques developed in the physical sciences, for, so the reasoning goes, if what has been done in physics is science, then every science must become like physics. There are those, too, who believe that symbols are used as a kind of make-believe in which we construct "wishing-books" under the rubric that if wishes were horses beggars would ride; and, finally, tribal magicians have come to life in urban guise as publicists who use communication to exhort us to do our share as heroic consumers of everything that money can buy.

In none of these views are symbols important as symbols; for, implicitly or explicitly, those who hold such views believe that symbols do not affect conduct because the springs of action in society are really determined by something "behind" symbols. Symbols are at best but masks of "interests"—sexual, economic, political, or religious, as the case may be—and we tolerate the mask in social analysis only so long as it offers clues to the "interests" behind it. But the popularity of this view of symbolic usage should not blind us to its inadequacies. For, when we tear off the mask in stern resolve to do away with the "distortions" of symbols, the "interests" disappear with the mask. We discover that what we thought to be only a mask was a form that determined the content of the mask, just as the content, in turn, determined the problem we had sought to solve in the creation of the form. The study of forms—the *ways* in which we communicate—becomes then the study of motives, just as the study of contents—*what* we communicate about—does also. The symbolic or formal phase of the act is, therefore, no less real than its motor phase. If we are to understand one, we must understand the other.

We may disregard the forms symbols take in communication, or insist that since we have discovered no laws of order in symbolic patterns there can be no science of symbolic analysis. But these attitudes are rooted in dogma over "proper" ways of practicing science or are the result of a confusion of science with mathematics as the mathematics of space. Obviously, if we believe that science is an attempt to solve problems, we will try to develop methods and techniques for doing so. For, if we do not, we soon end up studying problems for which we already have developed techniques, rather than attempting to solve problems we need to solve. The incredible neglect of Hitler's *Mein Kampf* and other such writings indicates that our failure to study symbolic phases of action may even threaten our very existence. The next Hitler will be armed with *both* nuclear and symbolic weapons.

But, whatever attitude we take toward symbolic analysis, it is impossible to read Burke unless we believe that the ways in which we communicate tend to determine the forms of our social relationships as well as, *per contra,* that the forms of our social relationships tend to determine the ways in which we communicate. As Burke says in his essay "On Human Behavior Considered 'Dramatistically,'" which appears in the Appendix to this edition of *Permanence and Change:*

> Man being specifically a symbol-using animal, we take it that a terminology for the discussion of his social behavior must stress symbolism as a motive, if maximum scope and relevancy is required of the terminology.[7]

But in the very next sentence he is quick to add: "However, man being generically a biological organism, the ideal terminology must present his symbolic behavior as grounded in biological conditions."[8] And in his parenthesis to this statement, he says: "This statement is *not* the same as saying that symbolism is *reducible* to biology. *On the contrary."*[9] That is, we cannot say that words are but sexual puns, for if we

[7] *Permanence and Change,* this edition, p. 275.
[8] *Ibid.*
[9] *Ibid.*

do, we explain everything about courtship except why it involves love. Sex is not simply an "outlet," and woman is not merely a "sexual object." Those we love (and hate) are partners in a social relationship, and if we are to understand what is "sexual" about it, we must take this relationship into account, just as we must take into account what is "sexual" if we are to understand what is "social" in the relations between men and women.

To some it may seem like flogging a dead horse to belabor this point. But those of us who have been trying to work in the Burke tradition, and, like the writer, trying to stay within the guild of American social scientists, have discovered that our greatest difficulty comes precisely at this point. Some people simply do not believe that the study of communication is relevant to the study of social relationships. Others say that we have no "proof" of the kind familiar to them in the sciences of motion, and in terminologies grounded in sensory perception. Such attitudes have forced the communication theorist into a kind of scientific purgatory and have made it difficult for him to get on with the very necessary task of analyzing the social aspects of communication. And worse, this attitude reduces the reading of Burke to an interesting but irrelevant pastime. Those who see (and hear) society as The Great Machine that "gears" and "meshes" into fitful moments of "equilibrium" have even gone so far as to hint that readers of Burke are heretics who must be stamped out of the community of Big Science.

4

Serious critics of Burke do none of these things, of course. They point out that even if we take the first step toward an understanding of Burke and admit that symbols *are* motives, we have only begun our quest. The obvious next question is: *How* do symbols affect motives? It is Burke's answer to this question that marks his greatness. To describe Burke's complete answer would involve statements by experts from many disciplines, for Burke has been very careful to relate his theory of symbolic action to the resources of language itself as well as to many theories of social action. Therefore, *any* specialized view of Burke's work must be only a restricted perspective. The view taken here is that of the sociologist; therefore, readers who have interests in literature, philosophy, psychology, anthropology, history, art, or religion have every right to resent the heavy sociological weighting of Burke's viewpoint given in this introduction. But because *Permanence and Change,* as Burke himself says, is the book in which he places his greatest stress on the social aspects of meaning, there is some excuse for my heavy use of sociological views. It is impossible to understand *any* of Burke if we do not understand his view on social relations. Thus, *Permanence and Change,* and especially the present edition, with Burke's revisions, can serve as an excellent introduction to all Burke's writing.

As Burke makes clear, he came into his concern with social aspects of meaning through his study of meaning in literature. In *Counter-Statement,* which preceded *Permanence and Change* by four years, Burke considered the principle of socialization primarily in terms of literary form. He defines form in literature as "an arousing and fulfillment of desires."[10] A work has form "in so far as one part of it leads a reader to anticipate another part, to be gratified by the sequence."[11]

[10] See page 124 of the section entitled "The Nature of Form" in *Counter-Statement,* (Phoenix edition, Chicago: University of Chicago Press, 1957), pp. 124-128.

[11] *Counter-Statement,* p. 141.

This response occurs because the forms of art are not exclusively aesthetic. Purely formal properties are not unique to art; all experience is distinguished by them.

> The accelerated motion of a falling body, the cycle of a storm, the gradations of a sunrise, the stages of a cholera epidemic, the ripening of crops—in all such instances we find the material of progressive form.[12]

Thus, "though forms need not be prior to experience, they are certainly prior to the work of art exemplifying them."[13] When one turns to the creation of form by the artist, or to the enjoyment of it by an audience, "a formal equipment is already present, and the effects of art are involved in its utilization."[14] In sum, the forms of art can be said to have "a prior existence in the experiences of the person hearing or reading the work of art."[15]

Thus, while Burke, even as early as 1931, began to define the principles underlying the appeal of literature as literature, he also concerned himself with the question *how* people *use* art in their attempts to relate to each other. Burke is careful not to reduce art to sociology or to explain away the struggle of the artist to create forms that will help him to make sense of his relationship to his physical and social environment. In the section of *Counter-Statement* entitled "Lexicon Rhetoricae," he offers thirty-nine propositions on the function of art in society. In proposition 20, "The Symbol," he defines the symbol as "the verbal parallel to a pattern of experience."[16] A poet who suffers from undeserved neglect may express his emotional response in self-pity, outrage, self-hate, or hatred of

[12] *Ibid.* p. 141.
[13] *Ibid.*
[14] *Ibid.*, pp. 141-142.
[15] *Ibid.*, p. 143.
[16] *Ibid.*, p. 152.

he existing social order. His sense of outrage may be so great
nd may recur so often as to color his whole view of life. He
nds ever-new instances of man's depravity. Soon, outrage
t depravity becomes an organizing principle of the poet's
fe. As he expresses his outrage in his work, he makes it a
attern of experience. His symbolization of outrage is then
formula that he uses to order his relationship to his world.

If the poet's readers also feel dissatisfaction with the con-
itions of their lives, they will turn to the poet's expression
f outrage and make it their own. Symbols attain their
reatest effect when the artist's and the reader's patterns of
xperience coincide closely. In the music of Bach, composer,
rtist, and audience reach profound expression in a drama
f salvation shared widely and profoundly by all. Great art
roduces great moments of integration, but even on lower
evels of expression in art we use symbols to clarify an other-
vise unclarified complexity:

> It [the symbol] provides a terminology of thoughts,
> actions, emotions, attitudes, for codifying a pattern of
> experience. The artist, though experiencing intensively or
> extensively a certain pattern, becomes as it were an expert,
> a specialist, in this pattern."[17]

n general, symbols appeal "either as the orienting of a situa-
on, or as the adjustment to a situation, or as both."[18] We may
se symbols to accept a situation, to correct a situation, to bring
nto consciousness submerged or repressed experiences, to
ee us from the burden of symbols that are no longer relevant
o our problems, or to enjoy the play of symbols as such as in
ne enjoyment of "artistic" effects.

But symbols also have a power of their own; they cannot
e explained simply by social or other kinds of effects. "When

[17] *Ibid.* p. 154.
[18] *Ibid.* p. 156.

the poet has converted his pattern of experience into Symbolic equivalent, the Symbol becomes a guiding principle in itself."[19] It is a "generating principle which entails a selection of different subtilizations and ramifications."[20] This selection distinguishes the use of symbols in art from their use in the dream. The dream obeys no principle of selection, whereas art, "which expands by the ramifying of the Symbol, has the Symbol as a principle of selection."[21] This "principle of selection" by which art largely determines, as well as is determined by, the social relationship is no different from the selectivity of symbols used in science. If we use mathematics, we soon find that we are selecting problems that can be solved by mathematics. If we use mechanical imagery in describing the relationships of men, it is not long before we are treating men according to the imagery we have used. Men are related to the machine, and, as automation increases, it is the man, not the machine, who is unemployed.

5

In *Permanence and Change* Burke shifts from considerations of the ways in which the purely formal qualities of art induce an audience to participate in the work of art and of the factors that interfere with such appeals. Here, he emphasizes the differences of perspective that we find in a world of much occupational diversity. In the "Prologue" written for this edition of *Permanence and Change,* Burke raises the question:

> Why, in a world of many disparate perspectives, is the "poetic" perspective ("Man as Communicant") to be treated as foremost? Can the author make cogent claims

[19] *Ibid.*, p. 157.
[20] *Ibid.*
[21] *Ibid.*, p. 158.

that this particular perspective represents more than merely his special "occupational psychosis" as a literary man?[22]

Burke argues that the author can make cogent claims because "whatever the race of human beings may be in their particularity, they are all members of a symbol-using species."[23] Thus, he places man as communicant beside the sexual, political, economic, religious, and scientific models of man that we have inherited from the past and developed in modern times. Burke begins in *Permanence and Change* the construction of a model of symbolic action (a way for man to function as a communicant) in which the structure and the function of symbolic action are related within the act of communication.

If we say that man is a "communicant" and that in so far as communication is social it is a search for some kind of order in our relationships, we must create a model of the act of communication that shows how man (as communicant) does this. Granted that social order arises and continues to exist in communication, and granted that the content of experience depends on how it is expressed to become an experience, how are we to think about the structure of communicative action in terms of its function as a search for order in our relationships? And, even if we grant that communication is primary to all categories of experience, what is there about communication that makes this so? All Burke's writings attempt to deal with these questions, and nothing indicates more clearly the fertility of his mind and his great intellectual courage than the manner in which he keeps testing his theoretical constructions against the everyday, as well as the esoteric, facts of life. By 1945, with the publication of *A Grammar of Motives,* it was obvious that Burke had reached

[22] *Permanence and Change*, p. xxii; this edition, p. lvi.
[23] *Ibid.*

a clear understanding of the logics of linguistic forms considered as symbolic action. In 1950 *A Rhetoric of Motives,* which defined the rhetoric of linguistic structures, appeared. *A Symbolic of Motives* (the poetic dimension of language) is in progress. This will be followed by a fourth volume entitled *On Human Relations,* dealing with the ethical dimensions of language.

Permanence and Change was written in 1932–1933 and was published in 1935. *Attitudes Toward History* followed in 1937. Burke tells us that *Permanence and Change* considers communication in terms of ideal cooperation, whereas *Attitudes Toward History* characterizes tactics and patterns of conflict typical of actual human associations. In preparing this revised edition of *Permanence and Change* some thirty years later, Burke stresses the importance in this work of his analysis of metaphor as a kind of analogy, his analysis of "perspective" and "rebirth," and his analysis of the part played by "piety" and "impiety" in matters of "orientation." And while it is in his later works that Burke states explicitly that the principle of form typified in drama is the basic form of all relationships among men in society, his "dramatistic" theory of motives is implicit in *Permanence and Change.* The inclusion of Burke's essay "On Human Behavior Considered 'Dramatistically' " in the Appendix of this edition indicates how necessary to an understanding of his work he himself regards this dramatistic view of human relations.

A model of action based on man as a communicant must tell us what communication is doing for people as they act together, and in what forms communication can be studied. Burke calls his model "Dramatism." In the introduction to *A Grammar of Motives,* he raises the question of what is involved when we speak about what people are doing and why they are doing it. He answers by saying that *A Grammar of Motives* is "concerned with the basic forms of thought

INTRODUCTION

which, in accordance with the nature of the world as all men necessarily experience it, are exemplified in the attributing of motives."[24] These forms of thought are "equally present in systematically elaborated metaphysical structures, in legal judgments, in poetry and fiction, in political and scientific works, in news and in bits of gossip offered at random."[25] The structure of this dramatic act is composed of five terms. These are Act, Scene, Agent, Agency, Purpose.

In a rounded statement about motives, you must have some word that names the *act* (names what took place, in thought or deed), and another that names the *scene* (the background of the act, the situation in which it occurred); also, you must indicate what kind of person (*agent*) performed the act, what means or instruments he used (*agency*), and the *purpose.*[26]

What is this drama about as a social drama? How does it bring order in human relationships? Burke answers these questions very explicitly in the appendix of this edition of *Permanence and Change.* Here he states that the four basic motives arising in human communication are "Guilt, Redemption, Hierarchy, and Victimage."[27] By this, he means that in *human* relationships these four motives are the keys to the grand design of all human motivation. They "supplement and modify men's purely natural or biological inclinations . . ." and such "social, linguistically grounded motives can be said to 'perfect' nature, in a purely *technical* sense."[28]

[24] Kenneth Burke, *A Grammar of Motives* (New York: Prentice Hall, Inc., 1945), p. x.

[25] *Ibid.*

[26] *Ibid.*, p. xv.

[27] These terms are used in a long footnote to the first page of the Appendix, "On Human Behavior Considered 'Dramatistically,' " as given here in this text, p. 274.

[28] *Ibid.*

The specific contribution of purely social aspects of experience to motivation is hierarchy, the means whereby groups arrange themselves in some kind of rank order and at the same time transcend differences in rank through "social Mysteries" that infuse the lowest and the highest rank with their radiance. The private who salutes his superior expresses a difference in rank, but superior and inferior alike submit themselve to the flag and salute it together. As we say, we salute the office—not the man. By this we mean that, as the general and the private salute, they are saluting a principle of order that differentiates them into ranks at the same time that it transcends this differentiation through appeal to "mysteries" (country, flag, "land where our fathers died," and the like).

For Burke, order in society is not to be studied as some kind of regularity in a process, but as a distribution of authority. In the mutuality of rule and service in authority "with its uncertain dividing-line between loyalty and servitude, [authority] takes roughly a pyramidal or hierarchal form (or, at least, it is like a ladder with 'up' and 'down')."[29] Because of differences of sex, age, education, wealth, skill, and other conditions of life, different classes and kinds of people become remote and strange to each other. It is this estrangement that Burke means when he says that people become "mysteries" to each other.

> This condition of Mystery is revealed most perfectly in primitive priestcraft, which serves in part to promote cohesion among disparate classes, and in part to perpetuate ways that, while favoring some at the expense of others may at times thereby endanger the prosperity of the tribe as a whole.[30]

[29] This text, p. 276.
[30] *Ibid.*

But, however remote and strange the mystery of another may become, there must be some way of transcending this separateness if social order is to be achieved. Love may become a "sweet mystery," and our beloved may be a goddess we worship from afar, but, if the race is to continue, the mystery must lead us into, not away from, the sexual act.

Burke proposes that we accept "priestly stress upon Mystery" as a model for all social mystification. Such Mystery "attains its grandest expression in the vision of a celestial hierarchy loosely imagined after the analogy of a human social order." Celestial order becomes "secularized and distributed" among worldly social roles, "each of which treats the social Mystery after its fashion."[31] We all use such mysteries: the educator has his "testimonials of academic rank; the legislator has ways of identifying respect for himself with respect for the august body of which he is a member; the artist helps surround a system of social values with 'glamor,' as he finds tricks that transform the austere religious passion into a corresponding romantic, erotic passion; . . ."[32] Each institution strives to mystify us through surrounding its principle of order, and the roles in which this order is enacted, with its own glamor or what Burke calls "Mystery." Institutions also link their mysteries with the mysteries of other institutions, and with mysteries whose power is not rooted in social mystery. For there are mysteries of death, of birth, of aging, of dreams, just as there are mysteries of adventure and of love. Social mystery thus gains much in

. . . depth, persuasiveness, allusiveness and illusiveness precisely by reason of the fact that it becomes inextricably interwoven with mysteries of these other sorts, quite as

[31] *Ibid.*, p. 277.
[32] *Ibid.*

these other mysteries must in part be perceived through the fog of social Mystery.[33]

In his analysis of the reciprocal effects of social and linguistic symbols, Burke points out that nature (as communicated about) has her mysteries too. Although hens cooped up in a barnyard cannot be said to exist in nature, social rights among a flock of hens are ascribed to "nature" and then "derived" from it. Thus, in the "pecking-order" of the flock of hens observed by Schjelderup-Ebbe, we are told that in any small flock of hens there soon develops a rather firmly fixed hierarchy in which the top bird normally has the right to peck all the others without being pecked in return, and each of the others occupies a place subordinate to hers, usually in a linear series with respect to one another, down to the lowest bird, which all may peck without fear of retaliation. And in this ideal kingdom of dominance, as W. C. Allee tells us, the peck-right, once established, can be reversed only in the event of a successful revolt (which rarely occurs among chickens). Biological theories of this kind have been of great service to modern tyrants who find in such theories a "natural" ground for tyranny. Hitler called his version of the "peck-order" the "leadership principle," which, as Eichmann made clear in his trial, absolved from guilt anyone of lower rank who followed any order of a superior. But, as W. C. Allee, Adolf Portmann, and V. C. Wynne-Edwards (among others) have shown, despotic behavior is but *one* form of hierarchy among living organisms. Studies of the schooling behavior of fish living naturally show that dominance hierarchies are not found in many schools of fish. It seems to be characteristic of all fish schools that all individuals are of equal rank.

[33] *Ibid.*

6

As we learn from Burke, all types of social order rest on positives and negatives expressed in "thou shalt" and "thou shalt not." Even when we act as equals under rules of our own making, we are careful to define how the game must be played and to establish umpires to punish those who break the rules that we have agreed to respect. This characteristic of social order cannot be explained by hierarchy alone, and certainly not by recourse to biological views on hierarchy. Animals do not sit in court on each other. It may be that as we understand them better we will discover that culprits among animals are brought to trial as they are among us, but in the light of present knowledge, all we can say is that punishment among animals does not seem to be based on the kind of symbolization we create in laws, manners, and the other forms we invoke to punish those who have not done what those in power over them thought they ought to do. It may be that when we know more about animal play, which cannot be explained by theories of dominance or "adaptation," we may discover "disobedience" is as "natural" to animals as it is to man.

In one of his most significant essays, "A Dramatistic View of the Origins of Language," Burke locates the specific nature of language "in the ability to use the Negative."[34] Following Bergson, he argues that there are no "negative" conditions in nature.

> Bergson points out that there are no "negative" conditions in nature. Every situation is positively what it is. For instance, we may *say* "The ground is *not* damp." But the

[34] This appeared in *The Quarterly Journal of Speech*, XXXVIII (1952), 251–264, 446–460; and XXXIX (1953), 79–92.

corresponding actual conditions in nature are those whereby the ground *is* dry. We may say that something "is not" in such and such a place. But so far as nature is concerned, whatever "is not" here is positively somewhere else; or, if it does not exist, then other things actually occupy all places where it "is not."[35]

This use of the negative is not the only notable aspect of language. Classification, specification, abstraction also have their analogues in purely non-verbal behavior. But the negative is a peculiarly linguistic resource. And because it is so peculiarly linguistic, the study of man "as the specifically word-using animal requires special attention to this distinctive marvel, the negative."[36]

Nowhere is the linguistic and social interpretation of the negative more clearly shown than in the negative command, as in the Ten Commandments. For what are these but a list of "thou shalt nots" that function in conduct with all the force (perhaps, indeed, with more) of positive commands? That is, *both* the positive and the negative are commands that authority requires us to follow. All forms of authority are a kind of covenant between ruler and ruled that must be upheld if social order is to be maintained. But, unfortunately, there are no perfect covenants. At best, hierarchies have many incongruities that must be exposed to reason; at worst, many evils that must be exorcised. From the *technical* view of efficiency (that is the "efficiency" of authority), disobedience must be branded as evil. Yet when we ask how it is possible for an all-powerful and all-loving authority to "permit" disobedience, the paradox of all rulership becomes apparent. Authorities must bedazzle us with the majesty of their commandments and, at the same time, arouse guilt within us over disobedience of their "sacred" edicts.

[35] *Ibid.*, XXXVIII, 251.
[36] *Ibid.*

But if authorities control us through guilt, they cannot control us long if they do not assist us in expiating the guilt they have caused. An explanation of the way in which this is done is described by Burke in *The Rhetoric of Religion*. Here, as always, Burke makes clear that he is *not* "explaining away" religion as a mere matter of words. Burke tells us he is concerned not directly with religion, but rather "with the *terminology* of religion; not directly with man's relationship to God, but rather with his relationship to the *word* "God."[37] He points out that theological doctrine is a body of spoken or written *words*. "Whatever else it may be, and wholly regardless of whether it be true or false, theology is preeminently *verbal*. It is *'words'* about God."[38] And, furthermore, whatever we think of religion, we must admit that it offers us many examples of words "used with thoroughness." Hence, the "rhetoric of religion" furnishes us with a good model of "terministic enterprise in general."[39] On both social and linguistic levels, religious rhetoric offers many clues to human motivation.

Indeed, it is not too much to say that, for Burke, religious communication, and specifically Christian religious rhetoric, is the paradigm for all communication. As William H. Rueckert says in his excellent study of Burke:

> The notion that all men begin in a fallen state [of what Burke calls 'Categorical Guilt'], burdened by the hierarchic psychosis and categorical guilt, both of which belong to the Burkean hell—the pollution, war, division, disorder, corro-

[37] Kenneth Burke, *The Rhetoric of Religion: Studies in Logology* (Boston: Beacon Press, 1961), p. vi.
[38] *Ibid.*
[39] *Ibid.*

sion, disintegration, alienation, fragmentation cluster—is central to all of Burke. Without it, his own obsessive concern with pollution, guilt, and disorder, his almost monomaniacal emphasis on modes of purification, on mankind's vast and complex rhetoric of rebirth, and on redemption as an achieved state, would be meaningless—save, perhaps, as his own purgative-redemptive symbolic action. As it is, the categorical guilt and emphasis on pollution-purification-and-redemption indicate more clearly than anything else the fundamentally moral and ethical center of Burke. What he has finally done in his dramatistic theory, after many years of moving steadily in that direction, is to systematize a naturalistic, linguistically oriented, secular variant of Christianity. Burke has retained the principal ideas of Christianity and worked out dramatistic equivalents for them with astonishing thoroughness.[40]

In his discussion of the first three chapters of Genesis, in *The Rhetoric of Religion,* Burke says:

> The Bible, with its profound and beautiful exemplifying of the sacrificial principle, teaches us that tragedy is ever in the offing. Let us, in the spirit of solemn comedy, listen to its lesson. Let us be on guard ever, as regards the subtleties of sacrifice, in their fundamental relationship to governance.[41]

For if men can rid themselves of guilt only by making victims of themselves, as in mortification, or by making victims of others, as in sacrifice and all its variants, then we must study victimage in its purest form, namely, that of religious sacrifice, if we are to study it at all. For the Bible

[40] William H. Rueckert, *Kenneth Burke and the Drama of Human Relations* (Minneapolis: University of Minnesota Press, 1963) pp. 133-134.
[41] *The Rhetoric of Religion,* p. 235.

teaches us that victimage as redemption by vicarious atonement is intrinsic to the idea of guilt.

In his early discussions on sacrifice, and specifically on the use of the scapegoat (the purest form of sacrifice) in *Permanence and Change,* Burke warned that reducing the use of the scapegoat to magic, and then dismissing it as a "primitive" custom that man no longer needed, was highly dangerous. Whatever we may think of the sacrifice of the scapegoat, "we must remember that the technique of purification magnificently met the pragmatic tests of success. It was, for instance, quite efficacious in unburdening a people of their sins."[42] This was because the sacrifice of the scapegoat "was a formula and ritual whereby these sins could be transferred to the back of an animal, the animal was then ferociously beaten or slain —and the feeling of relief was apparent to all."[43] To us a theory that sins are transferable "may not seem . . . as justifiable as a theory that diseases are transferable . . ." and when primitive people try to exorcise plague by substituting goats for people it is easy enough for us to explain this peculiar type of thinking as "magic."[44] Or, we often say that the use of the scapegoat and all forms of vicarious atonement are only a "rationalization" of other motives (sexual, political, or economic).

But Burke's warning in this regard has been among many that went unheeded, and we have seen to our horror, in Hitler's use of the Jew and Stalin's use of the traitor in his purge trials, that the scapegoat is far from dead. The idea of a personal victim has had a long history, as we recall from the instance of Abraham's willingness to sacrifice his beloved son. We should not forget, says Burke, "that, in proportion as the idea of the *personal* victim developed, there arose the

[42] This text, p. 16.
[43] *Ibid.*
[44] *Ibid.*, p. 17.

incentives to provide a judicial rationale for the sacrifice more in line with the kind of thinking represented by the *lex talionis*."[45] Thus,

> . . . the idea of a personally fit victim could lead to many different notions, such as (1) the ideal of a perfect victim (Christ); (2) the Greeks' "enlightened" use of criminals who had been condemned to death but were kept on reserve for state occasions when some ritual sacrifice was deemed necessary; (3) Hitler's idealizing of the Jew as a "perfect" enemy.[46]

The closest analogue in daily life to the use of the scapegoat in religious ceremonies is to be found in mortification. For if we are right in assuming that a religious cult purges itself through the sacrifice of the scapegoat and that worldly orders purge themselves through "perfecting" victims whose sacrifice purges the community of evil, then we can assume that a similar process goes on within the individual. Mortification, and its variations, such as humiliation, vexation, and chagrin, is a punishment of an "unruly" aspect of the self. Mortification is never simply the result of "frustration" from without. It must come from within.

> The mortified must, with one aspect of himself, be saying no to another aspect of himself—hence the urgent incentive to be 'purified' by 'projecting' his conflict upon a scapegoat, by 'passing the buck' by seeking a sacrificial vessel upon which he can vent, as from without, a turmoil that is actually within.[47]

Where we cannot find easy outgoing relief or cannot project our guilt upon another, we circle back upon ourselves. The

[45] *The Rhetoric of Religion*, p. 217.
[46] *Ibid.*
[47] *Ibid.*, pp. 190–191.

goads of hierarchy—the embarrassment, shame, and guilt we are made to feel in learning to play our roles in society—are turned inward. Since we cannot punish others, we punish ourselves. Perhaps, Burke suggests, when we understand psychogenic illnesses better, we will discover that they are but "secularized variants of what might be called 'mortification in spite of itself.' "[48] Perhaps the secret to the analysis of the social pathology of everyday life, as well as the translation of the language systems of schizophrenes and psychopaths, lies in the study of mortification.

8

Enough has been said to indicate the range and intensity of Burke's analysis of motives. But his brilliance should not lead us to turn away from asking fundamental questions. Does Burke really tell us anything about the daily problems of living? Does he help us to make sense out of the many confusions that beset us? Each of us has his own private burden of woe, but if there is one affliction we all share it is our depressing need for *sharing* in the violence and hatred we visit upon ourselves and each other. We stand in terror before our greatly increased capacity to wound, torture, and kill. Why is man a "social beast of prey?" What need, individual and social, does our lust for violence satisfy? Unless we are willing to write the human race off as a hopeless joke, or as being composed of beasts who rose from all fours too soon, we must ask such questions. Our fate hinges on our capacity to answer them, and, thus, every "system" of human motivation must be measured by answers to such questions.

Burke began his answers in *Permanence and Change,* with his first analysis of "categorical guilt." He held that all hierarchies are infused with this type of guilt. The closest

[48] *Ibid.,* p. 190.

analogue to this kind of guilt is in the theological doctrine of original sin, where one's guilt is not the result of any personal transgression, but of tribal or dynastic inheritance. We are born into a status system, and the place assigned to us at birth is something over which we have little control. If our skins are black, we are born in "hierarchal," if not "original," sin. But insofar as we must live and face the world, there is little difference. Would any particular form of government (socialism or capitalism) *as such* do away with the "hierarchal psychosis" we now see in race relations in the United States? Burke does not think so. He takes it for granted that the pyramidal magic of hierarchy is inevitable in social relations because, in such relations, individuals, rightly or wrongly, become endowed "with the attributes of their *office*."[49]

Is there any hope for a symbol-using animal goaded by the spirit of hierarchy? If men must come together to share in the enjoyment of torturing and killing their hapless human scapegoats, what hope is there for ridding ourselves of violence and terror? If Christ's agony was not merely a historical event, but a paradigm of how the human psyche functions, is there any way out of human misery other than the religious way? And even if we accept the Christian way, what assurance is there that the future, like the past, will not see Christians torturing and killing each other in the name of God? If the reading of Burke were to sharpen these questions and focus our attention upon them, it would serve us well. But Burke goes far beyond this. There is hope if, *if* we learn to think about action in society as a kind of action that arises in, and continues to exist through, communication. What Burke offers— and it is the reason why so many of us turn to him for help— is a methodology, a *way* of thinking, and of testing our thinking, about *how* we act as human beings. We leave Burke's

[49] See pp. 278–279 of this text for discussion of this.

INTRODUCTION

wonderful books in sadness, but in this sadness is hope. If, in the suffering and horror of our time, we can develop a *method* for the analysis of what symbols do to us in our relations with each other, we may yet learn to lead a better life. Such is Burke's message to our time.

A Note on Reading Burke

The understanding of Burke has been greatly facilitated by the publication of William H. Rueckert's, *Kenneth Burke and the Drama of Human Relations* (Minneapolis: University of Minnesota Press, 1963). This contains an excellent annotated bibliography, divided into three sections listing works by Burke, works about Burke, and works in the Burke tradition. Although Rueckert's interest in Burke is primarily literary, this should not discourage those with other interests from relying on this book. Rueckert's book is indispensable, and while it would be idle to pretend that it "simplifies" Burke, it certainly serves as an excellent guide. The secondary literature on Burke, aside from this study by Rueckert, is neither notable nor voluminous. That a thinker of Burke's stature should have evoked so little serious and intense commentary is a sad reflection on American intellectual life.

But if Burke has not inspired many commentaries and glosses, he has been of great help to other writers in getting their books done, and in reaching some conclusion about the function of art in society. Francis Fergusson's *The Human Image in Dramatic Literature* (Garden City, New York: Doubleday Anchor Books, 1957); Stanley Edgar Hyman's *The Tangled Bank: Darwin, Marx, Frazer and Freud as Imaginative Writers* (New York: Atheneum, 1962); and the writer's *Language and Literature in Society* (New York: The Bedminster Press, 1961), and *Communication and Social Order* (New York: The Bedminster Press, 1962), are but four books which owe a great deal to Burke. Poets like W. H. Auden and Howard Nemorov; critics like Randell Jarrell, Malcolm Cowley, and Austin Warren; students of language such as Charles Morris and S. I. Hayakawa, are but a few of the workers in various fields who have made good use of Burke.

As I have indicated, the core of Burke's system is his dramatistic model of human relations. There are two ways toward an understanding of this. The first "way in" is through Burke's literary concerns in such books as *Counter-Statement* (second edition; Los Altos, California: Hermes Publications, 1958), and *The Philosophy of Literary Form: Studies in Symbolic Action*, also in paperback (Vintage edition, New York: Vintage Books, 1957). The second is in sociology through *Permanence and Change* and *Attitudes Toward History* (Beacon paperback edition, Boston: Beacon Press, 1961). These will prepare the reader for the later books, *A Grammar of Motives* and *A Rhetoric of Motives,* which have been issued as a single paperback by Meridian Books (Cleveland and New York: The World Publishing Company, 1962) and *The Rhetoric of Religion: Studies in Logology* (Boston, Beacon Press, 1961). But Burke must be read as a whole; it is impossible to understand what he says about language without knowing what he says about society. It is because of this that *Permanence and Change* serves as an introduction to all of Burke. For here in this book he talks about the *reciprocal* effects of language and society and thus prepares us for his later and more systematic statement of his dramatistic theory of human relationships.

Hugh Dalziel Duncan

Southern Illinois University
January 1965

PERMANENCE AND CHANGE

An Anatomy of Purpose

PROLOGUE

THIS BOOK, *Permanence and Change*, was written in the early days of the Great Depression, at a time when there was a general feeling that our traditional ways were headed for a tremendous change, maybe even a permanent collapse. It is such a book as authors in those days sometimes put together, to keep themselves from falling apart. Not knowing quite where he was, this particular author took notes on "orientation." Not being sure how to read the signs, he took notes on "interpretation." Finding himself divided, he took notes on division (or, as he calls it in this book, "perspective by incongruity"). Looking for some device by which to reintegrate the muddle, he asked about the possibility of a "resimplification" that would not be an over-simplification. In sum, being in a motivational quandary, he wrote on "motivation." The result is a kind of transformation-at-one-remove, got by inquiry into the process of transformation itself.

Though all decisions, because of their bearing upon the future, necessarily involve a measure of uncertainty, we can make a broad distinction here. Some decisions merely apply ways of thinking with which the deliberator was already quite at home. Other decisions, made at times of "Crisis" (which is but the Greek word for "judgment"), characteristically also involve an *unsettling*, an attempt (or temptation?) to think in ways to which the deliberator was not accustomed.

Either kind can be treated in terms of drama. An average decision is being treated "dramatistically," if it is discussed in such terms as "action," "purpose," "rôle-taking," and the like. But "Crisis" decisions involve "dramatistic" coördinates in a more specific sense.

Consider Macbeth's soliloquy in Act I, Scene VII, for instance: "If it were done when 'tis done, then 'twere well/ It were done quickly." This would be a "Crisis" decision. Criminal decisions in drama are particularly fitted to represent Crisis decisions generally, since decisions of the "unsettling" kind necessarily involve internal conflicts that are to some extent experienced as "guilt."

Such a moment may be "broken down" essayistically into a somewhat prolonged discussion of its components. "Dramatistic" *analysis* here would be almost the opposite of dramatic *synthesis* (though this distinction between analysis and synthesis should not be conceived too absolutely, since the essayistic has its modes of merger, and the dramatist gets his effects by a splitting of the total action into diverse rôles and step-by-step unfoldings).

However, the author would by no means here attempt to present his brand of "Crisis-thinking" in current Existentialist terms. For the reader would only too quickly discover that the book does not fill the bill. As a matter of fact, its original title was "Treatise on Communication," and it is written in that spirit. The author wrote in no country occupied by a foreign invader. Though he had an almost magical fear of destitution, he never passed up a single meal for lack of funds. He saw no new vision on a battlefield. He had not been tied in a cellar as a child, with rats crawling over him (though he had had a bad fall). If he was frightened, to a large extent it was by Hallowe'en pumpkins that he himself had hollowed out, and had carved with snaggle teeth, while the eerie glow he saw was something he had put there.

So, all told, concerned with words above all, when things got toughest he thought hardest about communication.

*   *   *

PROLOGUE

Since he also subscribed to the notion (as he still does) that communication is grounded in material coöperation, before publication of the manuscript he augmented it by five or six pages speculating on the form that such material coöperation should take. From the present edition these pages have been removed. Since, under present conditions, the pages could not possibly be read in the tentative spirit in which they were originally written, the omissions help avoid troublesome issues not necessary to the book as such. There is even a sense in which the omissions could be called a kind of "restoration," since they bring the text back closer to its original nature. The author would further justify the omissions thus:

Coöperation in human society is never an absolute, but varies with conditions of time and place. Any given mode of coöperation can be expected to have the defects of its qualities (with its apologists stressing only its qualities, and its opponents stressing only the defects). Any controversy as regards just what mode of coöperation best suits a given national or international situation cannot be resolved, or even properly confronted, in half a dozen pages of a work that is concentrated upon a much different though related topic. And the ease with which the pages can be dropped, without disruption to our thesis, is evidence enough that they are not necessary.

We do not mean that judgments about the political nature of a society's coöperative habits are in themselves unnecessary. On the contrary. We mean only that they are not necessary to the thesis of this present work, which needs but speculate on the fact that a system of ideal coöperation (whatever that might be!) would be a momentous material aid to the communicative medium, whereas communication is impaired to the extent that coöperation is impaired.

Even here, however, there is not a simple one-to-one correspondence. For in this world, communication is never an absolute (only angels communicate absolutely); and a deficiency at one point in a given communicative system may show as a proficiency at some other point (somewhat as persons deprived of sight may become more acute in hearing or touch).

*   *   *

To look over a book twenty years after it was first written is to discover that the author has been imaginative despite himself. That is, he has contrived to put himself in the rôle of a character not his own. He has imagined someone who stoutly averred things that he now would state quite otherwise. The book which he thought of as a monologue when he wrote it, has thus become in relation to his later books more like one voice in a dialogue.

Consider, for instance, the several references to what the text calls "Metabiology." At many points, by a "metabiology" the author seems to have meant that all "higher manifestations" of human culture are to be explained as "projections" of the body in its sheerly physiological nature. The author was exercised over the thought that technology takes men, at their peril, away from simple, natural ways of living. This fear is matched by a somewhat Gauguinesque notion of a gentle South Sea Island existence (without leprosy!) as the ideal norm of human living. At other times the reference to natural origins is used in an admonitory sense. Thus, pugnacity in human relations is thought of as directly deriving from the "biological fact" that the human organism, in its animality, is equipped by brain and muscle for survival in the natural warfare of the jungle.

But there is another kind of "Beyond-Biology" here, as in the many concerns with ethical quandaries *not* reducible to purely physiological terms. From the standpoint of these considerations, the book's references to animal experiments and the like are to be interpreted not as "scientific proof" of anything, but merely as a scientific-seeming kind of Æsop's fable, a metaphorical way of "revealing character." For an experiment with organisms that do not use language cannot tell us anything essential about the distinctive motives of a species that does use language.

Even on an empirical basis, a "Metabiology" needs the corrective of a concern with *social motives as such*. Thus, human kinds of domination and subjection must decidedly never be reduced to the strictly "natural" or "biological." The necessary discount is implicit in this book at many points. But it is not as explicit as the author would now have it.

*　　　*　　　*

A further point about the notion of the natural body as "warrior": While worrying, in this book, about the realm of "piety," a realm where poetic and ethical proprieties overlap, the author had been particularly concerned with linguistic speculations stemming from Jeremy Bentham, though perhaps he did not follow this line of thought in quite the ways that Bentham had intended. But at least, he was being Benthamite in distrusting the ready reaches of "moral indignation" by which so much public counsel is burdened (when issues that might have been rationally solved by deliberation and compromise are made agonizingly unwieldy by appeals to what Bentham called "interest-begotten prejudice").

About this same time, the author had had a plan for a kind of melodrama (or perhaps modernized morality play) constructed around two orders of motivation. In the foreground of the stage, there was to be a series of realistic incidents, dealing with typical human situations, such as family quarrels, scenes at a business office, lovers during courtship, a public address by a spellbinder, etc. In the background, like a set of comments on this action, there was to be a primeval forest filled with mythically prehistoric monsters, marauding and fighting in silent pantomime.

These two realms were to have no overt connection with each other. The monsters in the "prehistoric" background would pay no attention to the everyday persons of the foreground; and these everyday persons would have no awareness of the background. But the pantomime of the background would be in effect a "mythic" or "symbolic" way of commenting upon the realistic action of the foreground. Thus, each time some particularly "noble" or "delicate" utterance was made in the foreground, in the background some corresponding atrocity would take place. For instance, while characters appealed "sublimely" in the name of "justice," "virtue," "the noble spirit of self-sacrifice," and the like, the background might reveal two gigantic dragon-like creatures, with saw-toothed, gore-dripping jaws, locked in mortal combat. Such correspondences, it was intended, would indicate the "jungle motives" that underlie such practices as the use of an ethical vocabulary for goading men to the slaughter of one another.

Gradually, however, with increasing frequency, there were to be fleeting moments when the two realms seemed in more direct communication. And the play was to end with a sudden breaking of the frame, whereat the monsters of the background would swarm forward, to take over the entire stage, in a kind of Total Revolution that completely overwhelmed the powers of Reason, insofar as Reason was represented by the "normal" ways of moralized polemics. Symbol-wise, the author has never regretted that he was unable to carry out this project. He doesn't think it's the sort of plot one should be able to imagine convincingly. But, as a conceit, it does serve to indicate the sort of worry that lay behind his reference to "censorial words" as "the linguistic projection of our bodily tools and weapons," and behind the somewhat Nietz-schean statement that "morals are fists." And compensatory to such a view of moral judgments as a variant of "natural war," there was much tinkering with the thought of absolu-tizing Bentham's concerns with a "neutral" vocabulary, in a kind of *via negativa* that would be the linguist's equivalent of mystical discipline.

*   *   *

The author became concerned with thoughts of a Joining, a Categorical Joining, a Joining "in principle," a joining-at-one-remove by joining with the sheer Idea of Joining. And, in keeping with his "occupational psychosis" as a writer, he thought of such joining in terms of *communication*, which in turn was conceived specifically as ideal *poetic* communi-cation.

But whereas he had been mulling over the possibility of a *neutralized* language, a language with no clenched fists, he could not help seeing that Poetry uses to perfection a *weighted* language. Its winged words are weighted words.

The tangle was increased by the fact that such weighting of words arises from *group* relationships. However much the individual poet may transform language for his special pur-poses, the resources with which he begins are "traditional," that is: *social*. And such sociality of meaning is grounded in a sociality of material conduct, or coöperation.

Later, the author would be able to inquire into the ways whereby a poet can both exemplify group "weightings" in his use of language and "transcend" them, if the poem follows along a properly ordered series of steps (*gradatim et paul-atim!*) in which the reader sympathetically participates. At the moment, there was the clear fact that a communicative medium is grounded in a society's modes of coöperation, while our own nation's modes of coöperation at that time were in exceptional disorder (a state of affairs that at least had the advantage of revealing relationships not otherwise so noticeable).*

Consider, then, the "symmetry." One sets out to write on orientation, interpretation, communication, as affected by the resources of language. One goes through a "negative discipline" that aims ideally at the neutralizing of every moralistically weighted word. At this point, the very absoluteness of such a project drives one to the corrective opposite; namely: the thought of an ideally weighted vocabulary, grounded in an ideally ordered mode of material coöperation. And with such a non-existent ideal condition one joins "in principle."

Midway between an old weighting and a new weighting, is the realm we have called "perspective by incongruity" (a term that designates one way of transcending a given order of weightedness). The concept, as we see it now, was the other side of Remy de Gourmont's formula for the "dissociation of ideas." De Gourmont was concerned with the methodic blasting apart of verbal particles that had been considered insepa-

---

* Elsewhere, we have summed up thus the relation between the poet's use of weighted words and his way of going beyond such weightedness:

The "weighting" of words arises from extra-poetic situations in the social order. A relative fixity of conditions in the social order (what Malinowski would have called the "context of situation") makes it possible for a person to learn what Bentham would call the "censorial" nature of terms ("appellatives"). One learns it by hearing the terms used in contexts that imply moral judgments. However, one may next "play with" such terms, experimentally giving them a range of meanings that do not fit their orthodox use as sheer instruments of "social control." That is, *by setting up special conditions within a given work of art,* one might, without "demoralization," even bring things to a point where, in effect, terms for the loathsome could be applied to a most admirable person, and vice versa.

rable; "perspective by incongruity" refers to the methodic merger of particles that had been considered mutually exclusive. (The one was "fission"; the other, "fusion"?)

Anyhow, in accordance with our belief that dreams are sometimes hardly more than *caricatures* of one's serious concerns, we might mention the fact that, during his work on "perspective by incongruity," the author once dreamed of playing a new kind of card game. By the rules of this game, you could take a trick with a lower card than an opponent's, if you so renamed the card that its new name made it into a higher denomination than the face value of your opponent's card. (Thus, you could take a Jack with a deuce, if you renamed the deuce a Queen.) But the new assigned identity of the card had to persist from then on, and be remembered, until all the cards in the deck had been transformed. The dreamer awoke while the game was still in its earlier stages— but already it had become like a fever dream. Less drastically, the concern with "perspective by incongruity" could be likened to the procedure of certain modern painters who picture how an object might seem if inspected simultaneously from two quite different positions.

As for the subject of the "poetic" generally, much that is said somewhat dithyrambically about it has subsequently been discussed by the author elsewhere in terms of "symbolic action." Man justifies himself in the modes of socialization that go with his society (even "private enterprise" being an aspect of "socialization" in this technical sense). And such justification is so inspirited with symbolic motives that the most practical of careers should be analyzed in such terms (at those moments when one is brooding over the various kinds of "compulsion neurosis" that go to make up human conduct). In *Counter-Statement*, the author considered the principle of socialization primarily in terms of literary form. In *P & C* he widens the motivational orbit; but the discussion of "communication" that emerges, naturally retains many vestiges of the more specifically poetic concerns. *Attitudes Toward History* moves still farther from the specifically literary into the realm of human antics generally (with key terms akin to the concerns of a public-relations counsel, and accordingly treated as essentially "comic").

* * *

Another way of characterizing *P & C* would be to say that it lays primary stress upon the many differences of *perspective* that go with a world of much occupational diversity. But then the reader may ask: Why, in a world of many disparate perspectives, is the "poetic" perspective ("Man as Communicant") to be treated as foremost? Can the author make cogent claims that this particular perspective represents more than merely his special "occupational psychosis" as a literary man?

The question may be answered either specifically or "in principle." Specifically, not only are there obvious quirks of the author on every page; there are even many references local to one particular mood of our country, in the years around the beginning of F. D. Roosevelt's administration (a time when, on every side, there was the feeling that, for better or worse, an earlier way of life had come abruptly to an end).

But "in principle" we believe that this particular perspective *can* claim priority over the general run of perspectives, which are limited only by the range of men's occupations and preoccupations. For whatever the race of human beings may be in their particularity, they are all members of a symbol-using species. Accordingly, the author dares hold that the "Poetic" perspective is foremost "in principle."

To say so is not by any means to say that one expects such a perspective upon human motives to command authority. Political, military, and industrial powers are much more likely to "set the tone," so far as the "implementing" of per-spectives is concerned. But the perspective that views man in terms of his symbolic involvements may enjoy at least a uni-versally *corrective* function—or, if not that, then perhaps it may at least be found to go with the "brooding dimension" as regards human motives. And so one will constantly be coming upon it, even in the midst of the great pyramidal structures of authority that, while their strength is a mockery of the "poetic perspective's" weaknesses, are all prime exam-ples of its claims, since they all bear witness to man's great reliance upon language, terminology, *symbolism*.

* * *

Our treatment of perspective in terms of "metaphor" con-cerns what the social scientists now often discuss in terms of "models." In this regard, our references to "metaphorical ex-tension" touch upon a critical principle that has often been misused. We refer not just to its misuse in "analogizing," but rather to the misuse of the concept itself, when the critic is seeking to characterize the procedures of some particular work. He may say, for instance, that the "poetic perspective" or "metaphor" is merely being "expanded" beyond its proper frontiers, hence has but a "suggestive" value, being hardly more than a figure of speech prolonged to the point where it looks literal.

But he should be warned that the metaphor of expansion and contraction must itself be expanded and contracted, if we are to free ourselves of its limitations as a resource for the placing of a given problem.

For instance, often a position may be *arrived at* by the ex-pansion of an earlier position; yet when arrived at, it may bring up perceptions in its own right—so that, from there on, another position must take over. Or again, a position may be conceived in one set of terms, but may happen to be "jesuitically" recommended in another set of terms.

*　　*　　*

Here's one more matter that should be mentioned: In the Epilogue to the new edition of *Counter-Statement*, we referred to a somewhat ritualistic principle of development in *P & C*. The book begins on an image of depth (submergence) combined with an idea of caution, and ends on an image of height (emergence) combined with an idea of fear (while the middle "Incongruity" section features a transitional clashing of the two extremes). When reading over the book for this edition, we noticed another variant of such development—and we'd like to mention it because it gives us an opportunity to illustrate a point about verbal doings in general.

We noticed another kind of contrast between beginning and end. In the first section, where Interpretation is being discussed, the concept of the "scapegoat mechanism" was replaced by the Benthamite concept of "faulty means-selecting." But later in the book, when discussing ethical motives (as with our remarks on "piety," "impiety," and "recommending by tragedy"), we necessarily become involved with the paradoxes of sacrifice and victimage. Thus, the exposition somehow picks up another dimension as it proceeds from the opening section on "criticism" (or "judgment") to the closing section on the "poetry of action." And this amounts to introducing a variant of the "scapegoat" principle.

Technically, the "lesson" of this discrepancy between beginning and end might be formulated thus: "If you would analyze interpretation in terms of means-selecting, there is no need for such a term as 'scapegoat mechanism' to account for men's errors of interpretation. But some variant of the scapegoat principle *is* required, as soon as you turn to con-

PROLOGUE

der the sacrificial element in ethics." However, the most
omplete consideration of victimage is reserved for later work,
here we consider how the kinds of "guilt" intrinsic to the
ocial pyramid call for corresponding kinds of "purgation."

*   *   *

Many minor points should be corrected, if the author aimed
 make this book, which was written twenty years ago, be
actly what it would be if he were writing it now. For
stance, you may note here and there a certain "depart-
ental vindictiveness," such as members of one business
 profession sometimes permit themselves, when referring
ther to competitors in their own field or to persons engaged
 somewhat "alien" activities.

And a major reservation should be made with regard to
e section on "Magic, Religion, and Science." The stress here
ems much too "historicist" for the author's present prefer-
ces. Rather than thinking of magic, religion, and science as
ree distinctly successive *stages* in the world's history, the
thor would now use a mode of analysis that dealt with all
ree as aspects of motivation "forever born anew" in the
sources of language as such.

*   *   *

The topics of the book might be summed up thus: (Part I)
ow meanings take form; (Part II) Resources and embar-
ssments to do with the modification of meanings, once they
ve taken form; (Part III) Ideal New Order, as conceptual
sis for analysis of communicative problems and procedures,
d as corrected by the principle of *recalcitrance*, that gives
e to many unexpected developments, when any ideal pur-
se is translated into its organizational equivalents.

Each of the three sections is preceded by a more detailed
tement of contents.

K. B.

Los Altos, California
    April, 1953

PART I

ON INTERPRETATION

ON INTERPRETATION

w an "orientation" (or general view of reality) takes form.
w such a system of interpretation, by its very scope and
roughness, interferes with its own revision. Why terms
"escape," "scapegoat mechanism," "pleasure principle,"
"rationalization" should be used skeptically and grudg-
ly. (As we might state the case now: An overreliance upon
h terms keeps us from appreciating the positive virtues of
iven communicative structure in its internality.) How a
iety's ways of life affect its modes of thinking, by giving
to partial perspectives or "occupational psychoses" that
, by the same token, "trained incapacities." How complexity
ur contemporary ways of life has greatly increased the per-
tage of the problematical *in the terminology of motives.*
w this condition affects the nature of communication,
h scientific and artistic. The present overriding importance
the "technological psychosis" that has developed out of
gic and religion.

CHAPTER ONE

ORIENTATION

All Living Things Are Critics

W E MAY BEGIN by noting the fact that all living organisms interpret many of the signs about them. A trout, having snatched at a hook but having had the good luck to escape with a rip in his jaw, may even show by his wiliness thereafter that he can revise his critical appraisals. His experience has led him to form a new judgment, which we should verbalize as a nicer discrimination between food and bait. A different kind of bait may outwit him, if it lacks the appearances by which he happens to distinguish "jaw-ripping food." And perhaps he passes up many a morsel of genuine food simply because it happens to have the characters which he, as the result of his informing experience, has learned to take as the sign of bait. I do not mean to imply that the sullen fish has thought all this out. I mean simply that in his altered response, for a greater or lesser period following the hook-episode, he manifests the changed behavior that goes with a new meaning, he has a more educated way of reading the signs. It does not matter how conscious or unconscious one chooses to imagine this critical step—we need only note here the outward manifestation of a revised judgment.

Our great advantage over this sophisticated trout would seem to be that we can greatly extend the scope of the critical process. Man can be methodical in his attempts to decide what the difference between bait and food might be. Unfortunately, as Thorstein Veblen has pointed out, invention is the mother of necessity: the very power of criticism has enabled man to build up cultural structures so complex that still greater powers of criticism are needed before he can distinguish between the food-processes and bait-processes concealed beneath his cultural tangles. His greater critical capacity has increased not only the range of his solutions, but also the range of his problems. Orientation can go wrong. Consider, for instance, what conquest over the environment we have attained through our powers of abstraction, of generalization; and then consider the stupid national or racial wars which have been fought precisely because these abstractions were mistaken for realities. No slight critical ability is required for one to hate as his deepest enemy a people thousands of miles away. When criticism can do so much for us, it may have got us just to the point where we greatly require still better criticism. Though all organisms are critics in the sense that they interpret the signs about them, the experimental, speculative technique made available by speech would seem to single out the human species as the only one possessing an equipment for going beyond the criticism of experience to a criticism of criticism. We not only interpret the character of events (manifesting in our responses all the gradations of fear, apprehension, misgiving, expectation, assurance for which there are rough behavioristic counterparts in animals)—we may also interpret our interpretations.

Pavlov's dog had acquired a meaning for bells when conditioned to salivate at the sound of one. Other experiments have shown that such meanings can be made still more accurate: chickens can be taught that only one specific pitch is a food-signal, and they will allow bells of other pitches to ring unheeded. But people never tremble enough at the thought of how flimsy such interpreting of characters is. If one rings the bell next time, not to feed the chickens, but to assemble them for chopping off their heads, they come faithfully running, on the strength of the character which a ringing bell possesses for them. Chickens not so well educated would have acted more wisely. Thus it will be seen that the devices by which we arrive at a correct orientation may be quite the same as those involved in an incorrect one. We can only say that a given objective event derives its character for us from past experiences having to do with like or related events. A ringing bell is in itself as meaningless as an undifferentiated portion of the air we are breathing. It takes on character, meaning, significance (dinner bell or door bell) in accordance with the contexts in which we experience it. A great deal of such character can be imparted to events by purely verbal means, as when we label a bottle "Poison" or when Marxians explain a man's unemployment for him by attributing it to financial crises inherent in the nature of capitalism. The words themselves will likewise have derived their meanings out of past contexts.

Veblen's Concept of "Trained Incapacity"

Veblen had a concept of "trained incapacity" which seems especially relevant to the question of right and wrong orientation. By trained incapacity he meant that state of affairs whereby one's very abilities can function as blindnesses. If we had conditioned chickens to interpret the sound of a bell as a food-signal, and if we now rang the bell to assemble them for punishment, their training would work against them. With their past education to guide them, they would respond in a way which would defeat their own interests. Or again: insofar as our sophisticated trout avoided food of a certain shape or color because the bait that nearly hooked him happened to be of this description, his inadequate interpretation could be called the result of a trained incapacity. Veblen generally restricts the concept to the case of business men who, through long training in competitive finance, have so built their scheme of orientation about this kind of effort and ambition that they cannot see serious possibilities in any other system of production and distribution.

The concept of trained incapacity has the great advantage of avoiding the contemporary tendency to discuss matters of orientation by reference to "avoidance" and "escape." Properly used, the idea of escape should present no difficulties. It is quite normal and natural that people should desire to avoid an unsatisfactory situation and should try any means at their disposal to do so. But the term "escape" has had a more restricted usage. Whereas it properly applies to *all* men, there was an attempt to restrict its application to *some* men. As so restricted, it suggested that the people to whom it was applied tended to orientate themselves in a totally different way from the people to whom it was not applied, the former always trying to escape from life or avoid realities, while the latter faced realities. There may be such a distinction. At least, there are many critics who avoided telling us precisely what they meant by life, avoidance, and facing reality. In this way, through escaping from the difficulties of their critical problem, they were free to accuse many writers and thinkers of escape. In the end, the term came to be applied loosely, in literary criticism especially, to designate any writer or reader whose interests and aims did not closely coincide with those of the critic. While apparently defining a *trait of the person referred to*, the term hardly did more than convey the *attitude of the person making the reference*. It looked objective, as though the critic were saying, "X is doing so-and-so"; but too often it became merely a strategic way of saying, "I personally don't like what X is doing."

Or, otherwise stated: There were grave social dissatisfactions resented by poets; the poets symbolized their resentment in many ways; and any kind of symbolization that did not suit the critic's particular preferences was called an escape. The term thus tended to beg the question, as it apparently solved the very issue which should have been the subject of discussion. One could dismiss the account of a voyage into the rigors of Labrador as mere escape—or one could say that we are here as "escapists" from such rigors as those of Labrador. Accordingly, in its restricted sense the term seems worse than worthless as a device for clarifying the relationship between correct and faulty orientation. As it properly applies to *all* men, one cannot very well confine its application to *some* men without forever covertly drawing upon the correctives of private judgment. Hence we are relieved to think that Veblen's concept of trained incapacity may prove the restricted use of "escape" to be as superfluous as it is ambiguous. The revised account would run as follows:

Training, Means Selecting, and Escape

Whenever there is an unsatisfactory situation, men will naturally desire to avoid it. In a complex social structure, many interpretations and ways of avoidance are possible; and some of them are likely to be much more serviceable than others. Again; not all ways are equally practicable to all people. A school of disgruntled artists could migrate to Tahiti, but a whole nation couldn't. Many could "drown their sorrows in work," but the unemployed couldn't. And so on, *ad lib*. One's ideas of relationship obviously have a great deal to do with the selection of means under such circumstances. Savages could make fires by considering dry wood and friction as appropriate linkages in the process of fire-making. The serviceability of their orientation is less apparent when, because their Christian missionary and doctor wore a rain coat during storms, they linked rain coats with rainy weather, and accordingly begged him to don the rain coat as a medicine against drought. Irrigation would have been a more effective means, yet their attempts to coerce the weather by homeopathic magic were not "escapist" in the restricted sense. They were a faulty selection of means due to a faulty theory of causal relationships.

The problems of existence do not have one fixed, unchanging character, like the label on a bottle. They are open to many interpretations—and these interpretations in turn influence our selection of means. Hence the place of "trained incapacity" in the matter of means-selecting. One adopts measures in keeping with his past training—and the very soundness of this training may lead him to adopt the wrong measures. People may be unfitted by being fit in an unfit fitness. Thus: If the chickens, by their scheme of orientation, respond to the ringing of a bell as a food-sign, and if the experimenter has this time changed the rules, so that the bell is in reality a precursor of punishment, we need not introduce the notion of an escape mechanism to explain their "illogical" conduct as they come running in answer to the bell. We need not say that they have refused to face reality. We need only note—as seems experimentally verifiable—that their past training has caused them to misjudge their present situation. Their training has become an incapacity.

We thus have orientation discussible as either training or incapacity, depending upon its outcome in correct or faulty means-selecting. And our own judgments as to the adequacy of the means selected in any given instance might depend upon our particular sense of the appropriate. If a book pictured escape to Tahiti, for instance, we might object because we felt that this method of escape was too restricted, that writers should symbolize a means of escape (such as organized political revolt) which would be more serviceable to more people. Or we could praise this same book on the grounds that it symbolized in one set of imagery an attitude of dissatisfaction with our institutions, and we believed that such an attitude should be fostered. By the first orientation, the book would be an instance of faulty means-selecting; by the second, it would fall into the category of adequate means-selecting.

Closely allied to the misuse of the escape concept is the

notion of an especial "scapegoat mechanism," with its subsidiary term, "rationalization." It is doubtful whether either of these terms, when used disparagingly to designate some particular erroneous process, is critically defensible, though their great service in securing allies for one's position is unquestionable. Only by the acme of good taste can we distinguish our own wise selection of means from the scapegoat devices of the ignorant—and much deep sympathy is required to distinguish our reasoning from another's rationalizing. One may simply note in all orientation the process of linkage (involving certain linkages which, because we do not accept them as valid, we call scapegoat). Or one may note that, as people tend to round out their orientations verbally, we sometimes show our approval of their verbalizations by the term "reasoning" and disapproval by the term "rationalizing." Thus, these words also serve as question-begging words. Their high emotive value endangers their usefulness for criticism. Accordingly, if the question of orientation can be discussed without them, there is less likelihood of confusion. And I believe that they can be proved superfluous.

The Pavlov, Watson, and Gestalt Experiments in Meaning

The basic experiments in illustration of orientation by linkage are now classic, but we may restate them briefly. First, we have the work of Pavlov, who gave the vague associationist doctrines of speculative psychology a precise empirical grounding by his experimental establishment of the conditioned reflex. By ringing bells when feeding dogs, he conditioned the dogs to salivate at the sound of bells as they might at the smell of food. Watson, repeating similar experiments, noted the "transference" aspect of such conditioning. Having found that the violent striking of an iron bar produced fear in an infant, he noted that he could give a "fear" character to some hitherto neutral object, such as a rabbit, by placing it before the child each time the iron bar was struck; he next demonstrated that this conditioned fear of the rabbit was transferred with varying degrees of intensity to other things having similar properties (such as fur coats or cotton blankets). The Gestalt experiments established the fact that character could also be derived from relationships. A large receptacle *a*, habitually containing food, was set beside a smaller one *b* that was habitually empty. When the animals had grown accustomed to seeking food only in *a* (when *a*'s character as food-container and *b*'s character as non-food-container had been established), receptacle *a* was removed, *b* was put in its place, and a new and correspondingly smaller receptacle *c* was put in the former place of *b*. In size and position, *c* was to *b* as *b* had been to *a*. It was found that, although *b* was formerly neglected as a non-food character, the animals now went to it for food. This would appear to indicate that its character as a food-container was determined by its membership in a larger context. The distinguishing characteristic, in other words, is not an absolute, but a relationship to other characteristics, quite as one may recognize the North Star, not in itself, but by the pointers of Ursa Major.

Incidentally, though the schools of behaviorism and Gestalt have sometimes considered each other as antithetical, there seems to be no fundamental difference at this point between the "absolute" conditioning noted by the behaviorists and the conditioning to relationships, or "wholes," noted by the Gestalt experimenters. Even a so-called "single" sign (such as a specific pitch, or color, or form) is in reality a complex of events, interpreted by the senses as a unit. Such a unit as the ringing of a bell, for instance, can be subdivided by the physicist into a multitude of component vibrations individually different from the whole in much the same way as the Gestalt experimenters can subdivide an *ab* relationship into an object *a* and object *b* which, when isolated from each other, fail to have "fractions" of the meaning they have when presented together (as the letters *t, h,* and *e* are not fractions of their combination, *the*). A ringing bell is a multiplicity of events interpreted as one thing precisely as the relative position of two objects may be interpreted as one thing. Either of these "one things" can be subdivided into smaller components if one introduces a different "point of view." And the subdivisions will not suggest the "meaning" suggested by the whole. To use the Gestalt terminology: the meaning of the bell's individual vibrations is not "additive," not obtained as a sum of its parts but as a single totality, configuration, Gestalt. When one learns that water pours, not from a pitcher, but from its mouth, is this a Pavlov-Watson kind of conditioning, or the perception of a larger whole (a Gestalt), inasmuch as we determine what is the mouth of a pitcher by our perception of the pitcher as a whole?

In any case, as regards either the Watsonian transference or the Gestalt configuration, we must note that some judgment as to *likeness* is involved, and that likeness itself is not an absolute. A salad containing typhoid germs and a salad free of them may be wholly alike as regards gastronomic comparisons—or a good egg and a bad one may be wholly alike as regards their freedom from typhoid germs. A red square is like a green square when considerations of shape are uppermost, but considerations of color make a red square like a red circle. In the complexities of social experience, where the recurrence of "like" situations is always accompanied by the introduction of new factors, one's total orientation may greatly influence one's judgment of likeness. A good Catholic may feel that priests and guides are alike; a good Marxian may feel that priests and deceivers are alike. And since much of our means-selecting is done on the basis of comparisons (as when the man chose to sit on the chair with the tack because it looked like a chair without a tack), we see how orientation, means-selecting and "trained incapacity" become intermingled.

In a general way, we might say that events take character by a "linkage of outstanding with outstanding" (as the outstanding sound of the bell, in linkage with the outstanding experience of the food, imparted to the bell a food-character for Pavlov's dogs). The accumulation and interworking of such characters is an orientation. It forms the basis of *expectancy*—for character telescopes the past, present, and future. A sign, which is here now, may have got a significance out of the past that makes it a promise of the future. Orientation is thus a bundle of judgments as to how things were, how they are, and how they may be. The act of response, as implicated in the character which an event has for us, shows clearly the integral relationship between our metaphysics and our conduct. For in a statement as to how the world is, we have implicit judgments not only as to how the world may become but also as to what means we should employ to make it so.

The Scapegoat as an Error in Interpretation

Let us test the above statement of the case by considering a typical situation in which the "scapegoat" concept is often used by contemporary critics but may, by our terminology, be omitted. First, we have noted that the linkage of outstanding with outstanding is a fluctuant matter. With the dogs, the outstanding sound of the bell became linked with the outstanding interest in food. But when we turn to consider the outstanding economic misery of the Poor Whites in the South, with what other outstanding factor may we expect this to be linked? Now, by torturing rats under scientific conditions, savants have established it that the rats, though bewildered and not knowing how to escape, *do something with reference to the direction of the disturbing agency*. Thus, we may expect the Poor Whites likewise to do something in the direction of the disturbing agency.

But what is the disturbing agency? In the case of the rats, we may say that it was either the electric shock or the experimenter who applied the electric shock. The conditions of the experiment, however, do not enable the rat to perceive the experimenter's part in the enterprise at all. It is the *electric shock* itself which is taken as the disturbing agency, and the rat accordingly frames its conduct with reference to the location of this current.

Applying the analogy to our human victims: There is a condition of intense economic competition. There also happens to be an outstanding way of differentiating some competitors from others—the distinction by color. What, then, is the "direction" from which the misery of the Whites is coming? An interpretation of an economic structure is not very "outstanding" in comparison with a simple perception of a difference in color. Hence the ominous orientation: the Negroes being the rabbit that is presented as the iron bar is violently struck, they take on the menacing quality of the bar. And since orientation is a reading from "what is" to "what may be," the Poor Whites adopt intimidation by lynching as the adequate solution of their problem.

That this is a case of faulty means-selecting, we must agree with a shiver. But there is no evidence of an evasive process here distinguishable in its mental functioning from some non-scapegoat or realistic way of response. In this region, the outstanding color distinction could lead the response to follow along the line of color distinction, especially since the troubles are social and the color distinction has strong social counterparts. At other times, in other places, as in the contemporary distress in Germany, the linkage has followed theological or racial lines. But to call it scapegoat when we mean by the term some special way of functioning not common to all men would be like designating as scapegoat the food-bell linkage of Pavlov's dogs, the bar-rabbit-furriness linkage of Watson's infants, or the configuration-food link age of the Gestalt experiment.

All that can reasonably be said is that, as judged by a different scheme of orientation, from a different point of view a particular linkage is a deceptive one, making for faulty means-selecting. Those who call the attack upon the Negroe scapegoat, for instance, and mean thereby a kind of response from which they themselves are immune in their wiser moments, are simply approaching the question from a different orientation. This different orientation would entail a different way of linkage: It would link the outstanding economic distress with an outstanding defect in the economic system itself. A still wider historical perspective might conceivably provide a point of view from which the economic linkage also would seem scapegoat, itself being based upon too obvious a kind of association, just as was the approach to the issue through a largely irrelevant distinction in color.

As for the scapegoat mechanism in its purest form, the use of a sacrificial receptacle for the ritual unburdening of one's sins, here also we can avoid the hypothetical introduction of a separate mental process. The magical schema of cause and effect that generally went with the use of the scapegoat gave prominence to certain sins and suggested an appropriate homeopathic technique for castigating them. Insofar as we have developed a different orientation as to the nature of causes and effects, conduct based upon the earlier theory may seem inadequate. In some respects, however, we must remember that the technique of purification magnificently met the pragmatic tests of success. It was, for instance, quite efficacious in unburdening a people of their sins. All that was needed was a formula and ritual whereby these sins could be transferred to the back of an animal, the animal was then ferociously beaten or slain—and the feeling of relief was apparent to all.

16

ORIENTATION

A theory that sins are transferable may not seem to us as justifiable as a theory that diseases are transferable—and it is particularly when the savages attempted to exorcise plague by the same substitution of goats for people that we tend to explain their conduct by a special process. Faulty means-selecting, on the basis of an inadequate orientation, would seem enough to account for everything. The savage's very skill in magic (as a generally "successful" technique for making the sun shine, causing the rain to fall, insuring the return of summer and the fertility of women, and promoting co-operative responses among the tribe) would naturally blind him to the limitations of his method. The so-called scapegoat mechanism is merely an instance of his trained incapacity.

Connection between Rationalization and Orientation

The term rationalization, as distinct from reasoning, seems to have come from psycho-analysis. As soon as the Freudians had developed their special terminology of motives, they felt the need of a term to characterize non-Freudian terminologies of motives. Thus, if a man who had been trained, implicitly and explicitly, in the psychological nomenclature fostered by the Church were to explain his actions by the use of this Church vocabulary, the Freudians signified a difference between his terms and their terms by calling theirs "analysis" and his "rationalization." In general, he was thought to be concealing something from himself, especially if he put forward a noble or self-sacrificing set of terms to account for an act of his which the Freudian orientation could explain by a directly selfish motive.

His real motives were, by the Freudians' interpretation, hidden behind a whole panoply of distinguished and pleasurable virtues. They did not have in mind the deliberate deceptions of the crook, who tries to sell a bad bond as a good one. They referred rather to a process of self-deception, a rationalized

17

account of his conduct whereby a man could shut his eyes to the harsh realities of the case. He offered a highly presentable account of his conduct, whereas the Freudians detected at the roots of it precisely such interests and motives as his version so appealingly transformed. Why this man should have been suspected of self-deception when using the only vocabulary of motives he had ever been taught, will remain one of the mysteries of psycho-analytic rationalization. It would seem somewhat like accusing a savage of self-deception who, never having heard of Pasteur, attempted to cure his diseases without the orientation of bacteriology.

The topic of rationalization has carried us beyond orientation proper into the *theory of motives*. The Pavlov-Watson-Gestalt kind of approach confined itself in general to a description of the conditions under which simple responses are formed and altered. But man attempts to extend the range of his responses and increase their accuracy by deliberately verbalizing the entire field of orientation and interpretation. Whereas all organisms are critical, man seeks by verbalization to perfect a methodology of criticism. Such verbalization involves the attempt to reason, hence involves a consideration of the motives which he assigns for his acts. Accordingly, we have advanced as follows: (*a*) There is a sense of relationships, developed by the contingencies of experience; (*b*) this sense of relationships is our orientation; (*c*) our orientation largely involves matters of expectancy, and affects our choice of means with reference to the future; (*d*) in the human sphere, the subject of expectancy and the judgment as to what is proper in conduct is largely bound up with the subject of motives, for if we know *why* people do as they do, we feel that we know *what* to expect of them and of ourselves, and we shape our decisions and judgments and policies to take such expectancies into account.

CHAPTER TWO

MOTIVES

Motives Are Subdivisions in a Larger Frame of Meanings

SUPPOSE that I am a psycho-analyst who observes that *A* adopts an extremely ill-tempered attitude towards *B*. Suppose further that *A* is well versed in the vocabulary of virtue, old style, his resentment of *B* invariably taking the form of high moral indignation. *A* says that *B* has done some very mean things. None of these things, *A* assures me, has any connection with him personally, but it does make him impatient to see such things getting by. *B*'s conduct does not directly concern him at all, except that he cannot tolerate the sight of so despicable a fellow. *B* mistreats his wife and children; he has been involved in some shady financial transaction; he lies to his friends, as witness such-and-such anecdote. *A* dislikes *B* so much that he even dreams of him. For instance, *A* dreamed that all the clerks at the office banded together and asked that so unpleasant a character be dismissed. Ah!—as psycho-analyst I grow alert at this last detail. On further questioning I learn that *B* shows signs of becoming a formidable rival for *A*'s position. As psycho-analyst I am now at rest: I have found the real motive for *A*'s moral indignation, his fear of *B*'s enterprise—and *A*'s account, as he presented it, is put down by me as pure rationalization.

The case might look bad for anyone who would doubt the psycho-analyst's interpretation of motive here as contrasted with *A*'s. *A* explains the entire matter in the terms of moral indignation, of purely objective or disinterested judgments— and the details of the dream would be relegated to the sphere of the meaningless. The psycho-analyst would take the office rivalry as itself indicative, and the dream as almost conclusive, particularly if there were other dreams manifesting a similar pattern. (Note, incidentally, that the detection of a similarity in pattern would itself require the psycho-analytic theory of symbols. The dreams would not be alike in themselves. They would show great variety, and a framework of interpretation would be needed to disclose a common theme among them. Particularly important, in this respect, are the theories of transference according to which B might be symbolized by something associated with him, as his hat, his desk, a fast runner having some mannerism of B's, etc.) In cases where we ourselves are not involved, we have become so accustomed in a general way to the psycho-analytic theories of motivation that any other may seem self-deceptive to us. It is good, therefore, to remember that there are various theories of psycho-analytic interpretation, in violent disagreement with one another. Further, the scorn of the Marxians, with their brand of economic psycho-analysis, is evidence enough that the sexual rationalizations and individualistic neuroses of the Freudians can be in turn interpreted as a retreat or escape from the economic facts and the class struggle which are "really" at the heart of our motives. Such shifts in orientation (each with a different theory of motives and a different theory of self-deception to go with it) suggest that one school's reason is another school's rationalization.

Suppose our hypothetical A bred to a pre-Freudian terminology of motives. In the society in which he was raised, there were prescribed and proscribed rules of conduct, and a terminology of motives to go with them. He was conditioned not only as regards what he should and should not do, but also as regards the reasons for his acts. When introspecting to find the explanation for his attitudes, he would naturally employ the verbalizations of his group—for what are his language and thought if not a socialized product? To discover in oneself the motives accepted by one's group is much the same thing as to use the language of one's group; indeed, is not the given terminology of motives but a subsidiary aspect of the communicative medium in general? There is no pleasure principle involved here, as distinct from a reality principle. To explain one's conduct by the vocabulary of motives current among one's group is about is self-deceptive as giving the area of a field in the accepted terms of measurement. One is simply interpreting with the only vocabulary he knows. One is stating his orientation, which involves a vocabulary of ought and ought-not, with attendant vocabulary of praiseworthy and blameworthy.

Of course, if the conditions of living have undergone radical changes since the time when the scheme of duties and virtues was crystallized, the serviceability of the orientation may be impaired. Our duties may not serve their purposes so well as they once did. Thus we may no longer be sure of our duties, with the result that we may cease to be sure of our motives. We may then be more open to a new theory of motivations than we should be at a time when the ideas of duty were more accurately adjusted to the situation.

The Pleasure Principle in Orientation

In one sense, every orientation involves a pleasure principle, but not as something opposed to a reality principle. We characterize the signs of experience mainly with reference to pleasant and unpleasant expectancies. An orientation is a schema of serviceability. And as for the man who explained his conduct by the "best motives," we must recognize that moral goodness is usually linked with the serviceable. There is no need for trying now to trace all the elaborate network whereby the "good" and the "useful" become linked. We may note, however, that many of the highest virtues in a given society are such that, if they existed in all other people (though not necessarily in oneself) they would tend to make the sort of world in which one could be quite comfortable.

Such virtues are: industriousness, ability, frankness, kindness, helpfulness, generosity, cheerfulness, forgiveness — the "peaceful" virtues. We should love to have them all about us, hence they enjoy a certain categorical prestige with us; they seem desirable and admirable. Thus, we try to cultivate them in ourselves as well. Such a state of affairs is further re-enforced by the fact that it really does become useful to the individual to possess these qualities, partially at least, since they earn him the goodwill of his group, and Bentham has called goodwill the "promise of free service." In any case, we have enough here to suggest why one should naturally use morally serviceable words as supposedly technical terms for describing his mental processes. They would gain prominence in the environment—and one would simply be using the favored scheme of orientation in applying them to his own conduct.

Otherwise put: the signs of experience are orientated with reference to tests of service and disservice (benefit and danger). If, accordingly, the words that describe conduct and thought incline towards the eulogistic when referring to our enemies, this fact need not be explained by the workings of a pleasure principle as distinct from a reality principle, for the very gauging of reality in the first place is by reference to the tests of pleasure. Reality is *what things will do to us or for us.* It is expectation of comfort or discomfort, prosperity or risk.

To be sure, the characters which we formulate under the guidance of the *all-embracing* pleasure principle may be wrong or insufficient (as when the chickens, conditioned to the bell as a food-sign, came running when they were being assembled for punishment). But it could hardly be called a pleasure principle, as distinct from a reality principle, which led them to persevere in their earlier orientation "despite the realities of the case." They were obeying the only realities which their scheme of orientation equipped them to recognize. And were they to be repeatedly punished when the bell rang, the pleasure principle itself would lead them to alter their reading of this sign.

If people persist longer than chickens in faulty orientation despite punishment, it is because the greater complexity of their problems, the vast network of mutually sustained values and judgments, makes it more difficult for them to perceive the nature of the re-orientation required, and to select their means accordingly. They are the victims of a trained incapacity, since the very authority of their earlier ways interferes with the adoption of new ones. And this difficulty is increased by the fact that, even when a practice is socially dangerous, it may be individually advantageous, as with the individuals who reap profits from a jingoism resulting in great misery to the group.

The Strategy of Motives

All in all: when we see a man explaining his conduct by the favored terms of his social code, we may say that he is making exactly the same kind of rationalization as when he, having lived among psycho-analysts, begins discussing his interests solely in terms of libido, repression, Œdipus complex, and the like. This, too, is a rationalization, a set of motives belonging to a specific orientation—and it is even a serviceable set, since the frankness of those who express their motives thus humbly procures them the goodwill of persons who dislike the vastly more pretentious vocabulary of moral motivation prevailing before the "era of hypocrisy" came to a close. [Did it?!—*Addendum, 1953.*]

Yet, what is any hypothesis, erected upon a set of brute facts, but a rationalization? And what is the difference between a metaphysician and a simpleton, as regards matters of orientation, if not that the metaphysician merely goes farther afield in scanning the number and complexity of the facts to be rationalized? The metaphysician, not content to rationalize as the wind blows, attempts to apply stricter tests of coherence or compatibility among beliefs. Common sense spares itself such rigor, but the distinction between the two is mainly a matter of pressure. The metaphysician presses harder—usually too hard. As for the logical arguments of science, they are based upon elaborate rationalizations which seem to go beyond mere self-deception and come close to downright hypocrisy. For note the purest *diplomacy* in the choice of motives which the scientific author offers as grounds for his beliefs, when he seeks to make his point of view as appealing to the reader as he can.

Jean Piaget has speculated upon the differences between one's private way of following his thoughts and the order in which he presents them to others. Consider all the logical modulations which one adds in the attempt to socialize his point of view: consider how spontaneously he puts forward, as his grounds for belief, many points and progressions of thought which had never even occurred to him until he sat down to the business of motivating his argument for his public. The very considerations which are almost wholly elided during the inception of one's thesis often constitute the main burden of his efforts, once he sets about it to recommend his beliefs to others. In externalizing or impersonalizing his thesis, he seeks to translate it into a system of motivations which will be cogent with his readers because these motivations belong to the general scientific *Weltanschauung* of his times. He resorts to this trickery so spontaneously that he may even learn to think "naturally" in the terms of such motivations.

Any explanation is an attempt at socialization, and socialization is a strategy; hence, in science as in introspection, the assigning of motives is a matter of *appeal*—and the distinction between a Pharisaic account of one's motives and a scientific motivation of one's argument may involve merely a difference in the scope of the orientation within which the tactics of appeal are framed.

Further Consideration of Motive as Part of a Larger Whole

To summarize: Insofar as schemes of motivation change, one may expect a change in the very motives which people assign to their actions. A motive is not some fixed thing, like a table, which one can go and look at. It is a term of interpretation, and being such it will naturally take its place within the framework of our *Weltanschauung* as a whole. The process of rationalization with which the psycho-analysts were dealing was not centered where they thought it was. It was centered in the entire scheme of judgments as to what people ought to do, how they proved themselves worthy, on what grounds they could expect good treatment, what good treatment was, etc. The few attributions of motive by which a man explained his conduct were but a fragmentary part of this larger orientation.

Metaphysicians at one time began their works with a *philosophia prima*, which had to do with the structure of the universe in general. From this they proceeded to deduce their laws of history and psychology, of the good and the beautiful, their anthropology. Subsequent thinkers, noting the influence of the anthropological in shaping our ideas as to the nature of the universe, reversed this way of proceeding from the cosmos to man. They began with the study of purely human processes, and interpreted our views of the universe as an outcome of our psychological, physiological, ethnological, or historical responses. Instead of beginning with the universe and coming down to man, they began with man and worked towards the universe.

The new method gave much more pliancy to metaphysical discussion, but it served to disguise the fact that, however anthropologically grounded a given *Weltanschauung* may be, the introspective psychology that goes with it (and that is to be seen as well in the terminology of common sense or in the discoveries made by self-questioning and soul-searching) will take its place as a mere component of the larger whole. As regards the established scheme of orientation in general, including its institutions, customs, ways of livelihood, the psychology of motives will be a mere *imperium in imperio*. In an orientation, or rationalization, wherein it was held that all the purposes of living were directed towards the welfare of future generations, a man who was being starved might very reasonably attribute his resentment, or sorrow, not to his desire for food, but to his fear that his future progeny was being endangered.

Our objection to the psycho-analytic emphasis is that it would tend to accuse a man of self-deceptive rationalization if diagnosing his hunger-motive as an altruistic motive, whereas any set of motives is but part of a larger implicit or explicit rationalization regarding human purpose as a whole. The original Freudian scheme of motives, for instance, was but subsidiary to a strong sexual-bourgeois orientation already established in Western society, plus some prevalent common-sense distinctions between imagination and reality. Its terminology shows great indebtedness to romantic and scientific attitudes local to the age.

When justice was a pivotal word in the *Weltanschauung*, who can say that people did not give up their lives to the cause of justice? Indeed, they could even rush forward in behalf of the word's mere *syllables*. And lest any reader think it extravagant of us to imagine a hypothetical civilization in which the good of future progeny might be taken as a basic motive of human conduct, we may consider a simple anti-thetical case, the case of China in the heyday of her ancestor-worship, when the psychological motives for acts, the reasons for certain kinds of sacrifice, effort, discipline, censure, and praise, were built about the upholding of the ancestral digni-ties. One did things for dead men, since his welfare was in-volved in theirs. We may call this a roundabout system of causality, a dubious theory as to the relation between ends and means, but it is no more self-deceptive than would be the explanations of a man today who motivated his conduct by saying that he wanted work, whereas he really wanted the money that the work would bring and the goods that the money would bring.

The error is exposed in its fullest parochialism when the contemporary epigones of psycho-analysis set about to inter-pret for us the hidden sexual motives at the roots of such in-tense and brilliant theologians as Saint Augustine. The entire motivation by which Augustine lived and wrote is categori-cally discarded in favor of a few sexual impulses which can, at best, be shown to have been an ingredient in his motivation.

By what authority can one call them the essence of his motivation? Non-sexual interests may be interpreted as the symbolization of sexual interests—but then again, sexual in-terests may themselves be considered as the symbolization of non-sexual interests. That is: since sexual matters are of great importance, a pattern of thinking may reveal itself noticeably in the patterns of sexual thinking. What, except the strong sexual orientation of our society, in contrast with the strong religious orientation of Saint Augustine's society, determines which shall be called the true motive and which the symbolic accretion?

And as regards the case of old China, we could not even call their ancestor-worship an out-and-out case of faulty means-selecting. Since it stimulated certain social practices which were very beneficial to the obtaining and stabilizing of goods, it stimulated socially useful attitudes; and by conformity with this code, one procured the rewards of goodwill, with its tangible and intangible promises of free service.

Perhaps I am here trying to state a point of view which needs the clarity and corroboration of a different wording. Accordingly, I quote from *Mencius on the Mind* by I. A. Richards, a passage which seems to be handling the same general issue:

"It is a possible suggestion that we perhaps Think and Feel and Will because we have for so long been talking as though we did and that if language and tradition professed a different set of psychic functions we might be conducting our minds otherwise. This is an uncomfortable suggestion, since it would give to a change in popular psychological theory more consequence than we usually allow; and—not earth's foundations only—but the mind's foundations would seem in danger of fleeing. . . . The relevance of all this to Mencius, and of Mencius to such speculations, is through the absence of a theory of cognition in his psychology. But cognition, the concept of knowledge, is the category that 'response' psychology has most made shaky. For a Behaviorist, 'knowledge how' obviously replaces 'knowledge of'; and even for those who are violently not Behaviorists, awareness, instead of being a precondition of action, is often treated as a minor consequence at a resistance point of instinctive drives that are largely unconscious. On the whole, Western psychology is much more ready than it was a generation ago to consider seriously an account of the mind that omitted to discuss cognition. And readier too, I fancy, to conceive that a different society and language might develop different psychical functions. . . . The absence, in Mencius and his fellows, of a *theoretical interest* is the most evident of these differences. But even in attempting to adumbrate such differences we are compelled to use language which implies common coördinates—'interest', for example. There must clearly be a limit to our scepticism as to the basic assumptions we are using in our comparisons. Our question can only be whether *some* of the modes we currently assume to be common to all minds are absent in the mind that Mencius treated of."

Perhaps Richards' adventurous speculation can be summed up as a suggestion that a generally accepted account as to how the mind works can make the mind work that way. It would seem to carry the matter beyond the mere question of motives as implied in our rationalizations. In defense of his hypothesis, he discloses striking differences between the ethical approach of the old Chinese philosopher Mencius, and the clinical approach of the contemporary scientist, to the problems of psychology. My own thesis seems a stodgy step indeed, as compared with the latitude of the possibilities which he considers. I am merely attempting to suggest that a terminology of motives is not evasive or self-deceptive, but is moulded to fit our general orientation as to purposes, instrumentalities, the "good life," etc.

Motives Are Shorthand Terms for Situations

What are our words for motive, then, if considered in the light of associational linkage, of stimulus and response? When it is realized that the experiences of actual life do not have the simplicity of the laboratory experiments, being rarely of the obvious dinner-bell sort but presenting very complex matters for interpretation, must we not expect to find some indication of this fact in our introspective or moralistic vocabularies of human motivation? The discovery of a law under simple conditions is not *per se* evidence that the law operates similarly under highly complex conditions. We may

be justified, however, in looking for evidence of its operatio
in some form, as it either becomes redirected or persis
vestigially.

Now, there is general agreement that, whatever the so-calle
phenomenon of consciousness may be, it occurs in situatio
marked by conflict. It thus ranges from the simple consciou
ness of deliberate choice, through an indecisive weighing o
all the facts and consequences, to deep conscientiousness
the scrupulous fear that some important aspect of the ca
has been slighted, and thence to the aggravated crises of co
science. A distinguishing feature of consciousness is likewi
a concern with motives, and a feeling that we must consid
the motives for our choices.

Would not such facts all converge to indicate that our i
trospective words for motives are rough, shorthand descri
tions for certain typical patterns of discrepant and conflicti
stimuli? If we say that we perform an act under the motiv
tion of duty, for instance, we generally use the term to in
cate a complex stimulus-situation wherein certain stim
calling for one kind of response are linked with certain sti
uli calling for another kind of response. We act out of du
as against love when we finally respond in the way whi
gives us less immediate satisfaction (we do not throw up o
job and elope) though promising more of the eventual sat
factions that may come of retaining the goodwill of ir
parent or censorious neighbors. Linkages involving acqui
cent response to stimuli having a pleasure-character (t
thought of the elopement) are brought into conflict wi
linkages involving acquiescent response to stimuli havin
displeasure-character ("what will people say?")—and if o
finally decides to remain, on looking into his motives he w
find that he has acted out of duty. In such a case, duty w
be nothing other than his recognition of a particular patt
of conflict among his stimuli, a pattern recurrent frequen

ough in the experiences of his group for him to have at his
mmand a special word for it.

Or again: A man informs us that he "glanced back in sus-
cion." Thus, suspicion was his motivation. But suspicion
a word for designating a complex set of signs, meanings, or
muli not wholly in consonance with one another. The con-
ction is somewhat as follows: danger-signs ("there is some-
ing ominous about that fellow"); reassurance-signs ("but
body would try to rob me here"); social-signs ("I don't
nt to make a fool of myself if there is nothing wrong, but
ould just glance back along the pavement as though I had
opped something"), etc. By his word "suspicion" he was
ferring to the situation itself—and he would invariably
onounce himself motivated by suspicion whenever a simi-
pattern of stimuli recurred. Incidentally, since we charac-
ize a situation with reference to our general scheme of
eanings, it is clear how motives, as shorthand words for
uations, are assigned with reference to our orientation in
neral. And we may understand why *The Daily Worker* is
ever outraging the bourgeoisie by attributing such awful
otives to their politicians.

If our words for motive are in reality words for situation,
: may even observe perhaps the "words" of motivation in a
g—for we may note in his typical postures his recognition of
verse situational patterns. There is one posture for greeting
master, another when a stranger passes along the road, an-
er when threatened with a beating, a fourth when told to
home, a fifth when he has come upon a fresh scent, etc. He
s, let us say, a vocabulary of twenty or thirty typical, or re-
rrent situations, and we soon learn to recognize his utterance
them. A sleek young terrier in the country has a vocabulary
motives considerably different from that of a fat, coddled,
erfed poodle in the city, whose only adventures are con-
ed to candy and a constitutional on hard pavements.

This account of motives would go far to explain wh[y] many rival theories of motivation have arisen with incr[eas]ing frequency during recent centuries, to gain currency [for] a time among one group of specialists or one class of peo[ple] We have had people's conduct explained by an endless var[iety] of theories: ethnological, geographical, sociological, phy[sio]logical, historical, endocrinological, economic, anatom[ical] mystical, pathological, and so on. A particular form of [art] even came to flourish—the psychological or scientific nov[el] which devoted special attention to telling us *why* people [did] things, presumably because motivation had become a ma[tter] of extreme doubtfulness. Such art gave information on [the] subject of conduct, its style becoming less and less poeti[c or] ingratiating, and more and more trimmed to the need[s of] exposition and explanation.

In great eras of drama, the audiences *know* why charac[ters] act as they do. The characters themselves may be in a q[uan]dary, but the audience has merely to see them act and [hear] them talk, and the motives are taken for granted. But [we] even become muddled as to the motives in these ea[rly] dramas—hence our development of an art-form with mot[iva]tion as its specific subject-matter. This fact in itself sh[ould] indicate our growing instability; for in highly stable eras[,] recurrent patterns of life are highly stabilized, hence [the] combinations of complex stimuli become standardized, he[nce] the matter of motives is settled. At such times of cult[ural] integration a man may *lie* about his motives, but the su[spi]cion that he might not know them himself is unthink[able].

By our interpretation such an attitude is justified, sinc[e his] statement of his motives would simply name what partic[ular] pattern or combination of incompatible stimuli his situa[tion] appeared to contain. But in an age of marked instabilit[y,] great and shifting contrasts, typical patterns of stimuli w[ill] be less likely to run through the group as a whole, or ev[en]

ge part of it. Many of its stimulus-combinations will thus
unnamed (at least as regards this deepest kind of naming:
tainty as to motive, and universalization of the terms for
signating motive). In such vicissitudinous times as ours,
wever, with the advances of technology straining against
 political, social, economic, æsthetic, moral orientations
ablished at a period when the needs of society were radi-
ly different, is it not to be expected that the entire matter
motivation would again become liquid?

Our nomadism, our vast reversals from year to year in
nomic status, our cataclysmic shifts in the organization of
 nation under war, prosperous peace, and depression, our
le diversification of occupational habits, our total blank-
s of expectancy as to how the world is going or where we
y fit into it all five years from now, the complete disap-
rance of the "like father like son" attitude except perhaps
our rural districts—all such factors make for the *individu-*
ation of one's typical, or recurrent, patterns of stimuli, as
inst their highly *socialized,* or *universalized* character dur-
 a period of relative stability. This state of affairs should
eal itself barometrically in the question of motives, as
oes.

Indeed, it is worth noticing on this score that the attack
on introspective psychology was particularly popular in
merica. America is precisely the place where, on looking
 one's head, one is least likely to find a vast store of
ular, stabilized, recurrent experiences imbedded there, ex-
t for a few simple groups of stimuli, not highly complex
ll, such as the lure of a new refrigerator, the fear of losing
's job, the distinction of smoking a certain brand of cigar-
, etc. Thus, it is precisely here that the introspective search
motives might reveal something dangerously like total
otiness. Might this not be precisely the "culture" on which
ehavioristic psychology could rise and take form, with its

theories that education is not a drawing forth of insight fr
a vast store of possiblities, but a mere pumping of experi
tial content into an almost empty vat?

Perhaps the work most thoroughly embodying the te
ency to discuss motives as situations is the *Integrative F
chology* of William Marston and his colleagues. They po
late as the fundamental drives of conduct, the nutrit
sexual, and procreative. Our social activities in all their v
ety are interpreted as satisfying these drives either dire
or indirectly. The drives have derivative aspects: the hun
drive can be converted into commercial ambition, the se
drive can be expressed as a concern for the welfare of soci
the procreative drive can be turned into art, etc. The f
motivations of "unit response" are: Compliance, Domina
Inducement, and Submission. Compliance is the respons
yielding, against our will, to a force considered super
(The prisoner in his prison complies.) Dominance is
response of forcing things to be as we would have them.
is seen in infancy, as the child resists the attempt to w
draw a rod from his grasp.) Inducement is accomplishm
by wheedling, as in salesmanship, advertising, publicity,
tery, petition. ("The well trained child learns, during e
infancy, that he must *dominate things*, and *induce hu
beings and animals*.") Submission is to Inducement v
Compliance is to Dominance. The happy lover does
comply to dominance, but submits to inducement. The
tomer submits to the salesman's inducements. ("It w
seem to us that all spontaneous, naïve, imitative behavio
the part of both animals and human beings is motivate
Submission. The older instinct theories usually included
tation as one of the primary instincts. Moreover it w
seem that all imitative behavior must contain an elemen
submissive motivation even though the behavior as a w
may be controlled by dominant or compliant motives.")

f course, the opportunity for a simple "unit response" is rare
1 most cases of judgment. As soon as we come to complex
tuations, involving conflict among the drives, their deriva-
ve activities, and the four typical responses, we find that our
ocabulary for motives and emotions seems to characterize
timulus-response situations as complex as those of the "moral
ithmetic" which Bentham yearned to establish. The authors
ntatively analyze hundreds of complex situations which
opular speech names subjectively in the vocabulary of moves. The work also offers a neurological explanation of con-
iousness as it arises out of these conflicts in response, due to
ie conflicting character of stimuli.

The additional consideration which I am stressing con-
rns the character of the stimuli themselves. Stimuli do not
ossess an *absolute* meaning. Even a set of signs indicating
e likelihood of death by torture has another meaning in
e orientation of a comfort-loving skeptic than it would for
e ascetic whose world-view promised eternal reward for
artyrdom. Any given situation derives its character from
e entire framework of interpretation by which we judge it.
nd differences in our ways of sizing up an objective situa-
on are expressed subjectively as differences in our assign-
ent of motive.

But the question of motive brings us to the subject of com-
unication, since motives are distinctly linguistic products.
e discern situational patterns by means of the particular vo-
oulary of the cultural group into which we are born. Our
nds, as linguistic products, are composed of concepts (ver-
lly molded) which select certain relationships as meaning-
. Other groups may select other relationships as mean-
gful. These relationships are not *realities*, they are *inter-
tations* of reality—hence different frameworks of inter-
tation will lead to different conclusions as to what reality is.
Some things happen *in spite of* others, some *because of*

others, and some *regardless of* others. If we knew everythir
we should probably eliminate the *in spite of* and the *regar
less of*—but all finite schemes of interpretation differ mair
in their ways of dividing up these three categories. The nat
ralist, for instance, may say that *A* was hurt in an accide
regardless of his wickedness—the super-naturalist might s
that the accident occurred *because of A*'s wickedness. Shi
of interpretation result from the different ways in which v
group events in the *because of*, *in spite of*, and *regardless
categories.

Such shifts of interpretation make for totally different p
tures of reality, since they focus the attention upon differe
orders of relationship. We learn to single out certain relatio
ships in accordance with the particular linguistic texture in
which we are born, though we may privately manipulate tl
linguistic texture to formulate still other relationships. Wh
we do so, we invent new terms, or apply our old vocabulary
new ways, attempting to socialize our position by so manip
lating the linguistic equipment of our group that our pa
ticular additions or alterations can be shown to fit into tl
old texture. We try to point out new relationships as mea
ingful—we interpret situations differently; in the subjecti
sphere, we invent new accounts of motive. Since both the o
and the new motives are linguistically constructed, and sin
language is a *communicative* medium, the present discussic
has taken us from orientation, through motivation, to cor
munication. And the remainder of this section will deal wit
communication.

CHAPTER THREE

OCCUPATIONAL PSYCHOSIS

The Nature of Interest

IT IS NOT HARD to imagine that if a grasshopper could speak he would be much more readily interested in what you had to tell him about "Birds That Eat Grasshoppers" than in a more scholarly and better presented talk on "Mating Habits of the Australian Auk." The factor of *interest* plays a large part in the business of communication. Even if one speaks very clearly and simply on a subject of great moment to himself, for instance, one is hardly communicating in the desired sense if his auditor does not care in the least what he is saying. A philosopher, if he has a toothache, is more likely to be interested in dentistry than in mathematical symbolism. Communication cannot be satisfactory unless the matter discussed bears in some notable respect upon the interests of the auditor. Without the assistance of this factor, the entire paraphernalia of appeal—comprehensiveness, conciseness, cogency, construction, pliancy, and all the rest *ad lib.*—are wasted. The dullest sentences, exchanged between young lovers or between employee and employer, may be vibrant, whereas the results of many years' effort and engrossment may seem insipid. We interest a man by dealing with his interests.

To say as much, however, is to realize that the matter is much subtler. The Negroes in America before the Civil War must have been very much interested in the question of slavery, yet I do not know of a single Negro spiritual in which the topic is specifically mentioned. Despite the grave economic issues besetting him, the modern working man still seems to be more interested in society drama and adventure fiction than in proletarian literature, the latter kind being consumed mostly by sympathetic reformers, clerks, and bankers temporarily at liberty. The mere fact that something is to a man's interests is no guaranty that he will be interested in it. It is tremendously to the people's interests that they should understand the causes of war—but it is very hard to get them interested in the subject. The discontented will be less easily interested in an analysis of their discontent than in lurid fiction and crude newspapers. A racketeer who would not care *why* he was a tough would be spellbound by a prize-fight. A salesman, sick of the day's work and determined to think no more of it until tomorrow, will go to a motion picture and watch in delight the building-up of some character with precisely the brass, the ingenuity, and the social life which are the ideals of his calling. In this sense, he is not getting away from the matters of salesmanship at all, for he is watching the kind of character that exemplifies the ideals of his trade: the ideal fears, ideal hopes, and ideal methods that equip one for the business of selling.

I believe that John Dewey's concept of "occupational psychosis" best characterizes this secondary aspect of interest. Roughly, the term corresponds to the Marxian doctrine that a society's environment in the historical sense is synonymous with the society's methods of production. Professor Dewey suggests that a tribe's ways of gaining sustenance promote certain specific patterns of thought which, since thought is an aspect of action, assist the tribe in its productive and distributive operations. This special emphasis, arising in response to the economic pattern, he calls the tribe's occupational psychosis. Once this psychosis is established by the authority of the food-getting patterns (which are certainly primary as regards problems of existence) it is carried over into other aspects of the tribal culture.

Thus, a tribe which lives by the hunt may be expected to

reveal a corresponding hunt pattern in its marriage rites, where the relation between man and woman may show a marked similarity to the relationship between huntsman and quarry. The woman will be ritually *seized*. Also, the highly problematical nature of hunting, its continual stressing of the sudden, or unexpected, might instigate a cultural emphasis upon the *new*—and he cites examples of amnesty among warring Australian tribes that they may hear one another's newest songs. In stressing certain patterns of thought serviceable to the tribal occupations, the psychosis will come to have a kind of creative character which, when turned into other channels of action or imagery, will shape them analogously to the patterns of work. As further corroboration of this, we might note the contrasting emphasis upon the traditional, in the art and thought of agrarian cultures, which would naturally stress the periodically recurrent, the lore of the seasons, the astronomical fixities, etc., as basic to their productive system. And today, our psychotic openness to fads, the great cry for innovation engendered by competitive capitalism, could seem to be in keeping with the marked unstableness of our economic and social expectancies.

The artist deals largely with the occupational psychosis in its derivative aspects. He projects it into new realms of imagery. If a hunt psychosis leads to a prizing of the *new*, we may expect him to socialize his art by discovering all the possible devices by which he can suggest the experiencing of newness. Conversely, were he working in an agrarian psychosis, vowed to frame its productive schedule in pious conformity with the periodic movements of nature, he might well try to impress his public with the sound traditionalism of his contributions, as he kept alive for them a message that extended back through a mythical line of bards, to the bard that accompanied the founder of the tribe.

Even primitive societies, of course, do not have complete

occupational homogeneity. There are always at least some marks of a privileged class whose relation to the productive pattern is somewhat different from that of the tribe as a whole. But in a general way we might say that the artist works with the general tribal equipment by bringing outlying matter within the informing pattern of the occupational psychosis. He builds and manipulates the intellectual and imaginative superstructure which furthers the appropriate habit-patterns useful to his particular economic system. To equip themselves for their kinds of work, people develop emphases, discriminations, attitudes, etc. Special preferences, dislikes, fears, hopes, apprehensions, idealizations are brought to the fore. They are like little kegs of powder, and the artist seeks to light the fuses that will set them off. He is happiest when dealing with charged matter (that is, with the interests rising out of the occupational psychosis)—and insofar as his group is homogeneously charged, his work has the opportunity for universal appeal.

At the present time one can imagine various kinds of occupational classifications involving ways of livelihood different enough from one another to justify our search for corresponding differences in psychotic emphasis. These patterns of livelihood are not mutually exclusive; overlapping, they produce psychotic blends; yet a few outstanding occupational characteristics might be noted, with their probable psychotic parallels. (Incidentally, it might be well to recall that Professor Dewey does not use the word "psychosis" in the psychiatric sense; it applies simply to a *pronounced character* of the mind.)

Occupational Psychoses of the Present

There is the psychosis which might be variously called capitalist, monetary, individualist, *laissez-faire*, free market, private enterprise, and the like, the intensely competitive emphasis which has been gradually and imperceptibly disintegrating with the growth of corporations and monopolies (cartelization) and the corresponding growth of nepotism and seniority (rather than the stress upon the qualifications of a "live wire") as the basis of promotion among office-holders. Its psychotic force is probably best revealed in the professionalization of sports, and in the flourishing of success literature during the late-lamented New Era. The quota-system in salesmanship had its important place here, a device in the distributive scheme that corresponded with the belt or conveyor in the productive scheme—and, in keeping with the demands of both, "snap," "push," and "drive" became key virtues. Perhaps the subtlest, yet most effective, extension of this psychosis lay in the fact that, under its prodding, the earlier barter combination, thrift-and-small-income, crumbled before the newer purchase combination, waste-and-large-income. Great stress was placed upon the opportunity to get ahead, though as Veblen has pointed out, this might with as much justice have been discussed as the opportunity to fall behind. When no one but a savant with a mean streak in him could pause to notice such a possible rephrasing of the Faith, we may be justified in looking for the pressure of the psychotic.

There must be an agrarian psychosis as distinct from a metropolitan one, but today it is bastardized, or at least weakened, by its necessary acquiescence to the economic policies dictated by the great centers of population and finance. Taxation, interest, and the money crop have made impractical the barter mentality which once distinguished the agrarians; they are now simply the weakest, least effectual, most outlying members of the purchase economy.

There would seem to be an investor's or creditor's psychosis, as distinguished from the psychosis of the worker. It is not tied down to a concern with tangible, physical properties, manual or mechanical operations—but is a highly speculative occupation, dealing in such diaphanous things as forecasts, prospects, futures, such metaphysical bewilderments as valuation, and requiring a whole new astrology of graphs, statistics, indices, crop reports, and tables. No poet was ever so delicate and fanciful in his conception of the realities as those dreamers, those men of vision, whose imagination stems from the investor's psychosis. Here the superstructure of credit and interest is considered basic, quite as though one were to think of a transfer of goods as *incidental* and were to find soundness only in the paper on which the transaction was recorded. Actual physical properties are hardly more than a sign to be interpreted. A railroad is approached, not in terms of tracks, engines, roundhouses, repair plants, and working force, but through data as to its capital structure! There it lies, stretched over hundreds or even thousands of miles—yet it is not an *actuality*, but a *prospect*. Within the imagery of this psychosis, the world's problems of production, distribution, and consumption are naturally expected to be settled by going up in an elevator in a large city, shutting oneself and five or six of one's fellows away in a secret cabinet, and puzzling over some problems of belief (credit). Here, that deeply religious concept which once flourished as Providence does indeed seem to have been secularized, with all its spirituality intact, in strangely Ariel-like notions as to yield.

Often such people have been called materialists, but I can think of no charge more inaccurate here than that of materialism. If the proletarian psychosis in capitalist countries is to be as sharply divided as possible from this investor's psychosis, despite their common involvement in the competitive, I should suspect that the differences would reside precisely in the fact that the proletarians would be much more accurately materialistic in their aims and pleasures. For their imaginative patterns would arise from the direct *physical* aspects of our economic system. To them a yield would be a collection of definite, usable things. Lacking the spiritual joys of the financier, they could get little satisfaction out of cornering and hoarding promises (capital goods) and using these promises to corner and hoard more promises. Materialistically, they would have no understanding of promises. They would delight only in promises as redeemed in usable commodities.

If we may speak of a criminal psychosis, it would arise out of four principal groups. First, there are the *Lumpen*, the hoboes, the experts in receiving relief, the touch artists, etc. They are being improved now by the infusion of new blood, the technologically unemployed. There are the groups involved in organized political corruption: at its best we find here a somewhat puzzling morality based upon honest graft, systematized favoritism, reliability among the pack, conscientious fidelity to one's verbal bond (involving a contract too illegal for the risks of writing). It has given rise to a somewhat paradoxical use of the word "protection," as a way of designating immunity from interference by the police. There are the racketeers, who must develop fairly high cöoperative capacities, bolstered by a rigorous gang morality. In some ways this may be the most moral group of citizens we have, since their code is so clearly and directly shaped to meet the demands of their profession.

The fourth group arises from the gradual filtration of the cut-back system throughout legitimate business. It flowers in the high-handed tactics whereby the directors and officers of large corporations mulct their companies at the stockholders' and consumers' and workers' expense. If all these groups could be considered as one, there must be many millions of them contributing faithfully to a criminal psychosis, putting furtiveness, social cynicism, hatred of human betterment into the category of the psychotically needed.

PERMANENCE AND CHANGE
The Technological Psychosis

In and about all these, above them, beneath them, mainly responsible for their perplexities, is the technological psychosis. It is the one psychosis which is, perhaps, in its basic patterns, contributing a new principle to the world. It is at the center of our glories and our distress.

There seem to have been three fairly distinct rationalizations in human history: magic, religion, and science. Magic was the rationalization by which man got control over the primitive forces of nature. Though modern thinkers prefer to point out the errors in the magical theories of causation, it is obvious that magic did assist tremendously in schematizing man's ways of turning natural forces to his benefit.

Religion seems to be the rationalization which attempts to control the specifically *human* forces. As civilization became more complex, a highly delicate code of human coöperation was needed. Religious thought became the device in the mental sphere for ordering coöperative habits under such complex conditions.

We are now concerned with a third great rationalization, science, the attempt to control for our purposes the forces of technology, or machinery.

Its genius has been called experimentalism, the laboratory method, creative skepticism, organized doubt. It has an occupational morality all its own, though at present this is more forcefully revealed by its contribution to the break-down or cancellation of traditional moralities than by positive psychotic emphases. Though it is customarily traced back to the Copernican astronomy, Galilean physics, and the Baconian rationalization of the inductive method, the psychosis cannot be said to have fully blossomed until the time of the Utilitarian philosophers in England, the first country to feel the full shock of systematic technological development. The doctrine of use, as the prime mover of judgments, formally established the *secular* as the point of reference by which to consider questions of valuation. The transcendental accounts of moral origin, in accordance with which truth had been revealed by God to chosen representatives and thence transmitted through priestly ordination by the laying on of hands, now gave way to the notion that considerations of service or interest both *do* shape and *should* shape our religious, ethical, æsthetic, and even cosmological judgments.

Darwin was quite within the spirit of this psychosis when discussing the development of moral and intellectual traits as tools or weapons in the struggle for existence. Marx introduced the concept of coexistent moralities. Jeremy Bentham, in his *Book of Fallacies*, had patiently and caustically examined the devices in parliamentary debate whereby the utilitarian purposes of proposed measures were obscured behind the noblest concepts of moral grandeur. He had noted a striking difference between the thinking of the Ins and the Outs, as shifts in position changed their manipulation of the moral verities.

Marx broadened and deepened this classification by showing that these do not shift with the mere vicissitudes of political fortune, but tend to crystallize insofar as we get crystallized classes of Ins and Outs. He speculated upon the kind of psychosis that might distinguish such classes from each other; and like the Utilitarians, he tended to confuse the *is* and the *ought to be*, whereat we sometimes feel that class-consciousness is inevitable, and at other times feel that it must be coached. The difficulty here is probably the one we noted at the beginning of this section: the subtle distinction between *what is to a man's interests* and *what he is interested in*. Class morality may rise spontaneously, insofar as there are classes; but class-consciousness must be *taught* by accurate appeal to the class morality.

The position of Nietzsche in this genealogy of morals is remarkably complex. Whereas the other writers were essayists, he was a tragic poet. He was not interested simply in discussing the transvaluation of values, he wanted to *sing* of it, to give this great historical movement its prophetic, ritualistic accents. But since the poet is pious, and since the entire appeal of the pious is in the deep, unquestioned appropriateness of one's linkages, note the disastrous predicament with which he was concerned. He was questioning, down to the very last value, every pious linkage which man had derived from his cultural past. This nihilistic concern was his altar; accordingly he tried to surround it with all the symbolic devices appropriate to altars. These involved precisely the intensive use of linkages in the æsthetic category which he was corroding in the organically related ethical category. His magnificent equipment as an artist opened him constantly to the processes of piety; yet his sharply aphoristic intellect was turned upon the doubting of these processes.

The result is perhaps the fullest, most self-contradictory symbolization of the transition from the pre-technological to the technological psychosis which mankind will ever possess. We might call it the "pro-technological" attitude. Zarathustra, coming down to us from among the severities and strangenesses of lonely, snow-capped mountains, to hint of dangerous earthly and unearthly revels, and then piously to ritualize a kind of skepticism, of irreligious shrewdness, which is the very essence of the metropolis. No wonder that Thomas Mann, who acknowledges his debt to Nietzsche, uses much this same symbol, and for much the same ends, in his *Magic Mountain*. Nietzsche discredited some of his sharpest insights by extravagant statement—and he often appears as the prophet of the very jingoism which he, a *guter Europäer*, so consistently despised. But in the end the fertility of his work must be recognized.

OCCUPATIONAL PSYCHOSIS

Veblen is perhaps most responsible for bringing out the aspect of moral confusion now called the "cultural lag." In its simplest form, his doctrine is concerned with institutions which, developed as a way of adequately meeting past situations, became a menace insofar as the situation has changed. Naturally also, as long as the institutions survived, the ethical values that reënforced them would be upheld. It is easy to see how Veblen's concern with fossilized institutions fits with his concept of trained incapacity.

Such a problematical approach to questions of value seems clearly a part of the technological psychosis. And besides being substantiated by the documents of anthropology and ethnology, it is probably further stimulated by the occupational diversity that is part of this same technological framework. We have the doctor's point of view, as distinct from the lawyer's, the chemist's, the sandhog's, and the reporter's. Such interlocked diversification may be revealed psychotically in our emphasis upon intellectual tolerance, information-giving, works of popularization, outlines of knowledge—also perhaps in a kind of individualism which, if not the sort that we might expect from a pioneer psychosis wherein productive units were individualistically managed, is at least observable in the sense of departmentalism, intensive knowledge restricted to small groups.

Effects upon Literature

What effect do all such matters have upon the particular occupational psychosis that might go with the professions and trades of writing? For the present we may note three fairly distinct solutions. Some artists devoted themselves to emotionality, sexuality, adventure, excess, psychoses which men of all trades held more or less in common, since they were largely grounded in the occupational patterns of the human body itself. Others, insofar as writing was a profession with them, not an avocation, resorted to field work, historical and psychological research, human documents, and reliance upon the intensifying effect of issues temporarily made prominent by the press. In general, such tendencies led to the writer's cultivation of his marginal experiences inasmuch as they, by falling into other psychoses, are more likely to be widely communicative. One became adept at a kind of barometric response to the concerns of others. The type ranges from Broadway drama, through Hollywood, to simple reporting.

Paradoxically enough, perhaps the specifically writer's psychosis, as distinct from any other, is to be seen in *criticism*, though it is usually the critics who are plaguing the poets with the charge of specialization. To an extent they are justified in this, however, as the essayistic method of communication is most in keeping with the high value which the technological psychosis and its attendant phenomena have placed upon conceptualization and information-giving. Our communicative medium for purveying facts and making conceptual distinctions is in much better shape today than is the poetic medium, which aims to build its cogency, or appeal, out of stylistic ingratiation.

Though Dewey's conception of the occupational psychosis may serve admirably to indicate how imaginative superstructures rise above productive patterns, I do not believe that it could very well serve as the basis of critical discriminations. For still other psychoses can be readily imagined: Wherever one could note a distinction in ways of livelihood, one could reasonably look for a corresponding psychotic distinction, some special way of being interested in something or other.

Occupational Psychosis as Trained Incapacity

The reader may have noticed that one might manipulate Veblen's concept of trained incapacity quite like Dewey's occupational psychosis. By substituting Veblen's terms, we should see more clearly the *ambivalent* nature of an occupational pattern. Indeed, Dewey first proposed his term when objecting to the tendency among ethnologists to discuss savage thinking as a "failure" to obey the thought-patterns of the West. Dewey suggested that the emphasis should be reversed: the investigator should consider these thought-patterns as positive instrumentalities developed to assist the savage in his tasks. Seen from this point of view, the Western man may as well be described as failing to think like the savage. Dewey's concept contains implicitly the ambivalence which Veblen's contains explicitly.

Any performance is discussible either from the standpoint of what it *attains* or what it *misses*. Comprehensiveness can be discussed as superficiality, intensiveness as stricture, tolerance as uncertainty—and the poor *pedestrian* abilities of a fish are clearly explainable in terms of his excellence as a *swimmer*. A way of seeing is also a way of not seeing — a focus upon object *A* involves a neglect of object *B*. It is for this reason that we consider Dewey's and Veblen's terms as interchangeable. For our next topic, however, Veblen's explicitly ambivalent concept should be more serviceable. For we wish to discuss the state of the communicative medium (as affected by the "master psychosis," the technological)— and we want to consider it as though its *goods* and *bads* were obverse and reverse of the same coin. In other words, we want a term which helps us to observe in the medium of communication simultaneously both the defects of its qualities and the qualities of its defects.

Remembering the ideals of exposition, or information-giving, brought to the fore by the technological emphasis, we shall consider how this ideal has affected the use of *style* as a device for communicative purposes.

CHAPTER FOUR

STYLE

The Essence of Stylistic Appeal

IN ITS simplest manifestation, style is ingratiation. It is an attempt to gain favor by the hypnotic or suggestive process of "saying the right thing." Obviously, it is most effective when there is agreement as to what the right thing is. A plain-spoken people will distrust a man who, bred to different ways of statement, is overly polite and deferential with them, and tends to put his commands in the form of questions (saying "Would you like to do this?" when he means "Do this"). They may even suspect him of "sneakiness." He, conversely, may consider their blunt manner a bit boastful, even at times when they are almost consumed with humility. The ways by which the mannered speaker would ingratiate himself with mannered listeners, or the plain-spoken one with blunt listeners, may thus become style gone wrong when the two groups cross.

I have seen men, themselves schooled in the experiences of alcohol, who knew exactly how to approach a drunken man, bent upon smashing something, and quickly to act upon him by such phrases and intonations as were "just right" for diverting his fluid suggestibility into the channel of maudlin good-fellowship. The very rawness of the accomplishment reveals the process most clearly. Here was style or ingratiation successfully employed by the poet to produce a desired state of mind in his audience. I should have hated to see a Matthew Arnold tackle this job. He would have been too crude—his training would have been all incapacity. Even in America today, despite our mobility, one may come upon local sequences of statement and rejoinder, a rigidly observed pattern of remarks, gestures, and tonalities, which are repeated almost detail for detail whenever neighbors meet. Surely this is not mere psittacism, but a stylistic formula, a way of establishing mutual ingratiation by the saying of the right things.

Etiquette is French for label. Larousse says that it is put on bottles, boxes, sacks, to indicate the contents, the price, etc. Its derived meaning is, of course, court ceremony and ceremonious forms. Thus, obviously, the more homogeneous a society's ways of living and doing and thinking are, the more homogeneous will be the labels, hence the greater likelihood that artists will use these labels to their purposes.

When Mrs. Emily Post sold many hundred thousand copies of her book between the New Era years of 1925 and 1929, you can confidently look in your literature for a corresponding "problem of style." There will be forlorn Matthew Arnolds attempting to calm drunkards by reference to labels almost ludicrously inadequate. There will be tough, hard-boiled work which does manifest the tact of experience, does use the adequate labels required for producing the desired hypnosis under the circumstances. And there will be the superficial attempt to establish a set of labels by *fiat*: the literature of forced sentiments and hothouse elegancies, or of such quick allegiances that a proletarian movement in art can arise over night.

Of course, when used by a fertile and ebullient poet, the business of appeal by the saying of the right things becomes a highly adventurous pursuit. Shakespeare gives some indication how wide the range of conformity may be. In *Julius Cæsar*, for instance, we see him establish his conspirators as conspirators by the bluntest kinds of label. One plucks at another's sleeve, they whisper, they feign goodwill, they meet during storms and in the miasmal darkness of the night. In *King Lear*, the ingredients of such a character as Cordelia point to a subtler kind of ingratiation. Shakespeare first shows us how grossly she is misunderstood. Now, who among his audience was not both well-meaning and misunderstood? Hence, who among them did not open his heart to Cordelia, as the further purposes of the playwright made necessary? DeQuincey, commenting on *Macbeth*, reminds us that Shakespeare may go still deeper. When he has finished depicting Macbeth's murder of the King, and lets us hear a sinister knock at the gate, has he not here intermingled internal and external events, by objectifying something so private as the harsh knock of conscience, thereby implicating us in the murder not merely as *witnesses*, but as *participants*? It will thus be seen that the use of labels is no obsequious matter, but is best managed by the boldest minds.

It will also be seen that insofar as the structure of these labels is impaired, their serviceability for communicative purposes is correspondingly impaired. One does not hypnotize a man by raising a problem—one hypnotizes him by ringing the bells of his response. Change, heterogeneity of occupation, and instability of expectation have a radical bearing upon the range, quality, and duration of such linkages. Add geographical shifts, breakdown of former social stratifications, cultural mergers, introduction of "new matter"—and you have so many further factors to affect the poetic medium adversely. The people's extreme delight in the acting of Charlie Chaplin was probably due to the way in which his accurate mimetic style could surmount the social confusion. His expressions possessed an almost universal significance, since they were based upon the permanent certainties of the body, the eternal correlations between mental attitude and bodily posture.

Various Romantic Solutions

Some poets met the problem by observing once more the old linkages under glass. They recalled the ancient Mediter-

ranean lore. Like Anatole France, with a mixture of melancholy and irony, they "scribbled in the margins of books."
Others wrote for the elect, a vague quantity X of a public
who disliked the entire trend of events, and wished to have
their dislike confirmed by an aggressive symbolization of
better worlds. Closely connected with these were the writers
who hearkened unto themselves, to catch the linkages that
grew inescapably out of their own individual lives, hoping
that there would be enough overlap upon other lives to establish a bond. Others satirized the jerry-built linkages which
the exigencies of the scene were forever establishing over-
night, and which were particularly liable to ridicule when
judged from the point of view vestigially surviving out of
the past. Others socialized their art by quickly conforming
with the interests of the season, using a bias while it lasted,
selling a war play in war times, a vice play while the papers
were full of news about some minister involved in a scandal
with a member of his choir, etc. Connected with these,
though less opportunistic in their own eyes at least, were the
exploiters of new scientific discoveries, who might depict the
deadly ravages of syphilis or alcoholism at a time when much
talk of heredity was in the air.

Others made various attempts at neo-primitiveness, either
going off to live in regions still relatively unaffected by the
disturbances of the pro-technological West, or else trying to
disclose and exploit the new moralities that were spontaneously arising among the various groups formerly considered
from the standpoint of incapacity rather than from the standpoint of training: toughs, thieves, lumberjacks, whores, fish-
ermen, smugglers, miners, shopgirls, bullfighters, etc. Another
group of these neo-primitivists stressed sexual concerns as the
basis of the undeniable and universal.

Others met the issue by starting from the issue itself: Their
art became a methodology of art. Perhaps the most thorough

exemplification of this last solution is to be seen in the later works of James Joyce, who has subjected the linguistic medium to a severe process of disintegration, largely stimulated by researches in the laboratories of psychology. On a trivial plane, a somewhat analogous tendency is to be noted in the elaborate compound puns in which some of our nonsense comedians now specialize, though in their case the stimulus probably arises more indirectly, not from the laboratory, but from the need of reorientation which the many resources of applied science have led to.

But our concept of trained incapacity prompts us to look for the converse of this situation. The *dilemmas* of poetry must argue the *advantages* of something else. If one kind of communication breaks down, another kind will thrive on the ruins.

The *positive* side of this situation is to be seen in the development of the technological approach, with its low anthropomorphic content. The very change in the nature of our written vocabulary bears witness to this. The scientific terminology is conceptual, designed for the purpose of *naming*, whereas the spontaneous symbols of communication are hortatory, suggestive, hypnotic. It seems no accident that precisely the century which had so greatly confused its intuitive orientation should have developed, to a greater extent than has ever been known before, the *conceptual* use of language. Its very muddle as regards the subtleties of mimetic and tonal ingratiation would force us to *name* things rather than *respond* to them. Even the dominant music of the century became psychologistic, its programmatic genius strongly observable in the blunt onomatopœic qualities of Berlioz and flowering in Wagner's systematic reliance upon musical naming in his use of the leitmotif. The prestige of instruction rose as the prestige of suggestion fell. Style, beauty, form—these now had to be fought for; or where they prevailed, they were largely expended upon the eliciting of morbid response, so extreme as still to be unequivocal. Suasion was for cheap politicians, rhetoric became synonymous with falsity, and strict definition became the ideal.

The Need for Definition

The situation might be illustrated as follows: Suppose that a flock of birds, while consorting together, had developed a great variety in their ways of living. They now sought different foods in different places, so that the kinds and degree of danger which they incurred varied considerably. Also, their ways of food-gathering had altered their aptitude for escape: Some could get away more quickly than others, etc. Those feeding in trees met dangers which did not concern those on the ground or in the water.

Yet suppose that they still considered themselves a homogeneous flock, and still clung discordantly together, attempting to act by the same orientation as they had when living in a homogeneous culture. How would this cultural mongrelism affect them? Their responses would be thrown into a muddle. The startled cry of one member would lose its absolute value as a sign. The placidity of the group in a tree might not any longer be an adequate safety sign for those in the water. A cry of danger among those feeding on the shore might no longer indicate similar danger for those in the water or in the trees.

Suppose them at this point endowed with speech. Would they not immediately begin insisting upon definitions, in order that they might get this muddle cleared away? Words for danger, safety, food, etc., would not be enough. A scrupulously critical vocabulary would have to be introduced: danger under *what* conditions, food for *which* members of the flock, etc. Their old poetic methods of flapping their wings and crying out would lose prestige among the flock. Only the demagogues or the imbeciles would still resort to such procedures. The most intelligent birds would insist upon the perfection of a strict and unambiguous nomenclature.

In the Middle Ages, when the attempt was made to extend one system of communication throughout a culturally heterogeneous territory having hundreds of local symbolic systems, we had the development of the savants' tongue, learned Latin. It lacked the pliancy of colloquial speech; but it acquired a conceptual stolidity which the colloquial tongues possessed only insofar as they borrowed from the artificial medium. Is there not a striking analogy between the situation then and the situation now, when we find the attempt to erect a communicative medium that will lie across many diverse disciplines, distinct ways of living, different psychoses? Coexistent with the æsthetic departmentalism of the last century, did we not get the rise of a vast wig-wagging system, a *terminology* rather than a *language*?

Modern historians are fond of praising a writer such as Dante, who broke from the unpliant, catholicized medium of his day. The language which he renounced was shaped for saying in Northern Scotland the same things as one might say in Southern Italy. And learned historians praise him for turning from this conceptual speech (which was not the Latin of the Mass, but the Latin of the theologians) to employ a local medium. At the same time they distrust modern poets who take the corresponding step today, writing in the vernacular of their specific experiences—and they themselves proceed to perfect the same kind of medium as they praised Dante for abandoning. We do not mean to accuse them of inconsistency. The situation has altered. At Dante's time a Catholic period was drawing to an end. His shift from Guelph to Ghibelline sympathies parallels in the political sphere his shift from Latin to Italian in the poetic sphere. At that point, a poetic medium was *arising*, not *crumbling*, as a growing national unity of purpose was giving prestige to the colloquial.

We must note that the vernacular was not merely bad Latin, nor was learned Latin the vernacular perfected. They were two different instruments, for two different kinds of communication. The vernacular aims at the very kind of effectiveness which the block-like vocabulary of the artificial language omits. For we must remember that the conceptual terms are valuable mainly for what they *exclude*, what is left after *abstraction*. And though we usually think of abstraction as a very subtle process, from another point of view it may be considered a very blunt one. The scales abstract, for instance, when their dial registers their inability to distinguish a pound of feathers from a pound of lead. They judge by excluding all but their definitions of weight.

Today newspaper English probably marks the flowering of the technological psychosis as carried beyond strictly scientific communication. The appeal of the informative here is clearly bolstered by psychotically engendered needs, since people will pore over column after column of information so low-powered that, a few hours later, they cannot even remember what they had been reading. Yet their hunger continues, and must be continually fed. The same sentences, the same story, if offered to them in a book, would weary them. Except for the yellow journals and the columnists, the prose has arrived at a common denominator of statement wherein the last traces of stylistic ingratiation are eliminated. In the better papers not even the mimetics of the telegraphic style are sought. Effacement is total. The yellow journals still do cultivate the proprieties, though it is customary for the critic, approaching them from a Matthew Arnold locus of judgment, to accuse them of *lacking* propriety rather than *stressing* it. And one who loves the sound of words may get a perverse but genuine delight from the ringing tonalities of a scarehead editorial, whereas he may feel a strange repugnance if he tries to read a sober financial report with anything but the eye and the mind.

Disorders in the communicative medium may be met in part by an attempt to overcome them, in part by an attempt to go around them. One will either try to say his say despite his handicaps, or he will say the sort of things that can best be said within the terms of the handicaps. The poets (imaginative authors in general) represent the group who have been trying to persist despite the linguistic disorders, thus tending toward one or the other of two unsatisfactory solutions: either the profound exploitation of a restricted psychosis, or the superficial exploitation of a common psychosis. The scientists, technologists, represent the group that has turned the defect into a virtue. Their language, even much more than scholastic Latin, is devoid of the tonalities, the mimetic reënforcements, the vaguely remembered human situations, which go to make up the full, complex appeal of the poetic medium. To the scientist's symbols one can respond adequately by looking them up in a book. The very lack of pliancy helps to assist them in avoiding the appeal of pliancy. The language by which the third productive order (the technological) is being rationalized may largely surmount the temptations of the anthropomorphic by reason of its low anthropomorphic content. It is designed for machines.

CHAPTER FIVE

MAGIC, RELIGION, AND SCIENCE

The Three Orders of Rationalization

WE MIGHT close our chapter on orientation by considering more fully the three orders of rationalization: magic, religion, and science. Magic as the schema which stressed mainly the control of natural forces, religion stressing the control of human forces, and science stressing the control of the third productive order, the technological.

In *The Golden Bough* Sir James Frazer has made some interesting distinctions as to the similarities and differences of these three rationalizations. He notes that both magic and positive science assume a uniformity or regularity of natural processes, and attempt to harness these processes by the discovery of the appropriate formulæ. In magic and science, if the practitioner has observed the correct procedure, the desired results will follow of necessity. Should things turn out wrong, the assumption is that the coercive procedure was wrong, or alien factors had entered.

In either the scientific or magical schema, according to Frazer, the powers of the practitioner were limited solely by the limitations of his knowledge as to the workings of the natural agencies. "Both of them open up a seemingly boundless vista of possibilities to him who knows the causes of things and can touch the secret springs that set in motion the vast and intricate mechanism of the world." By the assumptions of either magic or positive science, nature operates through immutable laws. There are no accidents or caprices in nature; given a correct technique on the part of the practitioner, the invariable causality of the world can be made to do one's bidding. Errors in judgment can lead to perilous results, but the rewards of accurate judgment are infinite.

In contrast with this attitude, the religious rationalization is held by Fràzer to stress the propitiatory factor. The religious practitioner aims at "the conciliation of powers superior to man which are believed to direct and control the course of nature and of human life." The laws of the universe are not immutable; an *arbitrary principle* is introduced. Not knowledge and power (not a technique of dominance), but humility, obedience, ingratiation (the ways of inducement), become uppermost. If one has offended, there is no manipulation of causal law that can save him—but if one has earned favor, even the workings of natural law can be altered should the Superior Power so will it.

Or as we might say, the rationalization which aimed primarily at the control of the human productive forces introduced as the informing principle of Heavenly government the trait most distinctive of human consciousness, the principle of choice, the feeling that decisions are not wholly predetermined, but are ethical, creative, new. The illusion of liberty which characterizes man was reflected in his attribution of free will to the godhead. Not the incantations or laboratory formulæ of control, but the petitions of prayer, were requisite. For one "must dominate things, and induce human beings."

The magical and scientific rationalizations would thus be distinguished by the assumption of universal regularity which could be manipulated by the proper formulæ, whereas religion stressed an *arbitrary* principle which could not be *coerced* but had to be *propitiated*.

Frazer seems to think that the belief in the efficacy of magic broke down through the discovery of its errors. Yet the rationalization as he describes it was so totally consistent, and so well corroborated by "practical successes," that I do not see how it could possibly have lost prestige through disproof. The magician's ability to bring about the orderly progression of the seasons, assure the fertility of seeds, and promote the conception of children was on the whole astoundingly successful. And if a plague or a drought resisted him for a time, the assumption that a counter-spell was at work served to keep the rationalization beyond attack. As with the modern scientist when the manipulation of causal laws goes amiss, he could humbly admit that we still do not know enough.

It would seem to me that a system so self-sustaining could be attacked only *from without*. And I would suggest that the attack arose as a new point of view arose. This point of view emphasized, not the dominance of natural power, but the stressing of *human* coöperation. We may call this rising point of view the *philosophic corrective* to magic, with its brutal indifference to the sufferings of the victims it required for its success. Magic, modified by its corrective philosophy, gave us propitiatory magic. The tribal ceremonies were now designed to *please* an arbitrary power, and the sacrifices became more humanistic, with symbolic victims substituted for men.

This corrective philosophy gradually becomes metamorphosed into a new rationalization, religion. As the coöperative technique has become much more complex, and perhaps a *favored* group is established, the psychotic emphasis will naturally be placed wholly upon *propitiation*. The authority of magical regularity would thus be destroyed by the rise of a different psychotic emphasis, a different focus of interest: and the propitiatory pattern by which people were *induced* to serve "of their own free will" was read into the nature of the universe. There was a personal, arbitrary God, who could be pleased or displeased.

The religious rationalization thus lacks the well-rounded finality of the magical schema. There was now room for inconsistency in the management of nature, but one always

meets with it in management of people, who are forever sa
ing one thing and doing another.

It is probably the arbitrary factor in the religious orientati
which gave rise to the dual use of the word rationalizatio
rationalization as either the perception of the self-consiste
or the justification of the self-contradictory. But to place an
rational principle at the basis of a *Weltanshauung* isn't who
satisfactory either, since this way leads to a free-for-all
justification, superstition, quackery. The philosophic corr
tive of religious rationalization is usually called philosop
proper.

Significantly enough, the philosophic point of view ma
fested itself by an interest in mechanical invention. Af
various vicissitudes, partial eclipses, rebirths, it finally becar
enshrined as a totally self-sustaining order, backed by t
very nature of the productive plant which it had nurtur
It has long been written into the nature of the universe; a
eventually it must be written into the basic patterns of
State.

But as a point of view approaches the condition of alm
complete embodiment, it may naturally be expected to rev
more clearly and call forth the kind of correctives which
in turn requires. Those who look upon science as the final c
mination of man's rationalizing enterprise may be neglect
an important aspect of human response. Even a complet
stable condition does not have the same meaning after it
continued for some time as it had when first inaugurated.

Were science completely enshrined tomorrow by attaining
ultimate political equivalents, we might all the more ea
perceive precisely *what was lacking* in the scientific ideal
frame our corrective philosophy accordingly. At present,
matter is still problematical, and is further complicated
the fact that the technological methods of production h
nowhere been complemented for long by the political ins

mentalities which they require: hence the psychotic pressure in favor of science pure and simple is still stimulated by a definite social need for the completion of the scientific rationalization.

Perhaps for this reason the philosophical scientists, who have carried the study of scientific method to the point where it begins to undermine the key assumptions of science itself, are ridiculed as mystics and reactionaries by those who never forget that the most important aspect of the cultural lag (the inadequate political structure, whose means survive from an earlier orientation) is still to be remedied.

Such attacks upon the corrective philosophy of science are rarely based upon a careful scrutiny of the author's reasoning, but generally justify themselves *by appeal to the authority of the scientific rationalization itself.* The "mystics" are condemned for failing to abide by the established canons of positivistic science, quite as though science had never put itself forward as a deliberate and untiring questioner of any and all established canons. We begin to find that there are certain fixed Marquis of Queensbury rules for scientific combat, and anyone who would turn his skepticism against these vested interests of the scientific rationalization is suspected of a strong hankering to sink back into the Dark Ages of human thought.

Any point of reference by which a philosophic corrective of the scientific rationalization would be guided must almost necessarily show some superficial affinity with the religious rationalization. For man is essentially human, however earnestly he may attempt to reshape his psychological patterns in obedience to the patterns of his machines—and it was the religious rationalization which focused its purposes upon the controlling of human forces (the organic productive forces of the mind-and-body itself). Throughout the nineteenth century this search for a rock upon which the corrective

philosophy could be established led naturally to a stron
animalistic emphasis (the word is Nietzsche's). The chara
teristic era of increasing rational, scientific progress was al
the century that compensatorily stressed the glories of li
instinct, the unconscious, the impulsive, the primitive. Poc
sought to stress precisely the human qualities which the she
business of keeping the productive plant in operation l
people to neglect.

The church proper did not offer a very acceptable solutic
Those who attacked modern trends from the strictly orth
dox position did of course have an armory of resoundii
invective at their disposal. They wrote "powerfully," they h
the dignified backing of an "impersonal" cause, where
many abler and fuller men were forced into the weaker ta
tical positions of subjectivism ("I personally do not like it"
melancholy ("Oh, there were happy times"), and iro
("Very well, go your way"). Yet on the whole it was a l
ing fight. To begin with, the truly suasive genius of religi
had not been in its invective at all, but in its tactics of ing
tiation, or inducement. The champions of the One and Et
nal Truth must even be accused of a certain self-indulgen
for gratifying their resentments so unrestrainedly. Bertra
Russell has noted an element of malice in most mode
defenders of the Faith. Furthermore, the strict dogmas of t
Church retained in a fossilized state an enormous sup
structure of orientation which the shifts of history had ma
either inapposite or downright dangerous. And finally, t
True Church was so institutionalized as to be little mc
than a hippopotamus feeding in the miasmal swamps
time, while the deeply religious psychology of tragedy a
devotion had retired to the catacombs, left to the mourn
piety of "disorganized," "corrupt," and "atheistic" poets.

The Churchmen became merely the feeblest, most outlyi
group of scientists, vowed to an enormous number of usel

tics whereby they might make the older rationalization
ok like the newer one. They attempted to remould the
ligious structure by the criteria of rationality, or self-con-
stency, idealized by science. They too became advocates of
ogress, whereas the religious rationalization had been de-
gned for anything but progress. It had attempted to stabi-
ze a given coöperative system. It was implicitly ranged
ainst progress, since progress implied change. But so great
d become the prestige of progress, even Churchmen them-
lves found it hard to believe that any decent rationalization
uld have been developed for the purpose of maintaining a
atus quo.

The prestige of progress, however, must necessarily dimin-
. A point of view involves progress until it has been sub-
antiated, whereupon the desire is for stabilization, and the
agic lure of progress as a slogan is ended.

A Humanistic, or Poetic, Rationalization

A corrective rationalization must certainly move in the
rection of the anthropomorphic or humanistic or poetic,
ce this is the aspect of culture which the scientific criteria,
th their emphasis upon dominance rather than upon in-
cement, have tended to eliminate or minimize. The refer-
ce to poetry rather than to religion seems necessary for
any reasons. Perhaps foremost of all is the fact that poetry,
rough never having been institutionalized, does not stand
out as the Church does, like a big deserted building, with
oken windows and littered doorways. And the charge of
eversion" or "backsliding" cannot so easily be laid against
e poetic emphasis as against the specifically religious one.
ncidentally, it is worth remembering that the same charge of
version into abysmal darkness was laid against the alchem-
s, whose morbid experiments formed the link between the

vestiges of the magical rationalization and its refurbishme
as science.)

After all, the devices of poetry are close to the spontaneo
genius of man: in framing a corrective philosophy wi
poetic standards, we should have a point of reference whi
was in turn "biologically" grounded. In this respect, poet
could enjoy an authority drawn from the scientific psycho
itself, a criterion based upon pragmatic demands and n
offered as revelation. This is an important fact, since any ne
rationalization must necessarily frame its arguments as far
possible within the scheme of "proprieties" enjoying presti
in the rationalization which it would displace.

On the other hand, the poetic point of reference is wea
ened by the fact that the poetic medium of communicati
itself is weakened. The center of authority must be situat
in a philosophy, or psychology, of poetry, rather than in
body of poetry, until the scene itself becomes sufficiently s
bilized for linkages to acquire greater spread and permanen
throughout the group. If we are to revise the productive a
the distributive patterns of our economy to suit our sound
desires, rather than attempting to revise our desires until th
suit the productive and distributive patterns, it would sur
be in the region of poetry that the "concentration point"
human desires should be found. The corrective of the scie
tific rationalization would seem necessarily to be a *ration*
of art—not however, a performer's art, not a specialist's
for some to produce and many to observe, but an art in
widest aspects, an *art of living*.

PART II

PERSPECTIVE BY INCONGRUITY

PERSPECTIVE BY INCONGRUITY

The first section discussed "orientation" in general. The third will discuss the principles of a "new" orientation. This intermediate section will deal with the state of transition itself. Since the conditions of such transformation involve not merely intellectualistic problems, but also deeply emotional ones, the analysis is centered in a discussion of "piety" and "impiety." Piety, as the yearning to conform with the "sources of one's being," is shown to be a much more extensive motive than it is usually thought to be. Conversely, even the most conscientious of new doctrines necessarily contains an element of impiety, with a corresponding sense of guilt (though the doctrine may later become an orthodoxy, with its generally accepted code of proprieties and improprieties). The intermediate stage involves a shattering or fragmentation, analogous to the stage of "rending and tearing"(or sparagmos) in tragic ritual. (The equivalent of such a process in the Hegelian dialectic has been called a "logonomical purgatory.") Here reasons are offered for calling it "perspective by incongruity" (with the placing of special stress upon the kinds of hermeticism, or stylistic mercureality, that are got by the merging of categories once felt to be mutually exclusive). This is the realm of "gargoyles." Psychoanalysis in particular is viewed in terms of perspective by incongruity. For its cures are guided by a principle of inappropriateness, or "planned incongruity," or "methodical misnaming" (as the exorcist, to drive out demons, calls them by names unsuited to the nature that the sufferer attributes to them). But while the deep emotionality of the search for new meanings is considered (an emotionality extending even to bodily stigmata), the great importance of purely rational or "intellectualistic" elements is likewise stressed. Christ and Saint Paul are compared as types, with regard to the propounding of new meanings.

CHAPTER ONE

THE RANGE OF PIETY

Magical and Utilitarian Meanings

O NE CANNOT long discuss the question of meaning, as applied to the field of art, without coming upon the problem of piety. Santayana has somewhere defined piety as loyalty to the sources of our being. Such a notion should suggest that piety is not confined to the strictly religious sphere. It would as well be present when the potter moulds the clay to exactly that form which completely gratifies his sense of how it ought to be. The connection between our pieties and our childhood should seem clear, since in childhood we develop our first patterns of judgment, while the experiences of maturity are revisions and amplifications of these childhood patterns. An adult, for instance, may turn his thoughts from a father to a father-government; yet even in later life, should he take an axe and fell a great tree, we need not be surprised to find a strange misgiving permeate him as the noble symbol of shelter comes crashing to the earth. For however neutral his act, though the tree had been felled to satisfy the simple utilitarian needs of firewood, there may also be lurking here a kind of symbolic parricide. Not only firewood, but a parent-symbol, may be brought down in the crash.

It is possible that much of the anguish affecting poets in the modern world is due to the many symbolic outrages which a purely utilitarian philosophy of action requires us to commit. In primitive eras, when the utilitarian processes were considerably fewer, and more common to the entire group, definite propitiatory rituals seem to have arisen as a way of cancelling off these symbolic offenses. In the magical orientation (so close to that of poetry) if the felling of a tree had connotations of symbolic parricide, the group would probably develop a corresponding ritual of symbolic expiation. The offender would thus have a technique for cleansing himself of the sin he had committed.

The purely utilitarian attitude towards such acts, however, requires that one introduce a distinctly impious note: one cannot permit the symbolic overtones of meaning to function at all. If the tree falls, and one feels a strange uneasiness, one must shut off the queer remorse by an impatient "Nonsense! —this is only one tree, I needed it, and there are plenty of others to take its place." The non-utilitarian qualities of the act are dismissed—one must perform the act as a "new man" —and when a great oak falls, only the poet, bewildered and plaintive, may permit himself to feel that there is somehow a deeper issue here than the mere getting of firewood. (Whereat, thinking of modern "negativistic" trends, we might contrast "Woodman, spare that tree . . ." with the dictum of a contemporary poet who defined style imagistically as the resonance of the axe in the wood.)

Such considerations may be at the bottom of the tendency, often noted in æsthetic theory, to stress a direct antithesis between artistic and practical responses. For if our speculations are correct, it would follow that the purely utilitarian attitude could be upheld only by the suppression of those very overtones to which the earnest poet most resolutely exposes himself. And we may see why a writer of so deeply poetic a nature as Nietzsche felt that the purely rationalistic, utilitarian ideal required the perfection of a different breed, a superman who would be hard and brutal in the performance of his acts.

Perhaps an instance of the way in which the rational, scientific categories of linkage can run counter to the emotional categories may be seen in the classifying of the lion. The lion, if the usual psychoanalytic theory of symbolization is correct, is the male or father symbol *par excellence*. Yet the lion is scientifically included in the cat family, whereas the cat emotionally is feminine. In both great poetry and popular usage, it is associated with female attributes. Here we have, in our rational categories, an association which runs entirely counter to the associations of our emotional categories. A linkage emotionally appropriate becomes rationally inappropriate.

In such cases, where the rational order of symbols would establish a congruity wholly alien to the emotional order of symbols, is it not possible that intense conflicts could arise, with the result that anguish or unrest could follow any really thorough attempt to embrace the rational category? And might we see in Darwin's intense attacks of vertigo an evidence of precisely such a conflict? For Darwin furnishes the supreme instance of the tendency to construct rational categories which are at variance with the categories of linkage formed in emotional experience. His transference of man from the category of the divine to the category of the apes is, as the popular resistance to his new categories testified, the most obvious instance, though the same affront runs through the entire schema of biological classifications, as distinct from the linkages of the emotions. It is even recorded that women fainted when first being told of his conclusions (possibly because of the disturbing implication that they had been sleeping with apes). And for my own part, I shall never forget my great resentment as a child upon learning that lions were cats, whereas to me they were purely and simply the biggest dogs.

No wonder an intensity of purely illogical Symbolist linkages broke out in poetry precisely at the time when the rational schema of classification had come into full flower. Poets, whose logic is rooted in experience, were now faced with a contrary logic wholly the product of rational speculation, and their bewilderment was considerable. The fertilizer company has a much different attitude towards a dead dog than does the child who may have had it for a pet. The child's kind of linkage could be called poetic or magical, in contrast with the utilitarian linkage of the chemical concern.

It would be pious of a man to accept the full childhood implications of his adult performances, to take fully into account the need of expiation in case the tree which he was felling happened to be a parent-symbol as well as an aggregate of firewood. And much of the criminality in modern life might be explained psychologically as due to the loss of a definite, generally recognized technique for cancelling off these hidden offenses. Justification by success must replace the deeper-lying kind of magical justification — and since such success usually involves the strengthening of one's skill in precisely the act which contains the symbolic affront, the test of success must in time inure one to his rôle as malefactor. Such a possibility might lead us to look for equally devious modes of expiation among the practical-minded.

In any case, if piety is the sort of response we have described, it would seem to possess the following notable features: (1) It would show a marked affinity with childhood experiences, thus explaining, among other things, why poets living in a period of great change so often tend to become infantile. For it would suggest the deep connection between piety and the "remembrance of things past." (2) It would suggest why piety can be painful, requiring a set of symbolic expiations (such as martyrdom or intense ambition) to counteract the symbolic offenses involved in purely utilitarian actions.

Piety as a System-Builder

Furthermore, piety is a system-builder, a desire to round things out, to fit experiences together into a unified whole. Piety is *the sense of what properly goes with what.* And it leads to construction in this way: If there is an altar, it is pious of a man to perform some ritual act whereby he may approach this altar with clean hands. A kind of symbolic cleanliness goes with altars, a technique of symbolic cleansing goes with cleanliness, a preparation or initiation goes with the technique of cleansing, the need of cleansing was based upon some feeling of taboo—and so on, until pious linkages may have brought all the significant details of the day into coördination, relating them integrally with one another by a complex interpretative network.

If it is pious to exemplify a sense of the appropriate, there must be other aspects of piety not generally called such. Besides the pieties of love (birds and flowers for one's mistress— or the Elizabethan's promptness in getting from thoughts of young female beauty to the themes of honor and of *carpe diem*), there would be the less devout appropriatenesses of art: thus the villain of a bad drama speaks in sibilants; or a symphony, at an heroic moment, blares with its brasses; or the poet, writing of night, puts together all those elements that are his night-thoughts, the things that go with night as he knows it, and perhaps lying in his Paris room, he hears outside, lone crabs scraping on the street.

I would even go further in trying to establish this notion of piety as a response which extends through all the texture of our lives but has been concealed from us because we think we are so thoroughly without religion and think that the "pious process" is confined to the sphere of churchliness. Bentham discovered that poetry (a *poor* brand of poetry) is implicit in our very speech. For our words affect us and our hearers by drawing upon the wells of emotion behind them. We cannot speak the mother-tongue without employing the rhetorical devices of a Roman orator. And Bentham saw in the neutral vocabularies of science an attempt to eliminate this unconscious piety from speech. (He did not go on to ask whether this whole desire for a neutral vocabulary might be interpreted as one vast castration-symbol suspiciously expia tory in essence, particularly in the case of this crotchety old bachelor who formulated his neutral ideal with such avidity though such an ingredient would be more likely discoverable in a messianic temperament like Bentham than in the ordi nary run of his followers.) So if we are all poets, and if all poets are pious, we may expect to find great areas of piety even at a ball game. Indeed, all life has been likened to the writing of a poem, though some people write their poems on paper, and others carve theirs out of jugular veins.

As I call piety merely the sense of what goes with what, have opened myself to a *reductio ad absurdum*, thus: Suppose there is a flock of birds and that one of them, rightly or wrongly is frightened into flight; the rest of the flock rises also. In other words, the flight of the flock goes with the flight of the one By our definition, this gregarious obedience would be piety.

Piety is a schema of orientation, since it involves the put ting together of experiences. The orientation may be right or wrong; it can guide or misguide. If the bird saw an actual danger, the flock was right in rising with it. If the danger was not real, the flock was wrong. In either case it had been pious

Extending our term still further: If one is long unhappy and living alone with his unhappiness (as wounded animal slink off by themselves to die), and if he hears next door, at a certain hour each day, a peculiar nagging way of a door bell's ringing, he may even come to link the significance of his distress with the significance of this doorbell. He will connect his outstanding misery with the outstanding natur of the sound—and years later, should he survive his misery and be quite tough again, he may one day hear a bell ring next door, in a peculiarly nagging way, whereat an unspeak able heaviness will fall upon him. In this linkage, an outlaw appropriateness decidedly "Proustian," he will have commit ted a piety. Such are the pieties of moodiness, merging into insanity.

We are now prepared to carry our term to its limit. Refined critics, of the Matthew Arnold variety, assumed that exquisiteness of taste was restricted to the "better" classes of people, those who never had names ending in "ug." Yet if we can bring ourselves to imagine Matthew Arnold loafing on the corner with the gashouse gang, we promptly realize how undiscriminating he would prove himself. Everything about him would be inappropriate: both what he said and the ways in which he said it. Consider the crudeness of his perception as regards the proper oaths, the correct way of commenting upon passing women, the etiquette of spitting. Does not his very crassness here reveal the presence of a morality, a deeply felt and piously obeyed sense of the appropriate, on the part of these men, whose linkages he would outrageously violate? Watch them—and observe with what earnestness, what *devotion,* these gashouse Matthew Arnolds act to prove themselves, every minute of the day, true members of their cult. Vulgarity is pious.

These considerations force us to reinterpret what jurists or social workers often look upon as decay, degeneracy, disintegration, and the like. If a man who is a criminal lets the criminal trait in him serve as the informing aspect of his character, piously taking unto him all other traits and habits that he feels should go with his criminality, the criminal deterioration which the moralist with another point of view might discover in him is the very opposite of deterioration as regards the tests of piety. It is *integration*, guided by a scrupulous sense of the appropriate which, once we dismiss our personal locus of judgment, would seem to bear the marks of great conscientiousness.

Similarly with the "drug fiend," who can take his morphine in a hospital without the slightest disaster to his character, since it is called medicine there; but if he injects it at a party, where it has the stigma of dissipation upon it, he may gradually organize his character about this outstanding "altar" of his experience—and since the altar in this case is generally accepted as unclean, he will be disciplined enough to approach it with appropriately unclean hands, until he is a derelict. Like Holmes's chambered nautilus, which was always held up to us in our school days as an example of sound development, he will add one cell upon another, constructing an integer of wickedness out of deference to the norms of his times. He puts himself together by the social recipes all about him, his so-called decay being marked by as scrupulous and discerning a selectivity as in a poem by Keats.

There is, of course, a further factor involved here: the matter of *interaction*. Certain of one's choices become creative in themselves; they drive one into ruts, and these ruts in turn reënforce one's piety. Once one has jumped over a cliff, for instance, he can let events take care of themselves, confident in the knowledge that he will continue to maintain and intensify his character as one-who-has-jumped-over-a-cliff. To translate: Should a man given to crime or drugs become discouraged by the risks or distresses caused by his transgression, he might feel strong inducements towards apostasy. The altar of criminality or drug addiction might prove too exacting, so that he desired to reconstruct his linkages with some other less troublesome altar as the informing principle of his character.

Yet he may already have gone so far that other people are also helping him to continue in the same direction. He has become hypnotically entangled in the texture of his poem, as objectified in the external relationships he has already established. He can no longer retract his vow—hence, he is spared the trivial lapses that might otherwise have interrupted his devotion to the character of his offense; at times of weakness and doubt, when his own convictions are not enough to sustain him, he is kept under discipline by the walls of his monastery (that is, by the ruts which his experience itself has worn).

CHAPTER TWO

NEW MEANINGS

The Factor of Impiety in Evangelism

THE THOUGHT may suggest itself that an attempt to *reorganize* one's orientations from the past would have an *impious* aspect. For if our definition of piety first involved us in admitting that the gashouse gang is pious in its ways, we are now conversely pledged to grant the presence of *impiety* in something as pious as a new religion. The evangelist is asking us to alter our orientations. He would give us new meanings. Seeing his flock piously rise at the rising of one bird, an impious member (a "scientist") might ask: "Is that particular bird over-timid? Might he be stupid, frightening you from your hunting grounds at the sight of a man who, as a matter of fact, is a member in good standing of the Audubon Society? Or might this one flighty bird be moved by some perversity of motive not characteristic of your group, some quirk whereby he derives a morbid Napoleonic satisfaction from putting you all into the air by a few quick flips of his wings and a bird way of crying 'wolf'?"

Such questionings are usually considered the special property of science—but that may only be due to the fact that scientists, rather than prophets, are now trying to convert us to new meanings. Scientists and prophets may know themselves apart, but that does not matter. It is sufficient for our purposes to note that, by our definition of piety, the evangelistic aspect of science presents many similarities to the evangelism of any religious doctrine in its early stages.

In both the scientific and the religious doctrine, there is great emphasis placed upon prophecy or foretelling; in both it is held that certain important aspects of foretelling require a new orientation, a revised system of meanings, an altered conception as to how the world is put together; in both, it is insisted that, if we change our ways of acting to bring them more into accord with the new meanings (rejecting old means and selecting new means as a better solution for the problem as now rephrased), we shall bring ourselves and our group nearer to the good life. And there is even some indication (in such formulæ as the Logos and the Way) that the Christian evangelism started from questionings as intellectualistic as any that characterize science today. The formal philosophy out of which Christianity arose was highly skeptical.

In his study of language habits among children, Piaget has observed that children gradually learn to socialize their beliefs by logical proof as the result of quarreling. At first they state their differences merely as flat contradictions, of the "You did so—I did not" variety; but in time they learn how to offer "reasons" for their assertions. Seen from this angle, *cogency* becomes a mature form of *compulsion*. Thus the militaristic, or combative element, and the attempt to remould it into something qualitatively different, lies at the roots of civilization, though this fact is usually ignored in our philosophies of progress.

Such considerations may lead us to discern the same incentives behind evangelism and education or propaganda, despite the differences in terminology. For what does lie at the roots of an attempt to socialize one's position, to induce agreement in others? If a man takes great pains to obtain the approval of his group, does he not thereby give evidence that he *needs to be approved*? And is not such a need closely allied with guilt, in the sense that one will suffer unless he can induce others to corroborate him? As Richard Rothschild has written in his volume *Reality and Illusion*: "The religious notion of 'fear for one's soul' might lead into every field of human thought"—and he might have added: "into every field of human action." Justification by works still remains with us, lying behind the morality of toil in any form, however little acknowledgment it receives in our enlightened ideologies of today. For all effort is essentially protective, a structure of defenses, however sublimated our concepts of defense may be.

Necessitous and Symbolic Labor

We might make a distinction between *necessitous* and *symbolic* labor by suggesting that drudgery is purely necessitous labor, whereas symbolic labor is fitted into the deepest lying patterns of the individual. Symbolic labor is more pious. For instance, it would be "necessitous labor" if one climbed a mountain simply because he had to get somewhere and the mountain stood between him and his destination. The same act would be symbolic if the mountain happened to have some deeper significance to the climber, so that the *act of climbing* was in itself an accomplishment. If one has ever read the experiences of a confirmed Alpinist, he will appreciate the difference, for in the case of the Alpinist the incidental dangers are not merely *endured*, they are *courted*. A prodigy of attainment, in any kind of effort, artistic, scientific, political, or commercial, is probably a man in whom the necessitous and symbolic aspects are combined.

A Rockefeller was not merely a money-maker, for instance: in some way the entire Puritan code of morals was involved in his strivings, driving him to strain in his efforts at economic empire-building far beyond the demands of utilitarian necessity. He did not have a job—he had a calling. Similarly, in the case of a professional revolutionary like Lenin, his unswerving devotion to his work would suggest that the dictatorship of the proletariat was no mere instrumentality to him, but in some way was deeply allied with his most fundamental patterns of justification, or self-respect. It could probably be linked up with his childhood patterns of experience, quite as poor Gogol at an earlier date lost his mind when his satires met with such great success that he felt he had betrayed his loyalty to the little father. In Lenin's case, the clue is probably to be sought in his relation to his older brother, whose serious opinions Lenin adopted after the brother had been killed.

In sum: Where you discern the symptoms of great devotion to any kind of endeavor, you are in the realm of piety. Even the great disgust with their work manifested by many men of today, such as journalists, would indicate a kind of inverse piety—and I think it no accident that the more reputable newspapers are written in a purely serviceable style, whereas the yellow journals often display strong stylistic leanings, though of the gashouse sort.

Writers for the yellow journals have a pronouncedly moral element implicit in their efforts—for at bottom they greatly despise themselves, and such self-detestation is basically moral. Hence they possess an altar, to which they bring offerings appropriately unclean. Has one not noticed that a vile editorial actually *rings*, that it can be *read aloud*, that it has rhythm and spirit, whereas the daily output of the merely dutiful reporter on a respectable sheet falls under the category of a telephone directory? The purely serviceable style of the respectable paper testifies to a basic lack of engrossment—the writer is a mere observer. But if he works for a paper which he profoundly despises, he is constantly handling a *moral issue* when he writes, and his work shows the signs of this moral impetus if only by an eloquence in degradation.

Similarly, although psychologists have devoted themselves mainly to the works of poets as revealing the underlying patterns of symbolism in human work, I should imagine that our mechanical inventions could be found equally revealing. To Hart Crane, who suffered distinctly from a divided mind, the Brooklyn Bridge became a symbol of union—why should it not have the same non-utilitarian significance to an engineer who was profoundly and intensely a bridge-builder?

Reservations Concerning Logic

Distinctions between emotion and logic, intuition and reason, however well they may serve in other connections, need not concern us here. It was intuitive of the flock to fly when one of its members flew—and it was also quite logical of them to do so. They had responded to a character of events in a way which, generally speaking, assists in preserving them—and I cannot conceive of anything more logical, even though the one bird that set them off may have been wrong or perverse.

Should they learn to distinguish some subtler character here, they might make their responses a little more accurate. They might note, for instance, that young birds are flightier —hence the nervousness of a youngster might be partially discounted by those nearest him, and their irresponsiveness might reassure the group. In such a case, their reading of the signs would be more accurate, but it would hardly be more logical. By logic, as regards our way of approach, we would seem to mean: reorientation or verification by way of verbalization. That is: we are logical (*logos:* word) when we specifically state the nature of a problem and then go see within the terms of this specific statement. The birds' conduct would be logical in this sense if they actually could phrase some proposal for reorientation and try it out. But there is nothing illogical in our running away from a clothes-tree if, seeing it vaguely in the half-darkness, we happen to interpret it as a robber.

The nearest approach to a process distinctly illogical, in our sense of the word, may be seen in the following homely incident: A roguish son-in-law, gripping his tobacco pipe like a revolver, pointed it at the great-grandmother and said, "Hands up!" The ruse worked far better than was intended. The old lady was greatly frightened, shouting for him to put down the gun. The rogue then showed her that it was not a gun at all, but just his pipe—and she answered severely, "Yes, I know —but that's the way people get shot."

Her fear was logical—her resentment was logical—but as for her verbalization, I cannot imagine any scheme of orientation whereby it could be called adequate. She was giving her reasons why one should not point weapons even though one thinks they are not loaded; such weapons, she held, often prove to be loaded after all; hence, pranks with *weapons* often cost people their lives; hence, the justice of her fear and her resentment. But people don't get shot with tobacco pipes. Her reply was to the situation as originally characterized by her—not to the situation as recharacterized by him. It was illogical *only insofar as she ignored his verbalization*. It would not have been illogical if she also believed that guns can suddenly turn into pipes, and that this object may have been a gun while he pointed it, even though it was now obviously a pipe.

Most accusations of the illogical are of this second sort, where the hidden disagreement is over a matter of premises, whereas each of the opponents, accusing the other of being illogical, is in reality moving from premises to conclusion with the syllogistic regularity of a schoolman. We see this particularly in cases where Western investigators discover the lack of logic in the behavior of savage tribes. As a matter of fact the savages behave quite logically, acting on the basis of causal connectives as established by the tribal rationalizations. We may offer grounds for questioning the entire rationalistic scheme, as tested by our technique of testing—but we cannot call a man illogical for acting on the basis of what he feels to be true.

Let us, then, recognize the old lady as pious in her fear,

which properly went with the character of the events as she interpreted them. Let us call the son-in-law's demonstration that he held a pipe and not a gun an attempt to reorientate the situation as a way of showing her that her responses were ungrounded. In this he was naturally not successful, for though he offered a reason why, *from his standpoint,* she should not have been afraid, he could not possibly offer a reason why she should not be resentful, as the mere fact of her having been afraid was grounds enough for her resentment. Thus, her verbalization was illogical in the sense that it was framed to justify her resentment at being frightened, but was couched in words only apposite to her original fear.

What she was really saying, beneath her faulty symbolism, was: "I thought that it was a gun and I resent having guns pointed at me." But being a kindly old lady, who did not feel quite at home in resenting a prank proved harmless, she omitted the subject of resentment from her verbalization entirely, though exemplifying it by her attempt to strike him with a rebuke. Hence she misstated her case entirely, still trying, after it was all over, *to blame him for having pointed a gun, which was precisely the offense he had not committed.*

Thus, though we recognize the illogical in the sense that verbalizations may be inadequate even within the given speaker's scheme of orientation, we doubt whether the word can be of much help when discussing orientation in general. There seem to be systems of orientation by which certain events are singled out, with greater or lesser accuracy, as being of a beneficial, neutral, or dangerous character—and the man who acts disastrously on the basis of danger which we see but he does not is no more illogical in his conduct than the man who dies of poison because the bottle from which he drank was labeled medicine.

In this sense, any new way of putting the characters of events together is an attempt to convert people, regardless of whether it go by the name of religion, psychotherapy, or science. It is impious, by our definition, insofar as it attacks the kinds of linkage already established. It attempts, by rationalization, to alter the nature of our responses.

Thus, in the Jewish and Christian rationalizations, we see the earlier pagan practice of sacred prostitution reoriented as a sin. In a theory of dietetics, we similarly find a new set of injunctions and prescriptions, a reorientation as to our notions of the indifferent, the profitable, and the dangerous. In Marxism, we find new meanings serving to draw forth, for special attention, specific factors in the vast complexity of our productive, distributive, and moral network. All such attempts (and the nineteenth century threw forth thousands of new orientative devices, of greater or lesser scope in the range of matter on which they would convert us) are aimed at some aspect of our pious orientations, ferreting out the last ultimate assumption which we may have let go unquestioned.

Piety-Impiety Conflict in Nietzsche

Nietzsche was particularly significant in this movement owing to the totality of his exposure to it. His subject-matter was specifically that of reorientation (transvaluation of *all* values)—yet in facing the *problematical new* he spontaneously felt as a poet that he could glorify such a concern only by utilizing the *unquestioned old*. The essayist can be content to *name* a cause heroic. The poet can make it heroic only by identifying it with assumptions already established as to what the heroic is. Nietzsche's two most thorough disciples, Thomas Mann and André Gide, likewise faced this issue, glorifying the problematical in art, whereas the complete establishment of the problematical would make glorification impossible. On the whole, they all seized upon the same device: stressing the state of tension in itself, picturing the dangers and discomforts involved in maintaining it, hence relying upon the *basic* military equipment in man as their last source of appeal (though differing widely in their selection of the symbols which would serve as the channels in which this original biologic psychosis would run).

In reading Nietzsche, one must be struck by the pronounced *naming* that marks his page. Nietzsche's later style is like a sequence of *darts*. Indeed, at first I tried to explain it to myself as a simple conversion of his fighting, hunting attitude into its behavioristic equivalent. His sentences are forever striking out at this or that, exactly like a man in the midst of game, or enemies. They leap with a continual abruptness and sharpness of naming, which seems to suggest nothing so much as those saltations by which cruising animals suddenly leap upon their prey. I believe there is an element of truth in this —for Nietzsche's pages are certainly a battlefield of thought; and as men, having the same restlessness of insanity, but lacking its tenacity and brilliance, will convert their rooms into a replica of their own unsettled state, externalizing their moods in torn bedding and shattered furniture, so he vigorously constructed pages that put the raging of his brain before us. His mind seemed somewhat like that of a spring without a ratchet; it unwound with a whirr, except that it miraculously did this over many decades.

But however much the state of his mental or neurological structure may account for this dartlike quality of his page, an equally important source of it is revealed in his word "perspective." Nietzsche, we learn in his *Will to Power,* was interested in the establishment of perspectives. It was part of his program to give us these repeatedly. And in trying to analyze just what he meant by them, I came upon reasons for relating his cult of perspectives to his dartlike style. It was in the explanation of this that I came upon the term, "Perspective by Incongruity," which I shall now try to make clear.

CHAPTER THREE

PERSPECTIVE AS METAPHOR

Illustrations of Perspective by Incongruity

THE NIETZSCHEAN METHOD is perhaps best revealed by its excessive exemplification in the works of a disciple, Oswald Spengler, who clearly built his morphology of history upon Nietzsche's theories of decadence and of the eternal recurrence. It was this scheme that gave Spengler his informing concept of the contemporaneous, by which he meant, not things existing at the same time in history but things existing at corresponding stages in different cultures.

That is, the pre-Socratics of the sixth and fifth centuries of the Classical culture would be contemporaneous with Galileo, Bacon, and Descartes in Western culture; Socrates would be "contemporaneous" with the French Encyclopedists, Hellenism with Schopenhauer and Nietzsche, etc. By this method of establishing corresponding periods in different cultural cycles, he had a device for uniting under one head movements which were generally considered in complete isolation from one another.

Thus the "Spread of a Final World-Sentiment," as a culture decayed, was manifested as Buddhism in India, as Hellenistic-Roman Stoicism after 200 in the Classical cycle, as practical fatalism in Islam after 1000 (Arabian), and as ethical socialism from 1900 (Western).

Such a device quickly makes it possible to speak, let us say, of Arabian Puritanism, thus extending the use of a term by taking it from the context in which it was habitually used and applying it to another. We can discuss the Pergamene quality in Wagner, the Mozartian elements in Phidias, the calculus mathematics emergent in Gothic.

These are historical perspectives, which Spengler acquires by taking a word usually applied to one setting and transfering its use to another setting. It is a "perspective by incongruity," since he established it by violating the "proprieties" of the word in its previous linkages. The device as used in Spengler is, in a blunter way, precisely the same as it is used in Nietzsche—and this would explain the darting of his page. Nietzsche establishes his perspectives by a constant juxtaposing of incongruous words, attaching to some name a qualifying epithet which had heretofore gone with a different order of names. He writes by the same constant reordering of categories that we find in the Shakespearean metaphor.

Indeed, the metaphor always has about it precisely this revealing of hitherto unsuspected connectives which we may note in the progressions of a dream. It appeals by exemplifying relationships between objects which our customary rational vocabulary has ignored. Were we finally to accommodate ourselves, for instance, to placing the lion in the cat family, a poet might metaphorically enlighten us and startle us by speaking of "that big dog, the lion"—or were we completely inured to thinking of man as an ape, we might get a sudden flash, or perspective, from a reference to man as the "ape-God."

One must not think that this process is confined to such vatic thinkers as Spengler or Nietzsche. Mr. T. S. Eliot gave a perfect instance of perspective by incongruity during a recent visit to America, when he told a reporter that he noticed less "decadent athleticism" in American colleges than formerly. Now, by the pieties of the average American, this was a decidedly incongruous combination. The athleticism of our colleges is advocated precisely as the preventive of decadence. College alumni reassemble at the leading football matches of the season precisely that they may feel themselves wholesome. They cheer in lusty conformity; they exercise their muscles by vicarious atonement; they yield to their competitive psychosis with fervor. We need not here argue the merits of the case; it is enough to note that all such factors as these must have been in Mr. Eliot's mind when he, by planned incongruity, offered a casual moral revaluation or perspective by putting the wrong words together. Veblen's term, "trained incapacity," is of the same order. Our notions of what goes with training naturally suggest capacity rather than incapacity.

A flashier aspect of the transition was observable among sophisticated writers who mocked at the obedience to old verbal linkages. In particular the Oscarians of the *fin de siècle* movement made much capital out of holding platitudinous responses up to ridicule. This was an impious concern—and many of those engaged in such flouting of the national pieties "came to no good end." However, they only grazed the surface of their subject, confining themselves to the ridicule of linkages which were inadequate and inane enough for nearly anyone to appreciate their psittacistic nature as soon as it was pointed to. Meanwhile, the profoundest men of the century were engaged in this same *untergrabend* endeavor, with nothing more incongruous, as regards our entire vocabulary of moral judgments, than Darwin's formulation of man as an anthropoid. Nietzsche knew that probably every linkage was open to destruction by the perspectives of a planned incongruity. Throughout his life he "undermined," carefully qualifying his nouns by the juxtaposition of modifying matter that had the "wrong" moral inclination. The humorists, the satirists, the writers of the grotesque, all contributed to this work with varying degrees of systematization, giving us new insights by such deliberate misfits. The individualism of fiction and poetry was mild as compared with the individualism of science, ever in quest of new ways for characterizing and classifying events. The amusing moral perspectives offered us by the Oscarians found their counterpart a few decades later in the paradoxes of an Eddington, who outrages our old categories of orientation by carrying his incongruous perspectives into the very structure of the universe. Eddington's perspectives are written in the spirit of a cosmological Wilde.

Planned Incongruity in Bergson

The formulations of the philosopher Henri Bergson came nearest to a central statement of incongruity as a *system*. Nietzsche *exemplified* the procedure consistently enough—but he did not, to my knowledge, give us a specific rationalization of it. The rationalization is to be found at its clearest, I believe, in a volume entitled *The Misuse of Mind* (a work by Mrs. Karin Stephen), in which Bergson's doctrine is concisely rephrased. To attempt a brief résumé of a work which is itself a brief résumé of another's work, we might outline Mrs. Stephen's statement of Bergson's position:

The events of actual life are continuous, any isolated aspect of reality really merging into all the rest. As a practical convenience, we do make distinctions between various parts of reality, and by such processes of abstraction, we can even treat certain events as though they recurred, simply because there are other events more or less like them. Each temporal event is new, and cannot recur. We find our way through this everchanging universe by certain blunt schemes of generalization, conceptualization, or verbalization—but words have a limited validity. Their very purpose being to effect practical simplifications of reality, we should consider them inadequate for the description of reality as it actually is. Motion, for instance, is a total, single, or unified event. But Newton, for conveniences of calculation, conceptualized a planet's orbit by the use of two alternative forces acting against each other —one driving the planet out of its orbit at a tangent, the other pulling the planet towards the center of its orbit, the path itself being called the resultant of these two conflicting forces.

PERSPECTIVE AS METAPHOR

Bergson suggests that the great syntheses of the metaphysicians have been schemes for cosmically joining logical or conceptual distinctions which were not justified by the nature of the universe at all, but were merely verbal distinctions applied by us for our practical dealings with reality. Metaphysics in this sense, he holds, is the mere solving of pseudo-problems, as the metaphysician works out an elaborate system for reconciling differences which never existed in the first place, but were invented for purposes of convenience.

That is: A planet does not continually strike some kind of bargain between pulling away and falling back; *it moves in a path*—and this path is conceptualized, made available to astronomical calculations, if we compute it as a synthesis of tangential and centripetal forces. The actual motion *is* the synthesis, and it is never anything else. We conceptualize it as a union of antitheses, since speech is necessarily blocklike, pulling bits of reality apart and treating them as wholes; but a man solves a pseudo-problem who takes, not the *motion*, but the two *concepts* of centripetal and centrifugal forces, as the reality, thereupon devoting his energies to a scheme for uniting them into a synthesis.

An analogous procedure, where we do not have words already established, might be seen if we suppose that we had a special concept to designate the heart acting systolically, and a special concept for the heart acting diastolically. Some thinker might then come along and discover a grand synthesis whereby the two words could be united to form a single functioning heart. And Mr. J. M. Woodger's discussion of the quarrel over structure and function in biology would seem to expose a similar pseudo-problem, resulting purely from an aspect of speech. Structure, he says, is the word which applies to an organ when considered from a three-dimensional set of coördinates, the three dimensions of space. Function applies to the same organ considered from a four-dimensional set, the three spatial coördinates plus the time coördinate. One naturally makes different observations in accordance with the number of coördinates he selects to make them by— but this shift in the basis of his abstracting involves no legitimate material for a quarrel as to whether "structure determines function" or "function determines structure." The man who settles the issue in favor of structure or function will have massively solved a pseudo-problem resulting purely from the fact that one can assemble and classify data from many points of view.

As the nearest *verbal* approach to reality, M. Bergson proposes that we deliberately cultivate the use of contradictory concepts. These will not give us the whole of reality, he says, but at least they will give us something more indicative than is obtainable by the assumption that our conceptualizations of events in nature are real, and to be taken as fundamental enough for brilliant men to set about scrupulously treating these necessary inadequacies of thought and expression as though they reflected corresponding realities in nature. Instead of looking for an Hegelian synthesis that would follow thesis and antithesis, he would have us realize that the real course of events is necessarily, at all times, unified. We should not—as philosophers—speak of an anabolistic process in an organism as wholly distinct from a katabolistic one, thereafter plaguing ourselves to find a schema for joining them and getting metabolism. In cases where the synthetic word does not happen to be already given, he suggests we should get it by combining the antithetical ones (a proposal which seems to be accepted in such contemporary usages as space-time and mind-body).

The Function of Metaphor

"In order to get around this almost universal tendency to confuse abstractions with facts," Mrs. Stephen writes, "Berg-

n sometimes tries to get us to see the facts as they actually
e by using metaphor instead of description in terms of
stract general notions. He has been much criticised for this
t there is really a good deal to be said for attempting to
nvey facts by substituting metaphors for them rather than
using the ordinary intellectual method of substituting ab-
actions reached by analysis. Those who have criticised the
e of metaphor have for the most part not realized how little
moved such description is from the ordinary intellectual
ethod of analysis. They have supposed that in analysis we
ck to the fact itself, whereas in using metaphor we substi-
te for the fact to be described some quite different fact
hich is only connected with it by a more or less remote
alogy. If Bergson's view of the intellectual method is right,
hen we describe in abstract terms we are not sticking to the
ts at all, we are substituting something else for them just
much as if we were using an out and out metaphor. Quali-
s and all abstract general notions are, indeed, nothing but
arks of analogies between a given fact and all the other
ts belonging to the same class: they may mark rather closer
alogies than those brought out by an ordinary metaphor,
t on the other hand in a frank metaphor we at least stick
the concrete, we substitute fact for fact and we are in no
nger of confusing the fact introduced with the actual fact
which the metaphor applies."

Indeed, as the documents of science pile up, are we not
ming to see that whole works of scientific research, even
tire *schools*, are hardly more than the patient repetition, in
its ramifications, of a fertile metaphor? Thus we have, at
ferent eras in history, considered man as the son of God,
an animal, as a political or economic brick, as a machine,
h such metaphor, and a hundred others, serving as the cue
an unending line of data and generalizations. The attempt
fix argument by analogy as a distinct kind of process,

separable from logical argument, seems increasingly futi
The most practical form of thought that one can think
the invention of some new usable device, has been describ
as analogical extension, as when one makes a new machi
by conceiving of some old process, such as the treadle, t
shuttle, the wheel, the see-saw, the wedge, etc., carried ov
into some set of facts to which no one had previously felt th
it belonged.

The heuristic value of scientific analogies is quite like t
surprise of metaphor. The difference seems to be that t
scientific analogy is more patiently pursued, being employ
to inform an entire work or movement, where the poet u
his metaphor for a glimpse only. (Yet even here we may fi
a similarity; the complete works of the poet show signs o
unified attitude precisely such as may be summed up in o
metaphor: "He calls life a dream . . . or a pilgrimage . .
carnival . . . or a labyrinth.")

CHAPTER FOUR

ARGUMENT BY ANALOGY

Analogy and Proof

THE GREAT DANGER of analogy is that a *similarity* is taken
as evidence of an *identity*. Because two things are found
possess a certain trait in common which our point of view
considers notable, we take the common notable trait to indi-
e identity of character. A most obvious example of ana-
ical thought is the mystic symbolism of the Middle Ages,
described by the historian Huizinga:

Symbolic assimilation founded on common properties pre-
poses the idea that these properties are essential to things.
e vision of white and red roses blooming among thorns at
ce calls up a symbolic assimilation in the medieval mind:
example, that of virgins and martyrs, shining with glory,
the midst of their persecutors. The assimilation is produced
ause their attributes are the same: the beauty, the tender-
s, the purity, the white of the roses, are also the attributes
virgins, and the red is the colour of the blood of martyrs.
t this similarity will have a mystic meaning only if the
ddle term connecting the two terms of the symbolic con-
t expresses an essentiality common to both; in other words,
edness and whiteness are something more than names for
physical difference based on quantity, if they are conceived
essences, as realities. The mind of the savage, of the child,
d of the poet never sees them otherwise."

t is not so certain that the sophisticated mind does "see
m otherwise." The apparent difference in our ways of
nking today may be at bottom but a shift in our focus
interests. As C. K. Ogden has said in *The Meaning of
chology*, "The governing principle in association is the

direction of interest, and contiguity only works inside th
principle. Clearness and consecutiveness of thinking, in oth
words, depends primarily upon clearness in our interes
Perhaps most of the blunders of thought are due to confus
and mixed interests." And he adds, what most concerns o
discussion here: "The extraordinary views of many dement
persons can be traced to eccentricities of their interests."

Now, in those vast group insanities or eccentricities
interest which the various periods of history quickly reve
when all their varied certainties, their conflicting codes
heroism and indignation, are put bluntly side by side, do
really find a way of categorically distinguishing betwe
"logical" and "analogical" thought? Because the differen
between our interests and those of the Middle Ages makes
easy for us to deny any significant correlation between a v
gin and the color of a flower, are we using a different proc
of thought today, or merely searching for correspondences
our own in a different area? Is the difference one of form,
merely one of subject?

When a writer gives us a sequence of logical propositic
framed to show why he got to his conclusions, he is almo
reversing the actual processes of his thought. He prese
data which supposedly lead to a conclusion—whereas t
conclusion had led to the selection and arrangement of t
data. The *demonstration* is derived from the *demonstrandu*
Euclid's proofs are ramifications of his original thesis, or po
of view. From what we want to arrive at, we deduce o
ways of getting there, although the conventions of logi
exposition usually present things the other way round. T
debater suggests that his "facts" lead to his "resolved," but
know that his position was assigned him, and that he sele
his "facts" accordingly. To make us weep contentedly at t
final reunion of brother and sister, the poet hangs tellta
lockets about the necks of the little waifs lost in chapter o

When reading, we accept the final reunion as the logical conclusion of the telltale lockets planted in chapter one—but the order was exactly the reverse, the lockets in chapter one being the logical conclusion of the reunion in chapter last.

It is in this sense that we call a demonstration by Euclid merely additional matter created out of the principle of selectivity established by the nature of the particular proposition. The *true corollaries* of a proposition are usually called its *proof*. Applying which reversal to our mention of metaphor in science, we should say that the "data" evolved by those who would prove that men are machines, or the sons of God, or chemical compounds, etc., are observations moulded by the informing point of view.

There is nothing scandalous in this, unless one naïvely permits himself to assume that there is something absolutely right about this inverted order of statement, and feels that the very universe must be bungling and misguided unless it proceeds in accordance with the conventions of a barrister's plea. I do not see why the universe should accommodate itself to a man-made medium of communication, particularly when there is so strongly a *creative* or *poietic* quality about its goings-on, and we know from our own little bits of poetry that the preparations result from the ends prepared for. Perhaps because we have come to think of ourselves as *listening* to the universe, as waiting to see what it will prove to us, we have psychotically made the corresponding readjustment of assuming that the universe itself will abide by our rules of discussion and give us its revelations in a cogent manner. Our notion of causality as a succession of pushes from behind is thus a disguised way of insisting that experience abide by the conventions of a good argument.

Such considerations have bearing on Bergson's proposal that we programmatically combine logical opposites, on the ground that the conflicts are not in nature, but in the implements of logic itself. This proposal led us to consider the question of metaphor and analogy in thinking, and to ask whether there is any other kind of thinking, whether one can justly distinguish between *logical* and *analogical* thought

Tests of Success

One will note here that the medieval thinker was using precisely the general patterns of orientation we now follow He attempted to foretell events, and thus to guide his conduct, on the basis of a cosmological schema for characterizing the relationships in nature which he considered vital to his welfare. The Middle Ages must have found and correctly used many of these, as is evident in the fact that we, their descendants, are here today. If a people's growth and multiplication is not proof of a doctrine's rightness, what is? We cannot say that their doctrines were not tested, when there was daily corroboration in the satisfactions of prayer, popular festivals, and artistic exaltations. The scientific technique of isolating an experiment has given us different criteria for judging what success is—and when we consider the individualism that seems to have accompanied our technique of isolation, realizing that individualism can have a very bad effect upon the social body, we find reason to ask whether our own tests of success are wholly satisfactory either.

Much of our heuristic material offered now, to be sure, is of a sort wherein testing is easily made more accurate. Should one offer grounds for believing that man is an angel, empirical tests are tenuous. But should he hold, as would be more in keeping with our emphases, that man is a parachute, a few simple experiments with jumping from a housetop may convince him that the similarities between man and a parachute are slight as compared with their differences. That is, an analogical extension applied to the making of a new machine can soon disclose its inadequacies (though not always even here; the analogical extension from birds to flying machines was long proved false before it was proved correct).

In any case, the laboratory method of applied science should not blind us to the fact that most of our significant concerns with basic cultural matters lie in a territory where working models cannot possibly be made. The testing is as vague as with any medieval system of symbolic correspondence. People go on praising the objectivity of science despite the many significant rival analyses in any given branch of science. We usually tend to ignore this Babel of assertions, and to speak of science as though it were one thing rather than an assemblage of widely disagreeing scientists. And the success of science in some categories where analogy can be tested by working models has been permitted by analogical extension to carry over its prestige to categories where its analogies are open only to the vaguest kind of testing. If people believe a belief and live, the fact of their survival tends to prove the adequacy of the belief. This is so because wrong beliefs are not necessarily fatal—and because even dangerous beliefs may be of such a sort that they cannot easily be proved dangerous.

Even in those areas where the tests of success are made possible by experiment, it is only by a deliberate limitation of *interests* that we can establish such a test. Is the success of nitro-glycerine adequately tested, for instance, when a charge of it blows up an experimental rock, or when it has been distributed throughout the explosive social structure of the world? Are Pasteur's experiments proved "successful" by the prevention of one disease, or by the ultimate pollution of the bloodstream through all mankind which could result from the systematic extension of his methods? How many people today are rotting in either useless toil or in dismal worklessness because of certain technological successes? We do not here aim to discredit the accomplishments of science, which are mainly converted into menaces by the inadequacies of present political institutions. We desire simply to indicate that *the region where testing is of vital importance*, where the tests of success are in turn to be tested, is the region of *Weltanschauung*, of cultural, moral, political emphases, of ambition, concepts of the good life, notions of ultimate human purpose, where our opportunities to test the justice of our analogical extensions by reference to working models are not much better than at any other period in history.

Classification Dictated by Interest

One advantage our own era may have is the vast documentation of historical and psychological relativity itself. This relativistic attitude, be it in poetry or in the laboratory, has furthered the tendency to characterize events from a myriad shifting points of view: from the standpoint of an African explorer, of endocrine secretions, of the stenographer whose boss kept asking her to work after hours, of ethnology, geography, class conflict, physiological and psychological types, life in a Paris café, a Hindu pariah in love with a dissolute Englishwoman, a mother complex, primitive drives, etc., the causal systems of the scientists and the novelists here being indeterminately commingled.

The sum total of it all prepares for the maximum of Perspective by Incongruity, inasmuch as a given classification cuts across other classifications on the bias, and each new mode of classification produces new alignments incongruous with the alignments flowing from other modes of classification. If one wrote, for instance, "the princess, her courtiers, the ladies in waiting, and some pigs," one would have exemplified bathos, since pigs do not properly belong in this category. Yet when one speaks of "all living organisms," precisely

such bathos, as regards the *social* way of classifying, is implicit in his statement, which unites the princess and her pigs
under a single head.

Classifications are heuristic by reason of the fact that,
through the processes of abstraction and analogy, they dic-
tate new groupings, hence new discoveries. Thus a psychologist may couple a very great poet with a very poor one on the
grounds that both are *introverts*; systems of government as
unlike as Fascism, Communism, and monarchy may be
grouped on the grounds that they are all *dictatorships;* or
architectural structures as radically different as pyramids and
cathedrals may be grouped in accordance with a new concept
of *contemporaneity.*

When a philosopher invents a new approach to reality, he
promptly finds that his predecessors saw something as a unit
which he can subdivide, or that they accepted distinctions
which his system can name as unities. The universe would
appear to be something like a cheese; it can be sliced in an
infinite number of ways—and when one has chosen his own
pattern of slicing, he finds that other men's cuts fall at the
wrong places.

Interrelation of Analogy, Metaphor, Abstraction, Classification, Interest, Expectancy, and Intention

As soon as one tries to carry his pattern of cuts beyond the
classifications recognized in common speech, one strains at
the limits of "good taste," since good taste is manifested
through our adherence to the kinds of relationship already
indicated by the terminology of common sense. When attempting to extend one's classifications into new regions of
inference, one necessarily hits upon analogical extensions, or
linguistic inventions, not sanctioned by the previous usages of
his group. For instance, popular speech distinguishes between

vegetarians and meat eaters, but a thinker would affront the present barriers of vocabulary who attempted by analogical extension applying the same distinction to a description of literary styles, or to modes of conduct. We consider such metaphorical overlappings natural to poetry, but we do not generally recognize the presence of the same process in scientific or philosophic classifying. Both the poet's metaphors and the scientist's abstractions discuss something in terms of something else. And the course of analogical extension is determined by the particular kind of interest uppermost at the time.

Abstraction means literally a "drawing from." Whenever a similar strain can be discerned in dissimilar events ("drawn from" them) we can classify the events together on the basis of this common abstraction. And the particular strains which we select as significant depend upon the nature of our interests. The poet may be interested in the sea's anger, the chemist in its iodine. In the complexities of ordinary adult experience, an interest itself takes its shape from a prior body of classifications. Mr. A may be interested in cheating Mr. B, for instance, because he hopes to obtain a certain result which in the end will procure him something labeled desirable in the code of his contemporaries. And he is interested in using one trick rather than another by reason of various judgments as to the chances of success, degree of risk, personal aptitude, etc. The relationship between interests and classifications being interactive, there is no absolute starting point—but if we arbitrarily begin with interest for conveniences of discussion, we can extend the concept of metaphorical and analogical abstraction until it covers the whole field of orientation.

This particular thing is a *fire*, classified as dreadful by the burnt child, who will not get too close to it because it is to his *interest* not to be burned again. In accordance with this interest, its ability to burn rates high in his *expectancies*. The factor of expectancy suggests also the relationship between interest and *intention*. Intentions likewise disclose an abstract element. One who *intends* to build a fire, for instance, has dropped from the mind many specific details involved in the actual process of fire-building. He *intends* by recalling only certain "significant" aspects of his past experience with fire-building, thinks vaguely of wood gathering rather than of the particular events connected with the particular pieces of wood he had gathered in the past. We may thus note that in any educated action (action based upon expectancy involving past experience) one has necessarily *abstracted*. The child in Watson's experiment feared fur coats because it had abstracted from rabbits the quality of furriness—and since rabbits had conditionally become characterized as unpleasant, the rabbitness of a fur coat took on this same character.

Even a purely present act, such as that of a child learning to walk, has a strong suspicion of the abstract about it. The child gradually learns certain lowest common denominators of bodily balance, certain coördinations which apply *in a general way* to any act of walking. After he has learned to walk, even many years after he has become an accomplished walker, if you put him in a new situation, the abstractness of his walking becomes apparent. He has learned *a certain kind of walking* that is adapted to floors and streets, for instance, but poorly adapted to rough mountainsides—or the skilled sailor, having learned to walk by taking the roll of a ship into açcount, rolls when on firm ground.

Eventually one may meet such new situations by "analogical extension," adding some device from a different context, as when, accustomed to walking on level ground, one *invents* a forward swing of his hands for walking up-hill. Here he has projected certain balancing processes which were not thus extended in walking as he had learned it. He is an inventor, just as truly as though his new balancing device could be patented and monopolized.

It will also be observed that there is a certain bluntness in these accomplishments: The sailor, in learning an *adequate* stride for shipboard, made himself unfit for land. And it will be noted that such terms as analysis, synthesis, classification, and ideality are to be viewed similarly. One fears fires or intends to make fires by the singling out of certain characters: as, say, that fire burns. But acids can also burn. Hence, one's interests in this matter enable him to analyze both fire and acids as having a burn-character, which is an *ideality*—and by it he may produce a synthesis, may give us a classification of events in accordance with their burn-character, despite the many important differences between these events in other respects. And when he changes the nature of his interests, or point of view, he will approach events with a new ideality, reclassifying them, putting things together that were in different classes, and dividing things that had been together.

As for those who would doubt the great value of analogy, or abstraction, or bluntness, or stupidity in the assisting of human expectations, let them take a piece of litmus and read its message by "analogical extension," as it judges whether a chemical is acid or alkali by registering red or blue. So able is it in so classifying, that it can classify in no other way, as regards its response to liquids at ordinary temperatures. Our scales too are inveterate classifiers, since they record by one scheme of abstractions and no other. Thus also with our most delicate instruments of precision, which are mere extensions of our vocabulary, a way of making definitions on a dial.

Our senses themselves are similar abstracters, abstracting or interpreting certain events as having a sound-character, a taste-character, a heat-character, a sight-character, etc., for as Helmholtz pointed out, our very sensory equipment is a set of recording instruments that turn certain events into a certain kind of sign, and we find our way through life on the basis of these signs.

We even know that there are events not interpreted at all by our sensory equipment, ultra-violet rays for instance. Rather, we might have to modify this by saying that such events do not produce conscious interpretation. The response may be there nonetheless, as witness the rise in temperature which has been noted among some people working in broadcasting studios, though the actual rays that pass through them are not converted into signs in the sense that we consciously feel, see, or hear them. We may then learn to infer the presence of the rays secondarily, from the presence of the fever.

The Search for Analogous Processes

The business of interpretation is accomplished by the two processes of over-simplification and analogical extension. We over-simplify a given event when we characterize it from the standpoint of a given interest—and we attempt to invent a similar characterization for other events by analogy. The great difficulty with the method in the judging of historical events is that it requires the rectification of false analogies through trial and error, whereas the vast bungling complexes of history do not recur. For this reason, those who attempt to interpret history by ambitiously driven analogical extensions lay much emphasis upon the factors of history that can be called recurrent. But one can note the recurrent only by *abstracting* certain qualities from the given historical complexities. One must have special informing interests of his own. Hence, in the study of historic movements, one must violate the tenor of any culture as the members of that culture know it. Similarly, one must violate the tenor of one's own culture as the members of his culture know it. Hence the perspective by incongruity to which the historian or sociologist is automatically pledged.

The modern attempts to study *processes* can lead just as

surely to analogical over-extension as did the old medieva attempt to relate events by the search for their *essence*. The concept of process, for instance, involves precisely the notion that a given process may manifest itself in a surprising number ber of different guises, not all of which are identified in the vocabulary of common sense.

We have heard much of German *Schrecklichkeit*. We have also heard of German *Gründlichkeit. Thoroughness* and *terrorism*—one a word linked with all our *good* associations the other falling wholly in the category of the *bad*. Suppose I were to call them merely two different manifestations of an identical process, saying that *terrorism* is the word for *tho roughness* when applied to the category of warfare, and that *thoroughness* is the word for the militant, combative integ rity of terror when applied to the category of workmanship

Or suppose I similarly noted a connection between Englis diplomacy and the philosophy of *muddling through*. To *muddle through* is to be not over-exact, to let events shap themselves in part, to make up one's specific policies as on goes along, in accordance with the unforeseen newnesses that occur in the course of events, instead of approaching one problem with an entire program laid out rigidly in advance Is not this the ideal equipment of the diplomat?

Yet as soon as one attempts conversions of this sort, on faces the violation of linguistic and conceptual categorie already established. In the case of *Gründlichkeit* and *Schrec lichkeit*, it amounts to saying that one is terroristic in h industriousness and conscientious in his slaughter. Or tha successful diplomacy is a kind of bungling, while the Britis public is "diplomatic" in its present confusions. Such use c analogical extension similarly required us to admit that th gashouse gang was pious, while Christ, in offering new mear ings to the Jews, was asking them to commit a grave impiet a profound treachery against their entire orientation, with i established set of expectancies and motives. To characterize events by their *pattern*, alas! whereas an earlier age characterized them by their *essence*, merely commits us to different channels of extension.

To be sure, the breakdown in our categories of the "proper" is now so thorough that this transplantation of words into "inappropriate" settings is constantly with us. A man lays out an argument, point 1, point 2, point 3—and another answers him, not by taking up each point in turn and refuting it, but by saying simply, "The man is a bourgeois," or "He has a mother complex,"—or "He wants the job instead." In other words, recognizing the psychotic factor of interest, we immediately cut across the "proprieties" of the given discussion by a flat diagnosis of interests.

Our own proposal to cultivate so ambivalent a concept as that of trained incapacity clearly involves us in a clash with the vestigial congruities still upheld by language. For if one is interested in noting how a certain *insight* can be called a *bluntness* when approached from another point of view, one has necessarily vowed himself to conflicts with the classifications of everyday speech, which is primarily designed for calling things *good or bad, intelligent or stupid, this or that,* and being done with it. As soon as one attempts to trace a process through its observable manifestations regardless of the various ways this process happens to have been named or left unnamed, eulogized or condemned, in its different aspects, he will necessarily come into conflict with the accepted barriers of speech.

The language of common sense is full of abstractions, analogies, and double or triple names for the same thing. Thus, we call *obstinacy* in an enemy what we call *perseverance* in ourselves—or we call another man's frankness "incaution" and label as "caution" our own *lack* of frankness. And the language of common sense was never designed to trace processes through all their important metamorphoses. Any attempt to offer two concepts where the language of common sense had had one, or to offer a merger where the language of common sense had discriminated, naturally requires an artificial manipulation of the linguistic proprieties.

Perhaps one reason why mystics have so often outraged people of good taste is precisely because they stress the metaphorical nature of all speech. Their attitude towards the accepted categories of every day tended to give them blanket endorsement for retailing their unusual experiences in any metaphorical symbols they could manage, no matter how poorly their terms might fall together from the standpoint of "good sense." Inasmuch as mystics were concerned with precisely such aspects of experience as our technique of abstraction is not designed to handle, what more natural than that they should express themselves through a deliberate cultivation of logical disorders, turning by preference to the sharply Bergsonian oxymoron ("a sweet bitterness"—"painful, yet a delight"—"a brilliance wholly black")? For once you take words as mere symbolizations, rather than as being the accurate and total names for specific, unchangeable realities, you have lost the criteria of judgment which will tell you that it is "wrong," say, to describe a bullfight as a love encounter between the male toreador and the female bull, with the audience perhaps as peeping Toms.

Or perhaps, if you are a Hemingway instead of a Waldo Frank, you will prefer an even bolder technique of planned incongruity, describing gore and slaughter in a vocabulary heretofore reserved for such delicate operations as lens grinding, or astronomical measurement, or for the cautious removal of a diseased mastoid, or for such nice compliments as might be turned in a Jane Austen parlor. Much of Hemingway's power, in fact, is due to his discovering a vein of congruity still partially intact, the vein of our humanitarianism that went with the emancipatory aspects of the laissez-faire psychosis—and into this region he has introduced the most skilfully incongruous terms, gentle words, approbational words, highly Christian words, for events to which we habitually applied words of a wholly resentful order.

An Incongruous Assortment of Incongruities

The question of new meanings or heuristic is confused in its individual trends; and though many men would seem to have merely been breaking down old schemes of orientation, it is probable that with greater or lesser clarity they were doing so in accordance with a new schematization of their own which they were offering as replacement. In some brands of nonsense humor current today, it is hard to distinguish an informing principle other than a general dislike of our great complexity and confusion and indirectness of values, a dislike which the humorists convey by introducing a kind of artificial blindness, a complete vacuity as their new point of view—and the results are often as rich in perspective as are incongruities attained by more systematic methods.

Indeed, the nearest approach to a modern art which can appeal to the naïve and the sophisticated alike is perhaps this ambitious and creative nonsense. The explanation may be that the adepts of this organized stumbling are responding to a psychosis common to all. We are all necessarily involved in the momentous discrepancies of our present "order," generated perhaps from that basic economic freak whereby a "surplus" of productivity becomes a national and an international menace—and though we may disagree as to the ways *out of* such an irregular existence, even a paragon of orthodoxy must respond to these disorders as they manifest themselves in the remoter, but highly barometric region of our judgments, tastes, values, and expectancies.

There is, however, even a stage of planned incongruity that goes beyond humor: the grotesque, wherein the perception of discordancies is cultivated without smile or laughter. In comparison with the mechanisms underlying the appeal of the grotesque, even the most destructive nonsense is seen to be an upholder of things as they were. Humor still manifests its respect for our earlier categories of judgment, even while outraging them. Like blasphemy in the sphere of dogmatic religion, it reaffirms the existence of the old gods once more in the very act of defying them. And humor is most explosive when, besides throwing a shoe among the wheels of our machinery of judgment, it not only leaves one favored judgment completely intact, but deliberately strengthens it. It pits value against value, disposition against disposition, psychotic weighting against psychotic weighting—but it flatters us by confirming as well as destroying.

The grotesque is a much more complex matter, and gradually merges into something very much like mysticism. Humor tends to be conservative, the grotesque tends to be revolutionary. Aristophanes was a humorist, excoriating new ways with reference to traditional tests of propriety. Aristophanes was pious, but Socrates had leanings toward the grotesque and impious.

The gargoyles of the Middle Ages were typical instances of planned incongruity. The maker of gargoyles who put man's-head on bird-body was offering combinations which were completely rational as judged by his logic of essences. In violating one order of classification, he was stressing another. Considered in this light, Spengler's morphology of history becomes simply a modern gargoyle, a Super-Realist mural, a vast grotesque wherein the writer can soberly picture Kant walking the streets of ancient Athens or bring Petronius to a New York night club.

Such considerations also reveal a gargoyle element in

Marx's formula of class-consciousness. Class-consciousness is a social therapeutic because it is *reclassification-consciousness*. It is a new perspective that realigns something so profoundly ethical as our categories of allegiance. By this reinterpretative schema, members of the same race or nation who had formerly thought of themselves as *allies* become *enemies*, and members of different races or nations who had formerly thought of themselves as *enemies* become *allies*. The new classification thus has implicit in it a new set of ideas as to what *action* is, and in these ideas are implicit new criteria for deciding what means-selection would be adequate.

A kind of secular mysticism having a distinctly gargoyle quality is to be seen today in the paintings of the Super-Realists, who may show us a watch, dripping over the table like spilled molasses, not merely as an affront to our everyday experience with watches as rigid, but because a *dripping* watch gives us glimpses into a *different symbolism of time*. The outrageous watch is not *funny* at all—nor are those "humorous" death-bed scenes in *The Magic Mountain* funny. In their incongruity, they are even terrible.

The notion of perspective by incongruity has obvious bearing upon the grotesques of our dreams. Dreams (and dream-art) seek to connect events by a "deeper" scheme of logic than prevails in our everyday rationale of utility. The symbolism of both dreams and dream-art makes gargoyles of our waking experiences, merging things which common sense had divided and dividing things which common sense had merged.

Joyce, blasting apart the verbal atoms of meaning, and out of the ruins making new elements synthetically, has produced our most striking instances of modern linguistic gargoyles. He has accomplished the dangerous feat of dreaming most laxly while most awake. In the portmanteau words of his latest manner, he seems to be attempting to include within the span of one man's work an etymological destiny which may generally take place in the course of many centuries, as the rigidities of education gradually yield to the natural demand that the language of practical utility and the language of "unconscious" utility be brought closer together and their present intense duality be mitigated.

The concept of trained incapacity leads me to suspect that his disorders of sight are the reverse aspect of his accomplishments. The self-imposed blindness of Œdipus, who had outraged the most awesome pieties of his tribe, suggests a notable parallel here, since Joyce was profoundly Catholic in his youth, and his adult work, as judged by this Catholic framework, is one mighty monument of heresy. Modern medicine sufficiently recognizes a correspondence between our attitudes and our physical disabilities for one to feel justified in relating Joyce's misfortunes, as well as his attainments, to his intense skill at heretically disintegrating his childhood meanings, to which his exceptional personal sensitiveness (as attested in his *Portrait of the Artist as a Young Man*) had fully exposed him. This conflict between his earliest pieties and the reclassifications that went with his later perspective could, in a man whose responses are so thorough, result in a mental concern with disintegration which would have physical counterparts.[1]

---

[1] Such a line of thought suggests that, in some cases at least, a cult of perspective carried to extremes which far outstrip the possibilities of communication, or socialization, can have its roots in irrational emotional conflicts. For instance, we know that, if a man undergoes an intensely unpleasant experience, neutral environmental facts which happen to be associated with this experience tend to take on the same unpleasant quality. Someone who as a child was badly treated by a man with a wart may subsequently feel ill at ease with anyone who has a wart—or the mere sight of a town in which we were once very unhappy may restore the feeling of unhappiness.

Now, if one happens to have been thorough enough for *an entire orientation* to become associated in his mind with a painful experience,

ARGUMENT BY ANALOGY

We may also consider that semi-art, semi-science, *caricature*, which pursues the course of planned incongruity by a technique of abstraction. In caricature, certain aspects of the object are deliberately omitted, while certain other aspects are over-stressed (*caricare* "to overload"). Caricatures can almost talk in concepts. Many of Georg Grosz's earlier nudes were a simple choice of vocabulary: mug for mouth, bean for head, lunch-hooks for hands, can for buttocks. Caricature usually reclassifies in accordance with clearly indicated interests.

Dadaism, in many ways the movement out of which Super-Realism grew, revealed an organized hatred of good taste, courted a deliberate flouting of the appropriate, and thus is squarely in the movement toward planned incongruity. But Dadaism suffered from poor rationalization. Whereas it was

---

in attempting to obliterate the experience he may tend to wipe out the orientation associated with it. It is thus possible that even a wholly rational orientation, which is adequately serving its social purposes, may become discredited in one man's mind, since there are always the possibilities of individual unhappiness—and if the unhappy individual happens to have been so thorough as to associate his whole orientation with his unhappiness, the orientation will take on the unpleasant quality of the unpleasant experience itself. Pain is a great incentive to eloquence, since it provides one with an altar of preoccupation to which he must bring appropriate offerings—and eloquence is a strategy of appeal, a social implement for inducing others to agree with us. In this way individual pain may lead to radical evangelism, as the sufferer attempts to socialize his position by inducing others to repudiate the orientation painful to himself.

In classical eras, eras of pronounced social conformity, such anarchistic tendencies of the individual artist or thinker are corrected by the recalcitrance of the social body. In the very act of attempting to socialize his position, the artist is forced to revise his statements to such an extent that he himself is reclaimed in the process. But at times when an orientation is greatly weakened (and particularly under conditions when competitive demands place a premium upon the most notable or salient kinds of expression) such normative influences are lacking.

pursued by a group of very ambitious and serious-minded writers, many of them extremely well equipped in the traditional lore and especially interested in criticism, they allowed their movement to remain on the basis of mere waywardness, irresponsibility, refusal, which left it with too unpretentious a critical backing. This weakness was inevitable, since their attacks upon the old scheme of the pretentious would naturally apply to their own theorizings as well. But a movement so wicked was forever exposed to a sudden determination to reform. It would make inevitably for the resolve to put away childish things, to take up more serious matters—whereat it seems to have served as a mere opening wedge, a first draft, which some of its adherents later revised as Communism, and some as Super-Realism. Since both branches are concerned with new meanings, we can easily appreciate how the earlier systematized incongruities of Dadaism proper (with its cry of *"Rien! Rien!"*) were an integral step in either of these directions.

Incidentally, since the Dadaists traced their cultural descent from Baudelaire, we might recall an article "L'Erotologie de Baudelaire," by M. Jean Royère, who has noted the great prevalence of metonymy and "systematic catachreses" in the poems of Baudelaire. He discusses Baudelaire's "systematic use of the most illogical figure of speech, the catachresis (or mixed metaphor), which might be called the metaphor and hyperbole in one." Royère notes the effectiveness of the device particularly in the poem "Beau Navire," where Baudelaire likens a woman to a boat moving out to sea. The critic selects the word "perspective" to characterize the result.

In considering the profusion of perspectives, of course, we treat need and opportunity as interchangeable. The crumbling and conflict of values certainly puts new burdens upon the artist—but on the other hand, it facilitates certain kinds of artistic endeavor which, in a stabilized structure, might be possible to the wayward individual but would not be very highly rated by his group. In the confusion of a vocabulary (and of the social texture behind it) writers not only lose old effects but gain new ones. Grotesque inventions flourish *when it is easiest to imagine the grotesque*, or *when it is hardest to imagine the classical* (one may take either phrasing, as he prefers). One sees perspectives beyond the structure of a given vocabulary when that structure is no longer firm.

Historical conditions cannot wholly account for such a situation. Upon an individual, at any time in history, there may converge a set of factors which strongly differentiate his situation from that of his group. Great liquidity in one's personal life may lead one to see "unclassically" even in an era generally classical. And similarly today, some men have enjoyed cloistered conditions which enable them to retain fixities not there for most of us. The metaphor of the historic stream cannot be taken too literally, unless one is willing to judge a course by its direction through whole millennia, not decades.

Furthermore, there is always some quasi-mystical attempt being made to see around the edges of the orientation in which a poet or thinker lives. It is precisely in eras of classical drama, for instance, that the devices of dramatic irony flourish at their best. In cases of dramatic irony we see two conflicting sets of meanings acting simultaneously, as the *dramatis personæ* interpret their situation one way and the audience interprets it another. But in this device of classical drama (it flourishes best when a scheme of orientation is comparatively firm) there is nothing problematical about the audience's knowledge in the matter. The characters are *wrong* and the audience is *right*. The characters think they know, but the audience knows it knows. The characters may be bewildered as to motivation, but the audience is clear.

A Babel of new orientations has arisen in increasing profusion during the last century, until now hardly a year goes by without some brand new model of the universe being offered us. Such interpretative schemes, varying in their scope and thoroughness, seem limited only by the time and industry of the heuristically-minded—and our examples can be chosen at random. Out of all this overlapping, conflicting, and supplementing of interpretative frames, what arises as a *totality*? The only thing that all this seems to make for is a reënforcement of the *interpretative attitude* itself.

The vast documentation concerning new classifications and characterizations of the events about us may best serve as new case histories, material to be used for the closer study of classification and characterization in general. The myriad orientations will be tragically wasted, the genius of one of the world's most vigorous centuries will be allowed to go unused, unless we can adapt its very welter of interpretations as skeptical grounding for our own certainties. Such an attempt to utilize all past frames of thought, regardless of their apparent divergencies from us, is arising in the science of symbolism, as it extends all the way from new and sharper rigors of lexicography, through the various schemes of individual and group psychoanalysis (as writers like Bentham, Marx, Freud, Jung, and Burrow sought various devices for disclosing how the factor of interest bears upon our orientation) through the many attempts to found a language divorced from common sense (as with the adherents of symbolic logic, or Bergson's planned incongruity) to methodological speculations (mainly in physics and semeiotic) which lead one close to the edge of a mysticism as arrant as that of any "disorganized" medieval seer.

After all, the language of common sense was not invented for the extremes of heuristic forcing to which our contemporary eschatologists would apply it. Hence, any deliberate attempt at analogical extension can be accomplished only by going beyond the conventional categories of speech. The great emphasis upon the test of success is not so despicable as it might seem—for here we have at least a rough and ready corrective to the inventions of new classificatory alignments. The only trouble is, as we have said before, that success itself is a variable—and the tests by which the success of our process-thinking is proved may be as implicated in our ways of process-thinking as the tests of medieval essence-thinking were implicit in their ways of linking events by essence.

In any event, the confluence of scientific revelations, of minute and comprehensive schemes whereby we find new readings for the character of events, is in itself the evidence that Perspective by Incongruity is both needed and extensively practiced. Were we to summarize the totality of its effects, advocating as an *exhortation* what has already spontaneously occurred, we might say that planned incongruity should be deliberately cultivated for the purpose of experimentally wrenching apart all those molecular combinations of adjective and noun, substantive and verb, which still remain with us. It should subject language to the same "cracking" process that chemists now use in their refining of oil. If science would be truly atheistic or impious to the last degree, it should try systematically to eradicate every last linkage that remains with us merely as the result of piety or innate propriety, and not because of its rationally established justification.

An idea which commonly carries with it diminutive modifiers, for instance, should be treated by magnification, as were one to discuss the heinousness of an extra slice of beef, or the brain storm that rules when one has stumped one's toe. One should be prepared to chart the genesis, flourishing, and decay of a family witticism, precisely as though he were concerned with the broadest processes of cultural change, basic patterns of psychology and history thus being conveniently brought within the scope of the laboratory. One should study one's dog for his *Napoleonic* qualities, or observe mosquitoes for signs of wisdom to which we are forever closed. One should discuss sneezing in the terms heretofore reserved for the analysis of a brilliant invention, as if it were a creative act, a vast synthesis uniting in its simple self a multitude of prior factors.

Conversely, where the accepted linkages have been of an imposing sort, one should establish perspective by looking through the reverse end of his glass, converting mastodon into microbes, or human beings into vermin upon the face of the earth. Or perhaps writing a history of medicine by a careful study of the quacks, one should, by the principle of the *lex continui*, extend his observations until they threw light upon the processes of a Pasteur. Or do a history of poetry by going among the odds and ends of Bohemia, asking oneself why some monkey-jumper wore a flowing tie, and letting the answer serve as an explanation of Yeats or Valéry. Or allow the words of children, carefully charted, to humble us by their way of neglecting our profoundest sense of right—quite as though we had two social words for chair, an *A-chair* designating a chair sat in by negligible people, servants, children, and poor relatives, and a *B-chair* reserved for persons of distinction, such as the father and the mother—and as though a little child, with his "innate iconoclasm," had literally convulsed us by politely saying to the Bishop, "May I offer you this *A-chair*?"

Or by a schematic shift in the locus of judgment, supply eulogistic words to characterize events usually characterized dyslogistically, or vice versa, or supplement both eulogistic and dyslogistic by words that will be neutral, having no censorious quality whatsoever, but purely indicative of a process. For the friends of a man may discuss his devotion to his business, whereas his enemies may have the same activity in mind when they discuss his greed, whereby in talking to both we might discuss him somewhat as a stone rolling down a hill or as illustrating the diversion of man's generic militant, competitive equipment into the specific channels of effort that happen to be singled out by a particular orientation based upon commercial enterprise. Or, just as in the term xy, we may discuss x as a function of y or y as a function of x, let us move about incongruously among various *points de départ* for the discovery of causal connectives, whereby we learn either that free markets were a function of the movement towards emancipation or that the entire cry for emancipation was a mere function of the demand for free markets.

Or let us even deliberately deprive ourselves of available knowledge in the search for new knowledge—as for instance: Imagine that you had long studied some busy and ingenious race of organisms, in the attempt to decide for yourself, from the observing of their ways, what inducements led them to act as they did; imagine next that, after long research with this race which you had thought speechless, you suddenly discovered that they had a vast communicative network, a remarkably complex arrangement of signs; imagine next that you finally succeeded in deciphering these signs, thereby learning of all this race's motives and purposes as this race itself conceived of them. Would you not be exultant? Would you not feel that your efforts had been rewarded to their fullest? Imagine, then, setting out to study mankind, with whose system of speech you are largely familiar. Imagine beginning your course of study *precisely by depriving yourself of this familiarity*, attempting to understand motives and purposes by avoiding as much as possible the clues handed you ready-made in the texture of the language itself. In this you will have deliberately discarded available data in the interests of a fresh point of view, the heuristic or perspective value of a planned incongruity.

Which suggests that one may even programmatically adopt a postulate known to be false—for the "heuristic value of error" has already been established, as in the fertility of the phlogiston theory, a belief in "fire-particles" which led to the discovery of atomic combinations. So let us, perhaps, discover what is implicit in the proposition that "the presence of heat makes water dislike flowing downhill—and in order to avoid having to 'seek its level' it turns into steam." Let us found a mathematics—or an ethic!—by outraging the law of the excluded middle whereby, instead of saying "A is A; A is not non-A," we may say, "A is either A or non-A." Let us say with Lawrence that the earth's crops make the sun shine, or with James and Lange that we're sad because we cry.

Let us contrive not merely the flat merger of contradictions recommended by Bergson, but also the multitude of imperfect matchings, giving scientific terms for words usually treated sentimentally, or poetic terms for the concepts of science, or discussing disease as an accomplishment, or great structures of thought as an oversight, or considering intense ambition or mighty planetary movements as a mere following of the line of least resistance, a kind of glorified laziness; or using noble epithets for ignoble categories, and borrowing terms for the ephemeral to describe events for which we habitually reserve terms for the enduring. Let us not only discuss a nation as though it were an individual, but also an individual as though he were a nation, depicting massive events trivially, and altering the scale of weeds in a photograph until they become a sublime and towering forest—shifting from the animal, the vegetable, the physical, the mental, "irresponsibly" applying to one category the terms habitual to another, as when Whitehead discerns mere habit in the laws of atomic behavior—or like a kind of Professorial E. E. Cumming who, had he called man an ape, would then study apes to understand Aristotle. "Let us do this?" Everywhere, in our systems for forcing inferences, it is being done.

(The vocabulary of economists, with its abstract and staistical formulations for the description of human conduct, is perhaps the most outstanding instance of incongruity. A man may think of himself as "saving money," but in the economist's categories of description this man may be performing a mere act of "postponed consumption." The economist here says in effect that the savings bank carries in its window a sign reading: "Postpone your consumption, at 3% per annum." Similarly with an "insurance risk." Any particular man who takes out insurance is going to die at a certain date. This is simply a yes-or-no proposition. On such-and-such a date, he will or will not be dead. Yet as member of an insured group he takes on a wholly new attribute: the attribute of *probability*. The *probabilities* are three to one or four to one that on such-and-such a date he will be living or dead. He thus tends to think of himself as possessing this probability, which is solely a character possessed by him as a member of a certain abstract grouping, and does not at all apply to him individually. As an individual (the consideration that really concerns him) his case possesses no probabilities at all: he either will, or will not, be dead. . . . This deceptive attitude toward the whole subject of classification is at present observable in the intense critical battles over proletarian literature. A proletarian is defined, by abstraction, as a worker of a certain sort. But he is obviously many other things as well: a particular endoctrine combination, for instance, an "introvert" or "extravert," a man who did or did not have a bad attack of measles in his childhood, etc. All such non-proletarian factors are involved in his make-up—yet critics attempt to find some rigid distinction between proletarian and non-proletarian thinking that will serve as a schema for classifying *all* his expressions. No wonder they are forever detecting in him "bourgeois" or "feudalistic" vestiges.)

La Rochefoucauld says that some things should be seen close at hand and others from a distance. The doctrine of perspective would suggest that perspective is heuristic insofar as we see close at hand the things we had formerly seen from afar, and vice versa. Or Spinoza recommended that we see things *sub specie æternitatis*—but seeing by the ways of planned incongruity is a deliberate and systematic seeing of things *sub specie temporis*, though undertaken precisely for the ends which Spinoza had in view when speaking of eternity. And Leibniz, who is in many ways our father, has written: "The result of each view of the universe as seen from a different position is a substance which expresses the universe conformably to this view, provided God sees fit to render his thought effective and to produce the substance." God often does see fit—as witness the endless "substances" of the great century of New Meanings.

No wonder so many Nineteenth-Century writers were prodigious in output. A shift in the angle of approach must disclose an infinity of ways in which our former classifications can be reclassified. After a lifetime of productivity we find Bentham wishing that he could become a dozen selves, since his perspective showed him that he had work for all. Indeed he has in time become thousands of selves, as Darwin also has.

CHAPTER FIVE

SECULAR CONVERSIONS

The Fundamentals of Psychoanalysis

IN CLOSING this section, perhaps we should study that region in which *interpretation* and *therapy* most clearly converge: those secular bringers of good tidings, the psychoanalysts. From our standpoint, psychoanalysis can be treated as a simple technique of non-religious conversion. It effects its cures by providing a new perspective that dissolves the system of pieties lying at the roots of the patient's sorrows or bewilderments. It is an *impious* rationalization, offering a fresh terminology of motives to replace the patient's painful terminology of motives. Its scientific terms are wholly incongruous with the unscientific nature of the distress. By approaching the altar of the patient's unhappiness with deliberate irreverence, by selecting a vocabulary which specifically violates the dictates of style and taboo, it changes the entire nature of his problem, rephrasing it in a form for which there is a solution. Insofar as it is curative, its effects seem due to the fact that it exorcises the painful influences of a vestigial religious orientation by appeal to the prestige of the newer scientific orientation.

Even so virtuous a faith as Christianity situated the crux of conversion, not in *goodness*, but in *belief.* So we need not be surprised to find evidence that, in the secular rebirth engineered by the psychoanalytic seer, the processes of recovery from one's effective disorders are closely interwoven with a shifting of one's intellectualistic convictions, one's terminology of cause, purpose, and prophecy. *Theory* (literally, a *looking-at*, or *viewing*) plays a large part, not only in the technique of the physician, but in the patient's response. Psychoanalysis may be described as a new rationalization, offered to the patient in place of an older one which had got him into difficulties. The patient, with pious devotion, had erected a consistent network of appropriatenesses about the altar of his wretchedness, the thoroughness of the outlying structure thus tending to maintain the integrity of the basic psychosis. Yet the discomfiture itself laid him open *to the need of new meanings*, hence offering the psychoanalyst a grip within the terms of the psychosis itself. For one can cure a psychosis only by appealing to some aspect of the psychosis. The cure must bear notable affinities with the disease: all effective medicines are potential poisons.

Freud's great informing invention for the recommending of a kindlier, more Christian rationalization to replace the angry Jehovah of the earlier schemes was his doctrine of the six abnormal tendencies. These served as a remarkably accurate formulation for that kind of perspective by incongruity which we might call the opposite of magnification: conversion downwards—reduction of scale. The working of this device as a conversion *downwards* was really paradoxical—for on the face of it the device was of exactly the opposite sort. It seemed to be a universal slander, rather than a mitigating principle, for it said that *everyman* was in essence a pervert. Everyman, Freud assured his patients, had in him, and in the symbolism of his thoughts, speech, and actions, the six abnormal tendencies: autoeroticism, homosexuality, sadism, masochism, incest, and exhibitionism.

There were two extremely valuable aspects of this formula. In the first place, it is hard to imagine a single manifestation of human interests which could not be reduced to one of these six terms. A heterosexual interest, for instance, could be sadistic or masochistic, even down to the last subtle give-and-take of conversational repartee. And if one, at such a juncture, attempted to prove himself neither sadistic nor masochistic, by refraining from a retort of any kind, he was obviously open to the suspicion of an incipient autoeroticism, or perhaps a twisted kind of exhibitionism manifesting itself by blatant non-coöperation, or perhaps even a silently corroding incestuousness which was dragging his mind elsewhere. One can invent hypothetical cases at random, noting that the "six abnormals" will serve as well as any other terms to designate the underlying patterns of the mind. Such comprehensiveness of terminology, while offered under the guise of great specificity, had the signal virtue of catching all conduct in its net. Even a man who had been wholly bewildered by the "irrationality" of his conduct was given a scheme of motivations which promptly brought him back into the realm of "logic."

This gets us to the second great virtue of Freud's formula as regards the therapeutics of suggestion. If the six abnormals applied to everybody, it followed that everybody was abnormal, hence it followed that it was normal to be abnormal. Thus, as Marston has observed, the doctrine of the six abnormals seems to have rediscovered, under a technical or clinical terminology more in keeping with the anti-religious temper of the century, the old Church doctrine of original sin, which had long proved its curative value during the heyday of the Catholic rationalization. In a great century of progress based upon the doctrine of the innate goodness of man, or of his perfectibility through evolution, Freud reformulated the old doctrine of original sin to cure the people whom progress, in some form or another, was driving into hysteria. The pansexuality of Freud's formulæ seems to have been especially effective because sexual emphases were already outstanding in the orientation of his day, hence a sexual symptom could most easily recommend itself as the *core* of the entire situation, with all else as mere incidental by-products.

It is not our purpose here to refute Freudian theory or to choose among the various schools of thought that have de-

scended from it. We are interested simply in pointing ou
certain notable features of the conversion technique which
seem to characterize them all. These are primarily of two
sorts: the *conversion downwards* of the patient's distress by
means of an unfit, incongruous terminology—and the positive development of a substitute terminology until it has provided the patient with a brand-new rationalization of motives

As regards the first point, the procedure that most obviously serves the ends of impiety is that of sitting down and
talking the matter over—and every school of analysis seems
to stress the therapeutic value of this clinic-confessional
Freud, Adler, Jung, Rivers, and McDougall have all, within
the terms of their systems, found explanations for the necessity and efficacy of this practice. Essentially, it is at the very
roots of incongruity, bringing a professional, dispassionate
detached point of view to bear upon a subject matter which
has been surrounded with the pieties of intense personal devotion, awe, and silence (and authors, as well as mystics, have
testified to the accumulative power of silence).

It has been laid against Hegel that he tended to solve old
riddles of philosophy by simply redefining them, by approaching them in different terms, so that the earlier issues
were not so much *solved* as *dissolved*. History itself has a
way of doing likewise, letting old battlefields merge into a
single spot as the rise of other interests takes us remotely elsewhere—and likewise many private difficulties are better han-
dled by an *integral neglect* than by a direct attempt at recon-
ciliation. I do not mean that they are *suppressed*, I mean that
they are *allowed to languish*—and nothing is more destructive of beauties rising before bowed head and silence than a
competent, professional air, at once sympathetic with the
problem and unimpressed with its gravity.

Here is a fundamental incongruity, or impiety, proper to
all psychiatric methods—and often, as a matter of fact, the

pious sufferer resists it as such. Thus Freud mentions frequent violent antagonism on the part of the patient, Adler stoically asserts that the analyst may even have to accept physical blows as his reward for this impious affront upon the patient's sorrowful poem. For we must expect to meet with fury, when desecrating the altar of a patient's misery, to which he has brought the most pious offerings, weaving about it the very texture of his self-respect, developing an entire schema of motivations above this central orientating concern, profoundly stressing certain values and rejecting others according to their fitness for this integrative work, and clinging to the structure all the more passionately since, if it began as the *cause* of his distress, by the time the patient has finished building, it has become his only bulwark against distress.

McDougall's Modifications of Freudianism

In his *Outline of Abnormal Psychology*, McDougall specifically disapproves of Freud's approach on the grounds that Freud's terms omit precisely the factor in mental unbalance which McDougall considers the most important of all: dissociation. McDougall finds it remarkable that, whereas authorities like Janet and Morton Prince regard dissociation as the most important and far-reaching explanatory principle to be applied in interpreting neurotic disorder, Freud makes no use of this conception. He says that to his knowledge the word does not even appear in any of Freud's principal writings.

McDougall's theory is based entirely upon the stressing of this omitted concept. Like his fellow-countryman, the neurologist Sherrington, he stresses the need of integration, by which he means a single guiding principle, or purpose, which can coördinate tendencies more or less at odds with one another. He calls these minor conflicting tendencies "monads," after Leibniz, though seeming to differ from Leibniz' use of the term in the sense that there is not a pre-established harmony among them. According to McDougall, in fact, sane mental adjustment requires the *forcible* establishment of such a harmony. The minor monads are compelled to obey a *monas monadum*, which is the "self-regarding principle." This self-regarding principle, or "master principle," is the all-embracing personality which forces the various conflicting sub-personalities into line.

As an illustration of integration, McDougall uses the example of the British Empire, and as an illustration of the dissociative tendency, he cites the rebelliousness of Ireland. He thinks that the key to the problems of individual psychology is to be found in cases of multiple personality, in which some aspects of the individual so sharply conflict with others that they make different personality systems, and may even be felt by the sufferer as different selves. He cites various instances of split personality, most notably Dr. Morton Prince's famous case of Miss Beauchamp. His notion is that we are all examples of divided personality, that different degrees of hypnosis can serve to bring out one or another of our personality-systems, and that the content of our dreams reveals the workings of these other personalities even in normal people, while the breaks in the continuity of dreams may represent transitions from one personality to another.

All these sub-personalities are held together under normal conditions by an ideal personality, which coördinates the others in accordance with its supreme demands, as shaped by the self-regarding principle. But in times of stress or exhaustion, some of the submerged personalities may take the opportunity to exert themselves with extreme vigor, sometimes causing such marked division of personality that a sufferer has even been known to read a page as two selves, with one of his selves reading faster than the other, and reaching the bottom of the page before it. Thus may the personalities conflict, he says, quite as Ireland, always fuming under suppression, took advantage of the Empire's distresses in World War I to proclaim a distinct personality and demand autonomy.

McDougall cites this merely to illustrate his theory of motivations—yet might it not partially have instigated his framing of the theory itself? And might this very analogy with the Empire's political patterns make it more useful as a cure for specifically British sufferers? For if the individual's scheme of motives is but one aspect of a larger interpretative frame, it would be natural that the perplexities of an Englishman should be normalized or socialized by reference to meanings involved in the structure of the Empire as a whole. In offering the patient a theory of motives molded after the Empire, is he not reclaiming individual orientation by linking it with the general political orientation, thereby connecting the private pieties with the social pieties?

Note how he further exemplifies this "imperialist" sense of order when, under the heading, "The Appeal to Sentiments," he warns that the bringer of new meanings should not attempt "conversion" in the absolute sense which Nietzsche had in mind, a revaluation of *all* values, but should appeal to any normal standards which the patient still held intact. The physician is warned not to attempt a radical remaking of his patient, but to get whatever toehold he can upon the patient's past dispositions, not obliterating old systems entirely, but taking them over in sound imperialistic fashion and making them serve the purpose of the new order which he would impose upon them.

Poor Nietzsche, with his German *Gründlichkeit*, which either dominates or collapses, proposing to change everything *von Haus aus*: how different his scheme of conversion from that advocated by this diplomatic Britisher, who would "muddle through" the processes of cure! We do not make this point to cast aspersions upon Professor McDougall's theories. On the contrary, we are trying to suggest why these theories might be expected to have genuine curative effects. For in rebuilding the "master personality" along the lines of the nation's political pattern, he is socializing the patient's new mental structure by anchoring it to an obvious feature of the *group psychosis.*

As evidence that our suggestion is not excessive we recall in Professor Dewey's *Art as Experience* a discussion of the way in which our psychological vocabulary originated. He says that the words for describing the pattern of the mind were borrowed by analogy from the patterns of the state. "They were at first formulations of differences found among the portions and classes of society." He cites Plato as a perfect instance of this, saying that Plato openly borrowed his three-fold division of the soul from the situation which he observed in the communal life of the times. He observes that Plato is here doing consciously what many a psychologist has since done unconsciously, who divides up the mind in accordance with differences observable in the society about him while thinking that he has arrived at them by pure introspection. Plato, says Professor Dewey, formulated the sensuously acquisitive portion of the mind after the analogy of the mercantile class, his picture of the "spirited" faculty corresponded to the citizen-soldiers, while the "reason" was patterned after the group empowered to make the laws.

Our point of view should also explain why even a factor which McDougall considers so all-important as dissociation can be omitted entirely from a theory of human motivation without destroying the possibilities of cure. Freud wrote for a people who had, for many centuries, accommodated themselves to imperial decay—perhaps he wrote for something which we might call the "psychosis of the Strauss waltz." Hence, his devices for reorientation would be differently framed, to correspond with differences in the local orientation of his group.

Exorcism by Misnomer

Why is it so necessary that the patient be told the nature and origin of his disorder? Does one truly cast out devils by *naming* them? The notion of perspective by incongruity would suggest that one casts out devils by *misnaming* them. It is not the *naming* in itself that does the work, but the *conversion downward* implicit in such naming. Has one seen a child trembling in terror at a vague shape in a corner? One goes impiously into the corner, while the child looks on aghast. One picks an old coat off the clothes-rack, and one says, "Look, it is only an old coat." The child breaks into fitful giggles. Has one *named* the object which struck terror in the child? On the contrary, one has totally *misnamed* it, as regards its nature in the child's precious orientation. To have *named* it would have been to call out, "Away, thou hideous monster—thou cackling demon of hell, away!" and henceforth that corner would be the very altar of terror. One casts out demons by a vocabulary of *conversion*, by an *incongruous* naming, by calling them *the very thing in all the world they are not*: old coats.

The notion of exorcism by misnomer ("organized bad taste") may also explain away various other apparent conflicts among psychoanalytic treatments. Thus, Adler frames his cure from an entirely different point of view, stressing not the *amative* interests of Freud but the *combative* interests. He says that the patient is suffering from an attempt to compensate for early impressions of inferiority. Here too is a concept highly valuable in disclosing the rationality of conduct which had been labeled irrational. In the first place, just as it is quite obvious that everyone must love or hate something, so it seems inevitable that one should have been inferior to something, if only a mountain or a continent.

Much of Adler's technique is devoted to bringing out the antagonistic aspects of the patient's concerns until the patient is extremely resentful; then Adler undermines this resentment by a deliberately incongruous response, accepting the resentment as the *normal* and *expected* thing. This procedure, suggestive in itself as a method of conversion downwards, by making it clear that the patient's focal interests are really nothing to be so excited about, is also backed by the introduction of an alien vocabulary which is "unsuited" to the altar of the patient's distress.[1]

The conflict of exorcism by misnomer also has some bearing upon the insanity of such writers as Nietzsche and Swift, who were both preoccupied with the problems of conversion. These men devoted their energies to a *conversion upwards*, a one-way process of magnification, a *writing large* that lacked a compensatory process of *writing down*. Nietzsche keyed his concerns to the magnitude of the tragic, his typically schizophrenic dislike of normal laughter refusing to permit him any humor but the grotesque, sardonic kind. As a consequence, he lived enwrapped in loneliness, thinking in terms of grandeur, of vast historic sweeps, of long vistas as seen from the tops of cold and sterile mountains, a forbidding imagery which comes tragically to its perfection in his *Zarathustra*, a book which he adulated with all the reverence that a deeply pious nature could possibly bring to the honor of a Cathedral erected above his own profoundest misery. Yet

---

[1] The weakness in the various individualistic schemes of cure offered since the breakdown of the religious rationalization seems to arise from the fact that the resultant socialization is but partial. The texture of new meanings is not rich enough, and does not enjoy sufficient reënforcement from society as a whole, to make it soundly communicative. It is *compensatory* rather than *integral*.

he seems himself to have felt the need of a complementary process, since he tries repeatedly to put his poignant work forward as a "Happy Science." An aspect of this same feeling is to be seen in that eerie cult of exaltation which we find in the *Rausch* scenes of *Zarathustra*, the imaginary alchoholic indulgences and fraternizations of a man who testified that the slightest touch of liquor could set his mind into a painful whirl for many hours.

As for Swift: he too showed that he restlessly sought a technique of *conversion downwards*, some mitigating device which would enable him to call the monsters of his imagination old coats. As evidence that he felt this need, do we not have his simple reversal of relationship, from that of Gulliver big, Lilliputians little, to that of Gulliver little, Brobdingnagans big? But the true nature of his ways is revealed in the "synthesis": Yahoos crude, Houyhnhnms refined. To look at all three relationships is to realize that, whatever their reversals of proportion in the literal sense, they were all *au fond* the same: the *magnification* of human despicability, the emphasizing of greed, ignorance, coarseness, treachery, and the like, in sustained imagery. As a consequence, Swift lived among monsters—and to live among monsters is to live on the edge of hell.

Swift was, as Coleridge says of him with pointedness quite to our purpose, "*Anima Rabelaisii habitans in sicco*—the soul of Rabelais dwelling in a dry place." For it is precisely the ways of Rabelais that might best illustrate the fullness of a two-way process, the hearty shuttling back and forth between conversion upwards and conversion downwards, as he now approached the "spiritualities" of the Church through the terminology of gluttony and license, and then again "projected" the most riotous human appetites upward into their own noble, speculative and imaginative transmogrifications, giving us not only the swinishness that underlay the structure

of virtue, but also the wide reaches of understanding tha
grew out of this very swinishness.

Examination of a Case Described by Rivers

Though Rivers, like McDougall, had great respect for th
impetus which Freud had given to the study of "psychogenic
factors in functional disorder," he questioned the validity c
Freud's attempts to trace all motivations back to a sexu
origin. Such a state of affairs, he said, might well apply to th
neuroses that develop under peacetime conditions, but man
of the patients who were brought to him suffering fro
"shell shock" revealed little or no evidence of earlier sexu
irregularities or eccentricities. Rivers felt so outstanding
calamity as World War I, with its highly organized slaughte
and the frequent grotesqueness of the suffering which
caused, was a sufficient factor in itself to account for ment
disorders. Accordingly, he sought for the "traumatic origin" c
neuroses in war situations *per se*, and frequently found it ther

In his book, *Instinct and the Unconscious*, however, F
gives great space to a slightly different kind of case. Th
patient had been in no specific situation, such as a shell e
plosion or an attack under gruesome conditions, which mig
serve as a traumatic source—in fact, he suffered from a clau
trophobia which had plagued him from times long anteda
ing the beginning of the war. When he was confined
certain kinds of closed places, an uneasiness amounting
deep apprehension, and even terror, would come over hi
And although in the course of years he had mastered th
feeling as regards familiar surroundings such as the rooms c
his own house, the life in the trenches revived it in its mc
intense form. His horror of entering a dug-out was as gre
as the horror that someone else with a more normal set c
meanings might feel at *not* entering a dug-out. The patien

health finally became so bad that, after some weeks in a hospital in France, where he was given hypnotics without effect, he was sent to London, for treatment by Rivers.

A doctor himself, and interested in the theories of Freud, the patient collaborated in the attempt to disclose some possible childhood origin for this phobia—and finally, after the careful recording and analysis of his dreams, he did reconstruct an incident which he had completely forgot. He recalled a time when, at the age of four, "he had been confined in a narrow passage with no means of escape from a dog by which he was terrified." Yet the memory of this experience had completely escaped him for many years, and was only restored now after Rivers had employed his most astute psychological technique. Rivers took the case to prove conclusively that we do have significant experiences "shut off from consciousness in ordinary conditions," and that such experiences can continue radically to affect our lives. For the dread of confined spaces showed definite relations with the nature of the early experience and completely disappeared when the memory of this early experience had been brought to the surface.

To explain the "suppression" of this experience in conscious life, Rivers borrows Freud's concept of "active forgetting." By his interpretation, the organism aggressively surrounds an event with forgetfulness as a way of avoiding pain. He next has to explain how a way of avoiding pain can become the very factor that prolongs the pain over many years. He says that the experience was suppressed because of its *immediately* painful character, without regard for the ultimate effects of the process. Such suppressions cancel the unpleasantness of the moment, he says, but must ignore "future consequences." And though the suppression was designed for comfort, it can finally serve to perpetuate discomfort.

This anomaly is never fully explained. The issue is particu-

larly difficult because suppression is also recognized as a nor
mal and serviceable procedure when it works. Like the gir
with the curl in the middle of her forrid, when it is good it i
very very good, and when it is bad it is horrid. Rivers cite
other cases where loss of memory seems to successfully oblit
erate the effects of pain. In contrast with such case, however
Rivers' victim of claustrophobia seems to have responded loy
ally to the painful event of his childhood every single day of
his life for thirty years, recalling the mood with Proustiar
piety, and faithfully reconstructing the early state of terro
whenever some detail of environment (like the enclosure of
a dug-out) suggested the pattern of the original stimulus.

Responses of such depth can probably be established in two
ways: by abruptness or by duration. "Trauma" is the term
generally used when a meaning is established by abruptness
A terrifying accident is *traumatic*. And some psychologist
also lay great emphasis upon the "trauma of birth," a shock
ing revolutionary experience when the organism leaves it
placental heaven, where it had led the life of Riley, and
bursts into the harsh world of combat. At times of shock
some attendant circumstance may become associatively er
dowed with all the meaning of the experience itself. Synec
dochically (by the principle of the "part for the whole") thi
association may even serve to restore the quality of the expe
rience. Thus, a certain kind of wallpaper, or a certain tone of
voice, or the gleam of a surgeon's instrument, may remai
forever endowed with "affect" because of its accidental asso
ciation with the informing experience itself. Such traumatic re
sponse may be seen less spectacularly in the fact that a ca
after having his toes pinched by a suddenly opened doo
learns to move back from the door when he hears footstep
approaching.

The commoner educative method, by *duration*, is to b
seen in any technique of conditioning, of either the Pavlov o

the Gestalt variety. Its Proustian nature is observable when, if one felt a pervasive mood at one period in his life, any sound or odor that marked this same period may partially or wholly restore the mood.

We are trying to suggest a different explanation for the sufferings of the claustrophobic patient, whose constancy of response to a situation "learned" in childhood seems very different from the oblivion that goes with cases of total amnesia. It neither removes the pain, nor does it in the least cancel off the "educative" effect the patient had experienced in his childhood when finding himself trapped and confronted by a vicious dog. Rivers, it will be noted, feels that he has got at the "true" situation when he finally hits upon the incident of the dog in the alley way—precisely as Proust, in his remembrance of things past, seeks to trace back the exact details of his early experience which fall together, awaking in him so specific a mood as he hears the tinkling sound of the teacup. Proust seeks the content of this mood by recalling all the events that coexisted with it during its formative period, just as the victim of claustrophobia recalls the details of the formative traumatic experience.

But why does Rivers feel that he has hit upon the truth when he has disclosed that the original trauma was concerned with a *dog in a passageway*? What was the therapeutic value in this disclosure? Why did this meaning henceforth remove the terror of closed places? Why did the decision that the claustrophobia so originated serve to cast out the devil that had beset this man for thirty years?

To begin with, we can avoid the somewhat legalistic concept of suppression, particularly since the sufferer showed signs of remembering his early training constantly. We shall note that the patient's training (his claustrophobia) was not acquired as the response to a *thing* (the dog) but to a *situation, the situation of being confined in a passageway without*

an exit at a time when a danger sign (the dog) was present
Is not this enough to account for the patient's response? Had
he not learned the meaning of a situation quite as the chick
ens of the Gestalt experimenter do when they learn that the
larger of two objects contains food and the smaller is empty

The traumatic experience had left its mark upon the pa
tient. An associative meaning for closed places had been
branded upon his mind. Closed places had been given
danger-character, hence his dread whenever he was forced to
enter one. Hence the justice of his breakdown under war
conditions—for now the pattern was complete, there being
not only the confinement of the dug-out to take the place of
the closed alley way, but also the nearness of the enemy to
take the place of the dog. Response to this danger-situation
by a sense of dread seems, except for the matter of intensity
to be precisely like a child's responding to the intonations of
its mother's voice with a sense of reassurance. The child had
not *suppressed* its specific understanding of the mother's in
tonations. It had *never really noticed* them as such—as a con
sequence, in most cases, it responds to their suggestiveness
without even being aware of the fact that the intonations are
a factor in evoking the response. The matter becomes a prob
lem only when the response is very painful or when one is
Marcel Proust.

Again, who is to say what the nature of attention is under
great strain? Must we assume that it is precisely identical
with the kind of detailed inventory-taking that we might
permit ourselves if we are noting circumstances for report
before a Commission? In his remarkably fruitful volume
Pleasure and Instinct, A. H. Burlton Allen cites from Dr
R. W. McKenna the case of a soldier who recalled his experi
ences immediately preceding his first entry into active com
bat. As this man marched to the trenches, every detail of
sense perception was sharpened: the grass became a mor

vivid green; each flower he passed seemed unusually beautiful; the song of birds took on a new, more penetrating sweetness; and the clouds were not merely white, they were miraculously white. And one who has read accounts of mountain-climbers (one of these also is quoted by Mr. Allen, but I recall an exciting account by Garrett W. Service, an indifferent writer who this once became eloquent) will have reason to believe that the "visions" rewarding the seers do not derive merely from the view, but rather from the constant dread that animates them as they pick their loose footing above the abyss.

We are trying to suggest that the matter may not be one of *active forgetting*, but may involve *the nature of attention* in the first place. We are proposing that the metaphor be tentatively shifted from a legalistic one suggesting repression to an optical one suggesting focus. We are bringing up the possibility that, under conditions of terror, the nature of attention itself may change, just as one may forget so *real* an event as a raging toothache for a few moments if some sudden excitement breaks in upon his concerns. Has he "actively forgot" his toothache in order to "suppress the pain" of it, or has he simply shifted the focus of his interests elsewhere?

In any case, whether one chooses to believe such a possibility or not, one can refer to the chickens of the Gestalt experiments as evidence that an organism can be conditioned to a *relationship* as well as to an *absolute*, which would suggest that one can be made to respond to *confinement-in-closed-places* as a fear-sign just as well as to *dogs from which one cannot escape*. In this sense, the terrified child can be seen to have learned his lesson, and remembered it faithfully for thirty years, responding quite as automatically as one does with the multiplication table, or as people are said to do who, having become accustomed to hypnosis, fall asleep at some merely incidental movement on the part of their doctor, even

when he had no intention of hypnotizing them at all. Th
have come to take one of the adjacent characters, an in
dental feature of the doctor's movements, as having the san
suggestive content as the movements by which he conscious
prepared to induce the hypnotic state. Similarly, a bur
child dreads the fire, not because it has *suppressed* the mer
ory of the time when it was burnt, but because it has fait
fully abstracted the nature of the experience, and responds
new fire-situations accordingly.

If this interpretation is correct, it would also account for t
sudden conversion on the part of the patient, who treache
ously abandoned his deep piety of response, as soon as t
informing incident or trauma was disclosed. For here was
case of exorcism by misnomer. A mere dog in an alley w
the cause of all this dismal devotion! What grown ma
would submit to such an awesome attitude towards a do
The vague shape had thus been renamed the old coat—ar
the demon was effectively cast out by the impious devices
incongruity.

Conversion and the Lex Continui

Conversions are generally managed by the search for
"graded series" whereby we move step by step from sor
kind of event, in which the presence of a certain factor
sanctioned in the language of common sense, to other ever
in which this factor had not previously been noted. T
thinker attempts to establish a continuity for arriving at co
clusions which might seem abrupt and paradoxical if the tv
ends of his series were juxtaposed abruptly, without the int
polation of a gradient. Thus, in harmonic theory, the con
poser Arnold Schoenberg takes us step by step from t
methods of classical music to the methods which he emplc
—and if we follow his gradients we are imperceptibly eas

from a region of sound where the logic of composition is generally apparent into a region of sound which might have seemed to the uninstructed hearer as chaotic. The ideal gradients are found in the recordings of the physicist, as when he shows us by thermometer readings the quantitative critical points at which water is converted into substances so qualitatively different as ice and steam. In the psychological realm, the search for gradients is more complex and dubious—but the clear assumption of the *lex continui* is to be seen in both animal and abnormal psychology, where the thinker notes the workings of anguish or training as revealed in clinic or laboratory, and seeks to infer the presence of the same basic processes in normal human life. We have attempted to obey the *lex continui* in our treatment of piety by a series of steps moving from religion (where the presence of piety is linguistically acknowledged) to the habits of the gashouse gang (a kind of conduct from which common usage had excluded pious ingredients).

The significant shortcoming of this method as a way of understanding human nature lies in the fact that it omits the critical points. It may show the presence of the same factor in normal human life that we discern in animal or abnormal psychology; but it cannot state, with the precision of the thermometer, the exact stage at which the *qualities* of the experience change. It is better adapted for showing that water, steam, and ice are all H_2O than for discovering the important readings of temperature at which H_2O undergoes such significant transformations. And human experience being essentially qualitative, this failure to name the critical points is admittedly a grave fault. In mental happenings, a *quantitative* increase in complexity may cause a complete *qualitative* transformation as distinct as the difference between water and ice. And the *rationale* of pre-evolutionary thought, which refuses to consider things in the light of their genesis, is founded on the feeling that, unless you can name the critical points at which qualitative transformations take place, your account of derivations is too truncated to be of real service. This would be the basis of a theologian's refusal, for instance, to accept Marxian or psychoanalytic explanations of the genesis of religion.

But let us make up a sample set of gradients (having in mind our technique of conversion) to illustrate the full scope of the choices which the principle of the *lex continui* can place before us. In his *Nature and Life*, Whitehead has written: "Philosophy is the product of wonder." It so happens that Veblen situated the origin of philosophic, or scientific speculation in "idle curiosity." Now, if you key up *idle curiosity*, you might get *curiosity* pure and simple. If you key up *curiosity*, you get *interest*. Key up *interest*, and you get *wonder*. Key up *wonder*, you get *reverence*. And so to *awe, fear,* and *dread*. Thus, by conversion upwards, we can modulate from Veblen's formula, through Whitehead's, to an assertion that "Philosophy is the product of terror."

The gloomier colors of our spectrum would suggest an element of hypochondriasis in scientific speculation, and might explain why one of our earlier star-gazers was actually awe-struck as he turned from his telescope and announced, "I have found a hole in the heavens!" It so happens that he had not; the heavens were still intact; he had merely found a dark nebula that blotted out the stars behind it—but this feature need not detain us here. It is his awe, verging upon fright, that is relevant to our sample set of gradients. Furthermore, Rivers has noted the fact that patients may reconcile themselves to their disease by becoming engrossed in its symptoms. He calls such adjustment hypochondriasis. We may clearly discern its presence in the speculations of *Hamlet*, Job, Ecclesiastes, Jeremiah, and Eliot's *The Waste Land*. Might we not also note it among scientists who announce that they are "merely diagnosing our social difficulties, merely facing the facts, without regard for a remedy"?

Further extensions are imaginable. For instance, we could convert downwards, going from *idle curiosity* to *play*, thereby getting to a choice which particularly distinguished many theories of the Nineteenth Century following Schiller. Or we might project *fear* at a tangent, getting by continuity to such exegetic possibilities as *defense*, since fear suggests the need of self-protection. *Defense* (or *combat*) in turn could be split into the dichotomous concepts, *courage* or *cowardice*. Our choice along the path of gradients now runs:

Philosophy is the product of play
                     idle curiosity
                     curiosity
                     interest
                     wonder
                     reverence
                     awe
                     fear   } defense (combat)
                     dread
                     terror } cowardice; courage.

Note that the establishment of the series itself does not automatically provide a clue as to which point we should select as the *essence* of the entire scale. One's choice usually flows from other aspects of his orientation, or from the particular purpose which his series is designed to fulfil. We have already noted the therapeutic reasons that influence choice, in the curative device of conversion downwards. But we should also note that a certain degree of conversion upwards may be curative on occasion. *Wonder*, for instance, is much more in keeping with the usual standards of decency than *play*, unless one hastens to broaden the concept of play until play itself has been converted upwards, magnified beyond its ordinary connotations. And a man whose general scheme of values would lead him to balk at the choice of *fear* or *cowardice,* might find no trouble in selecting *defense* or *courage.* That doughty warrior Nietzsche might have preferred another aspect of defense, *combat*—and Piaget's researches into the development of logic from *quarreling* would seem to provide some justification for this choice.

Another interesting attempt to find the source of complex mental structures is suggested in the literature of mysticism, where there so often recurs the compelling image of the *abyss,* some aweful internal chasm (Eliot: "we are the hollow men"), a sense of distance, division, or vertigo which has at times been verbalized by reference to a "geographical" place, the bottomless pit of hell. This image may arise from some neural dissociation which, involving the two lobes of the brain, is sensed by the "shut in" type of mind but not interpreted with complete accuracy. In any event, we note the presence of the image strongly in Milton's epic, with its startling pictures of inter-stellar space—and it was Milton who distinguished between his poetic glorifications and his prose vituperation by the metaphor of the *right* and *left* hand.

Our contemporary mystic poet, Hart Crane, seems to have revealed a similar sense of the abyss in his choice of the *bridge* as his key symbol. Socially, the division was observable in his unhappy conflict between homosexual and heterosexual leanings. And it may be more than a coincidence that this symbolist ended his life symbolically, by plunging into the great abyss of mid-ocean. In any event, it is conceivable that a purely subjective sense of the abyss could be converted downwards by actually going into high places and gazing from them, thus bringing the experience within the negotiable realm of factual objects. The curative effect of such a process might account for the almost mystical exaltation we have noted in the descriptions of mountain-climbing—and conversely, it might justify us in looking for an "abyss-motif" behind the cult of flight.

CHAPTER SIX

MEANING AND REGRESSION

Pure, or Unmixed, Responses

THE THOUGHT that piety responds to analogies of *situation* or *relationship*, and not merely to analogies of *objects* may throw some light upon the phenomena of *regression* which psychiatrists note as so prominent a feature of pronounced mental suffering. We may begin by noting that any intense experience is regressive in one respect: It is more characteristic of childhood simplicity than of adult complexity. In maturity our experiences are usually mixed, lacking the purity they may have in childhood when the range of response is more limited. If, on the other hand, you restore a primitive stimulus, would there be anything surprising in your eliciting a primitive response? From this standpoint, instead of calling the intense response a *disease*, we might consider it quite accurate.

Mr. Squib is a very mild and tolerant fellow, distinguished for a certain humorous charitableness, harboring no grudges, worried over the fate of mankind, and really doing much good for those with whom he comes into contact. Suppose, however, that you arrange a situation whereby Mr. Squib, when thoroughly exhausted, is prevented by constant torture from falling asleep. You know that after a few hours of such treatment he would be a very demon of regression, a savage beast or a pathetically whimpering child. Now suppose that Mr. Squib happens to place upon certain aspects of experience a value which results, though more subtly, in precisely this same state of affairs. Meanings, as they exist for him, imply that the situation in which he finds himself is one of intense torture, as ingenious in its disturbing of his rest as any scrupulous Chinese nagging of an exhausted prisoner. Suppose that, in accordance with his orientation, he is persuaded that he stands beneath a Damoclean sword, or that he bears a Bellerophontic letter, or that his hungers are being fed by the mocking mimetics of a Barmecide feast. If some primitive response arises under such a situation, are we not really dealing with something so *intellectual* as a matter of interpretation, and is not the affective response (the primitivism of terrors, vengeances, or collapse) quite in keeping with the meaning of the situation as it presents itself to him?

In noting that the rational is shaped by the affective, psychoanalysts did great service—but too often the discovery led them to underrate the fact that, once the rational has arisen and taken form, it brings forward demands of its own, and guides us as to what the affective response should be. Consider the highly intellectual equipment required, for example, to be terrified at a gun the first time in one's life a gun is pointed at one, and without ever having been shot. If one shows remarkable affective responsiveness under such a situation, he does so precisely because of the meanings he attaches to this instrument which, as regards "natural" conditions, is as neutral as it would be to a grasshopper sitting on the barrel. By the concatenations of meaning, however, it can become so *pure* a stimulus as to call forth the most primitive forms of action. Thus, even though one grant that the original formative factors of the rational are affective, one cannot jump to the conclusion that henceforth all rational manifestations must be considered as a mere phosphorescent glow arising above the affective. Instead, our interpretations of the signs, be they true or false, can instigate the most intense affections.

The probable fact that our rationalizations of events arise out of purely affective tests (pleasure, displeasure, neutrality) does not account for the workings of a rationalized structure once it is erected. One may build a house for shelter, but one may hurt his hand because he is building a house. The tendency to refer always back to *origins* would be somewhat like saying that the man hurt his hand for shelter. Our characterization of events is admittedly rooted in considerations of affect (as the baby's nurse becomes *lovable* through ministering to the baby's wants and wishes). But we must realize that purely *derivative* factors enter (when the baby reads the signs to the effect that someone is trying to take its bottle from it, it may set up a wail accordingly, though this highly affective response may have arisen purely from an error in interpretation, the "menacing agent" perhaps merely having taken the bottle for the purpose of refilling it).

Thus, though our orientation rises out of the affective, it in turn calls forth affective states. Otherwise stated: meanings and stimuli merge—and you may assume that, if a certain stimulus has rightly or wrongly a danger-character, a danger-response will result. We do not persuade a man to avoid danger. We can only persuade him that a given situation is dangerous and that he is using the wrong means of avoiding it. Danger-stimulus and fear-response are one—and to remove the latter you must redefine the first.[1]

[1] To be complete, this discussion of the relationship between meaning and affect should also consider at great length the mind-body parallelisms suggested by such sciences as endocrinology. Some research which I did in drug addiction leads me to suggest that the interaction between intellectual interpretations and the secretions of the "body's drug factories" (the endocrines and their neural channels) would be as follows: Such a response as fear arises from our interpretation of a situation as dangerous. This fear response also sets up in the body a glandular constellation which can make for extreme wakefulness (since alertness is biologically part of our defensive equipment, being precisely the sort of attitude that would best help us protect ourselves against the thing or situation interpreted as a fear-sign). If such wake-

MEANING AND REGRESSION

In *The World as Will and Idea*, after having quoted with
approval Seneca's *velle non discitur*, Schopenhauer, for all his
emphasis upon the priority of the instinctive, goes on to quote
with approval a scholastic formula to the effect that we are
not moved by the *reality* of a cause but by our *interpretation*
of it (*causa finalis movet non secundum suum esse reale; sed
secundum suum esse cognitum*). He next proceeds to warn
us that even imaginary circumstances can operate as real:
"For instance, if a man is firmly convinced that for every
worthy deed he is rewarded a hundredfold in the life to
come, such a conviction has the same validity and effect as a
sound long-term investment—and he can be charitable from
egoism just as, with another perspective (*Einsicht*) he might
be greedy from egoism." He refers also to Spinoza, and on
turning to the relevant passage in the *Ethics*, we find that
will and intellect are one and the same" (*voluntas et intel-
lectus unum et idem sunt*). Similarly Nietzsche, who was if
possible an even more confirmed philosopher of the will than

---

illness is prolonged, the state of exhaustion adds new factors to be
interpreted as danger-signs.

Now, if we reverse the process, beginning with the endocrine constellation (which may arise purely from some physical glandular infec-
tion), we find the organism in a state of alertness—and since extreme
alertness is part of the danger-equipment, it may in turn lead the sufferer to interpret his situation as a danger-situation. In this way his
endocrine disorder may lead him to discern fear-elements in events outside him which would not be so interpreted if the disorder were removed (as it can be temporarily, for instance, by a sedative).

But we should also remember that in the devious ways of the mind
the simple correlation between danger and fear can be greatly altered
by the insertion of shuttle-terms. For *solace* belongs as much to the
danger category as fear does. Hence wakefulness may also lead to an
elaborate structure of solace, as in the case of scientific, religious, or
poetic insomniacs who may convert the burden of sleeplessness into
output.

Schopenhauer, was an intellectualist in his recognition of the part played by meanings in channelizing the expression of the will.

On this point, even extreme rationalists and extreme voluntarists are in agreement. The thought may suggest the possibility that primitive or regressive elements in the conduct of the insane may be called *normal* in the sense that any normal person would be similarly agitated if he placed a similar interpretation upon events. A greater normality of response arises from a real or imagined security which a normal man derives from *his* reading of the signs.

Errors of interpretation would account for certain forms of irascibility, vindictiveness, etc., to which some people are exceptionally given. There is still a tendency, despite our sophistication, to feel that a response like vindictiveness arises from some special mean streak in a man, an unusual kernel of deviltry which is forever revealing itself. Yet any normal man is vindictive when endangered—hence, the excessive vindictiveness of our maligned individual may be due to the fact that he interprets an unusually large number of situations as danger situations. He is menaced in multifarious ways: Certain remarks seem likely to affect his chance of holding his job, certain ones have for him the character of lowering his reputation in the eyes of his family, certain expressions imply the ridicule of values which he considers of great weight, etc. hence his vindictiveness. Add the fact that such a trait as vindictiveness may easily become *creative*, may entangle the man in a texture of situations which really do endanger him, hence calling for further vindictiveness, and you have the usual vicious circle we have noted in the interrelationships between the outward and inward ministrations to one's "altar."

We may connect the phenomena of regression with the more clearly Proustian aspect of piety. When a new situation arises which, because of some marked similarity with the

riginal informing experience, reawakens the emotional char-
cters that went with this earlier experience, we have already
he rudiments of regression. The process is the same as when
fire in the neighborhood sets all the neighbors to exchang-
ig tales of fires they saw in the past, or when this Christmas
alls up other Christmases.

Thus if a man happens, during a period of adolescent lone-
ness, to have indulged in some distinctive practice, such as
ealing, stamp-collecting, or the writing of anonymous let-
rs, a lonely period in adult life might "properly" permeate
is thoughts with imagery strongly suggestive of the earlier
lolescent pattern. Regression under strong emotion is appro-
riate because one's informing experiences do generally take
lace in early years, when the very sparsity of experiential
quipment tended to make the earlier experiences purer
ure delight, pure terror, trust, hope, wonder, etc.) whereas
ie adult usually meets new situations with a multiplicity of
sponses conflicting in their affective tone.

Considered from this point of view, regression is hardly
ore than the carrying of connectives beyond the symbolism
words, thoughts, moods into the symbolism of overt be-
vior itself. Were the hypothetical man's new loneliness to
come aggravated until it formed the very core of his pre-
cupations (were his "vow" to be backed by the "enclosing
alls of a monastery") his regressive imagery would proba-
y lead to an actual resumption of his earlier practices. If
ese practices happen to have been in the criminal category
uch as stealing) his respect for the meanings of his group
ay become an added factor in the building of his poem or
tar, until he has caught himself in a hopeless texture of
eanings, from which only the impieties of drastically new
eanings, with their conversion downward, could possibly
tricate him.

Yet in all this process we are dealing with nothing exceptional, with hardly more, in fact, than students of recidivism in crime or drug addiction have continually taken into account: How, after cure, a return to old conditions may stimulate relapse, by the doubly hypnotic process of vow and monastery, as the old surroundings suggest once more the "rightness" of the earlier practices, while these in turn have been interwoven with the man's way of livelihood, companionship, etc.[1]

[1] Once a set of new meanings is firmly established, we can often note in art another kind of regression: the artist is suddenly prompted to review the memories of his youth because they combine at once the qualities of strangeness and intimacy. Probably every man has these periods of rebirth, a new angle of vision whereby so much that he had forgot suddenly becomes useful or relevant, hence grows vivid again in his memory.

Rebirth and perspective by incongruity are thus seen to be synonymous, a process of conversion, though such words as conversion and rebirth are usually reserved for only the most spectacular of such reorientations, the religious. The evangelizing tendency that usually accompanies rebirth, the need to tell others what one has seen, is interwoven with the whole problem of socialization, the tendency to justify one's change by obtaining the corroboration of others. Evangelization is the obverse side of guilt—and when we realize that the new way of seeing often vows one to a divergency from his group, we can understand why the founders of a line may often seem not merely to endure persecution, but to court it.

The artist is always an evangelist, quite as the religious reformer is. He wants others to feel as he does. And the anguish of an artist whose work is condemned by his contemporaries arises from the fact that his symbolic justification is never completed until his work has been accepted. (Considered from this point of view, the doctrine of Art for Art's Sake can be seen as a compensatory attempt on the part of writers to so change the rules of the game that a symbolic justification which had failed to communicate itself to the group could nevertheless be felt to have performed the justificatory function. Justification was situated in the individual's *performance itself,* rather than in the *endorsement* of this performance by the group.)

MEANING AND REGRESSION

Conversion and Regression in Religion

In his work, *Some Aspects of the Life of Jesus*, George Berguer remarks that in the life of Christ as we know it we do not have the exact reproduction of the conversion process. Christ's conversations with the theologians at the age of twelve, and the calm assurance to his parents that he must be about his Father's business, synchronize with the awakening that generally takes place at puberty, as the individual, perhaps under the stimulus of new endocrinal factors then coming into his life, feels the direct need of deliberate orientation. However, in Christ's case there is evidence of a *confirming*, rather than a *rebirth*. Similarly with the incidents of the Temptation, a scheme of values already established is temporarily *threatened*, but there is no *transvaluation* such as distinguishes conversion proper. Rather, the direction already chosen is momentarily checked, perhaps by the exceptional imaginative fertility of watching and fasting, and is then resumed.

Christ seems to have developed into a slowly increasing mastery of a *method*, much as an artist might develop his technique with the years. He was concerned with matters of strategy, of presentation, apparently being certain from the start that his point of view was "correct." To this end he utilized with great effectiveness the analogical extension provided him by the parable—and in the simple paradox, as it is most clearly crystallized in his Sermon on the Mount, he offers a basic conversion concept for a total transvaluation of values whereby the signs of poverty were reinterpreted as the signs of wealth, the signs of hunger as the signs of fullness, and present weeping was characterized unmistakably as the first symptom of subsequent delight. By this translating device, danger-situations were not merely converted downwards: They were rephrased precisely as *comfort-situations*.

Berguer singles out, as the unusual feature of Christian exhortation, "the *affirmative character of his manner of teaching*." Jesus phrased his admonitions as invitations.

It is in Paul that we find the phenomena of conversion at their intensest, particularly as they are telescoped into a period extraordinarily brief, accomplishing in a few seconds a symbolic reconstruction that may sometimes require years, and even generations. It is conceivable that, in a man so given to outward action as Paul was, the phenomena of rebirth (the "conversion hysteria") would not be confined to the symbolism of moods and imagery, a metaphorical way more proper to the contemplative type of person. Rather, the forceful collapse of his earlier orientation might be expected to call forth its exact mimetic counterparts, precisely as any good actor supplements his words by the adoption of bodily postures in keeping. When a man of Paul's temper, both practical and deeply pious, is in some way "struck down," responses may indicate their appropriateness by actual disorders of muscle and vision (particularly since the slightest sense of guilt or dejection will show itself, even in ordinary persons, as a drooping of the spine or a shifting of the eyes). When a man so vigorous as Saul had of a sudden ceased to be Saul, in that dramatic interim between the loss of his old self and his rebirth as Paul, we may expect to find his structure shaken to its very roots.

Approached purely from the secular standpoint, his revelation, as regards its rationalized counterpart, was marked by a radical shift in his scheme of values. Old linkages were ripped apart, new linkages were welded, brutally, in accordance with the new creative device which had suddenly come upon him precisely as if the pattern of a new invention had sprung into his head, although in this case the invention was a way of seeing whereby the categories of his thinking were reassorted so that the men he had hunted became his allies, and his former allies in the hunt became his pursuers.

MEANING AND REGRESSION

After such an experience one might well be "marked," for how can one forget a day on which former monsters suddenly became sweet and the formerly familiar was transformed into the monstrous? A shift in something so integral to one's welfare and one's conduct must remain outstanding in the memory, traumatically becoming the altar of one's concerns, so that one's purposes seem to flow from this source henceforth, and one possesses *certainty* in the sense of possessing a *vocation*, and one possesses a vocation in the sense that he has had a personal experience which he must socialize. We glimpse somewhat the reasons for the double meaning which mystics attach to their statement that they are "wounded" by their insight, as though pain and endowment were interchangeable. (Verlaine: *"Mon Dieu, je suis blessé d'amour"*; The *New Yorker*: "When I had my operation"; we may also recall the brutal initiatory rites of many savage tribes; and I remember the words of a political agitator who insisted that one held one's doctrines with a deeper loyalty after having felt the crack of a policeman's club against the skull.) There is left the scar of a branding—stigma, vocation, preoccupation, obsession, trauma, wound, and revelation thus all designating the same event from different points of view.

Hence arises the notion that something like "the way" has been discovered (and indeed it has, so far as the individual is concerned, since he now has a confirmed method, an attitude, which may be turned upon any new matter with creative results). We need not here decide whether it is, in any given case, correct or incorrect. We need simply note that where it has occurred, one thenceforth has purposes which have been "revealed" to him—and regardless of how they may have come about, he may even be expected in time to reconstruct from them, out of his memories as revised, some appropriate setting that corresponds in function to the incident on the road to Damascus, or to the "heuristic" ascent of some "magic mountain" on which engraved tablets were discovered (Moses; Zarathustra; *Das Kapital*).

We may liken the selective process of the chosen to the writing of a great poem, or of a bad poem, as we prefer, but in either case we find the two aspects of the poet's certainty: The poem is a sudden *fusion*, a *falling together of many things formerly apart*—and the very force of this fusion leads one to seek further experiences of the same quality. Such is the kind of "stigma" that might well be found, after death, to have engraved itself by some actual markings upon the body. Since passing anger can be externalized in a curl of the lip, why cannot the exaltation of any prolonged "insight" be found finally in the very shaping of the organs, if we but know how to read the characters there? The stigma will not, of course, be of the literal sort described by the ancient martyrologists, who felt that a piety profound enough could actually reproduce a pious image upon the heart. The connectives would be remote, like the relationship between emotionality and glandular change. But they would be there nonetheless, in the physical parallelisms of the mind.

CONCLUSION

A Historical Parallel

Throughout this section we have frequently shown much respect for the "errors" of past systems. Even the extreme mystic is unquestionably talking about *something*, though one may disagree with his ways of interpreting and verbalizing the signs which he has seen. Hallucination itself is real in the sense that actual physical events must occur for the hallucination to arise. And we have been deliberately indiscriminate in scrambling magical, religious, poetic, theological, philosophical, mystic, and scientific lore. Insofar as the individual mind is a group product, we may look for the same patterns of relationship between the one and the many in any historical period. And however much we may question the terminology in which these patterns were expressed, the fact that man's neurological structure has remained pretty much of a constant through all the shifts of his environment would justify us in looking for permanencies beneath the differences, as the individual seeks by thought and act to confirm his solidarity with his group.

Indeed, when looking over the scene today, we find much evidence to believe that our situation is in notable respects analogous to the era when the Christian rationalization first took form as a universalizing attitude. The Christian doctrine arose at a time of pronounced cultural mongrelism, when many distinct cultural integers had been brought into vital contact by the political unification of Rome. This economic relationship required its spiritual counterpart to complete the workings of the *pax Romana*. There were many discordancies of evaluation, many conflicting schemes of spiritual order, leading to much the kind of imperfect overlaps we find in perspectives today. There was also a highly tolerant group of thinkers who took the very confluence of rival certainties as their point of departure, and were seeking to erect a philosophy of tentativeness precisely at the moment when a new authoritarian doctrine was beginning to gain power. The analogy seems even closer, as there were many rival "saviors" in the earlier era, corresponding to the various scientific bringers of new meanings who now call out to us. I was about to say that their manner is altered. But I am not even sure; for much Christian theory having to do with "The Word" shows signs of stemming from precisely such methodological concern with the basic devices of communication as has arisen once more. Prophecy and quackery were then, as now, hopelessly intermingled, since the breakdown in the machinery of orientation had brought matters of expectancy again to the fore, leading to a psychotic emphasis upon *foretelling*. The situation now is not different in essence, when our experts at forecasting happen to be called not prophets but "knowists."

In the earlier confusion, the golden rule seems to have been brought forward as a lowest common denominator of appeal. It was a truly "catholic" basis of reference, or sanction for human values, which might unite all cultural integers despite their many differences. It formed a rock-bottom of communication, having about it sufficient self-evidence as a desirable end to gain it at least acceptance in principle among people of many sects and cultures with wholly distinct systems of piety or customs.

There are even grounds for suspecting that the doctrine had a double qualification. For besides its validity as a universal criterion, a basic formula for spreading a single cultural reorientation across a host of economically united but spiritually disunited cultural integers, it had roots in the patterns of vindictiveness. Was it not the "tooth for a tooth and eye for an eye" formula rephrased? Had not the *lex talionis*, so basic to human notions of justice, been simply lifted by the golden rule out of the vindictive category and placed in the *caritas*-category?

Bentham was so confirmed an adversary of religion that he regularly referred to the Bible as the "Jugg Book," having in mind the many forms of unintended self-immolation into which this Juggernaut had led the Faithful in their search for benefits. Yet it is the Utilitarians, and Bentham foremost among them, who offered the clearest formulæ for a reconstituted ethics by which judgments of goodness were held to arise from judgments of usefulness, and judgments of evil were held to arise from judgments of disservice. Was not this desire to found our morality, and in particular our political expedients, upon a clear reference to the tests of *utility* much the same sort of reduction to a lowest common denominator of sanctions? Was the corollary, the test by the "greatest good of the greatest number," much different from the original catholicizing device which informed Christian teaching, though it was restated this time in the terminology of economics, anthropology, philology, and the like?

And does not the scientific ideal of a "neutral" vocabulary show marked similarities with the pre-Christian skepticism, particularly as manifested in Christ's dislike of vindictive judgment? Such hesitancy in pronouncing judgment is most natural to eras when the matter for ethical digestion is, for one reason or another, extremely complex and conflicting. And the financial empire-builders greatly intensified such disorders in the modern era, which was also bewildered by the new ways of life arising with the introduction of machinery. The documents of ethical relativity supplied by anthropology and similar sciences contributed vastly to the same confusion. Beset on so many sides, the orientation necessarily was broken, giving rise to the skepticism and eclecticism which Nietzsche and Spengler noted, and to an attempt at resimplification.

Such doctrines of ethical causality as Bentham's and Marx's, enunciated at a time when the perplexities of our society were first coming sharply to the fore, are distinctly in line with the earlier connection between resimplification and skepticism. Ogden and Richards have also unearthed in the few surviving pages of Ænesidemus evidence that the present linguistic skepticism was astutely formulated in Rome just prior to the time when the new exaltation provided by the Christian orientation swept it from the scene. Meaning or symbolism becomes a central concern precisely at that stage when a given system of meanings is falling into decay. In periods of firmly established meanings, one does not *study* them, one *uses* them: One frames his acts in accordance with them. Seen from this angle, the whole scientific program of organized doubt belongs to the "dark ages," a period of transition between one schema of certainty and another.

For in the last analysis, men do not communicate by a neutral vocabulary. In the profoundest human sense, one communicates by a *weighted* vocabulary in which the weightings are shared by his group as a whole.

Towards a Philosophy of Being

To avoid the possibility of confusion, let us specifically state that we are not offering these observations as evidence that the earlier magical or religious rationalizations were "right" and should be restored. We wish simply to emphasize the fact that, insofar as the neurological structure remains a constant, there will be a corresponding constancy in the devices by which sociality is maintained. Changes in the environmental structure will, of course, call forth changes in the particularities of rationalization, quite as we must employ different devices for salvation if we fall into water than if we are sliding down a cliff. But the essentials of purpose and gratification will not change.

If we choose to emphasize the shifting particularities, we approach human problems *historically*, as in the philosophies of *becoming* which seem to have reached their flowering in Nineteenth Century thought (Goethe, Hegel, Marx, Darwin, Nietzsche, and the vast horde of lesser evolutionary or revolutionary thinkers). If we choose to emphasize the underlying similarities, we return through symbolism to a philosophy of *being*, the Spinozistic concern with man *sub specie æternitatis*. We replace the metaphor of progress (and its bitter corollary, decadence) with the metaphor of a *norm*, the notion that at bottom the aims and genius of man have remained fundamentally the same, that temporal events may cause him to stray far from his sources but that he repeatedly struggles to restore, under new particularities, the same basic patterns of the "good life."

The whole idea of progress, when approached from such an angle, seems to have cloaked one long hysterical attempt to escape from a grossly mismanaged present. That it was grossly mismanaged is now apparent. A sound system of communication, such as lies at the roots of civilization, cannot be built upon a structure of economic warfare. The discordant "sub-personalities" of the world's conflicting cultures and heterogeneous kinds of effort can be reintegrated only by means of a unifying "master-purpose," with the logic of classification that would follow from it. The segregational, or dissociative state cannot endure—and must make way for an associative, or congregational state.

A sound communicative medium arises out of coöperative enterprises. And the mind, so largely a linguistic product, is constructed of the combined coöperative and communicative materials. Let the system of coöperation become impaired, and the communicative equipment is correspondingly impaired, while this impairment of the communicative medium in turn threatens the structure of rationality itself.

PART III

THE BASIS OF SIMPLIFICATION

THE BASIS OF SIMPLIFICATION

Part I dealt with the "reading of the signs." Part II dealt with the intermediate stage between an old and a new way of reading the signs (a stage of unsettledness that attained its corresponding affirmation in the cult of "stylistic gargoyles," with their peculiar kind of visionary aptitude). Part III concerns the "solution," insofar as a new fixed way of reading the signs is deemed necessary. The complexities of the problem are reviewed (the confusion due to a welter of solutions). Since the stress here is to be upon a "poetic" solution (in accordance with the profoundly emotional nature of a response to meanings), we call attention to the fact that the poet uses weighted *words. Review of Bentham's linguistic exercises, for transcending any given order of weightings (and application of his principle to the point where we can discern emotional weightings hidden even in nouns apparently "neutral"). But such weightings in themselves are not poetic but ethical (being derived from the partisan nature of practical action, which is guided or deterred by "censorial" terms). And such ethical grounding of poetic communication splits into two aspects: (1) Things* materially profitable *can be interpreted as* spiritually "good"; *(2) Such ethicizing of the utilitarian can lead to notions of propriety that operate in their own right, even at the cost of material advantage. (The "good" thus advances from means to end, so that one can "sacrifice" for "the good," dying for things that he hoped would make him prosperous.) The ethical in this sense involving character, or personality, we consider the character of men who socialized themselves*

*by a "poetry of action". What was their purpose? The question
invites us to note how an over-all, or "statistical" term for
motives transcends the particular localized motives (based
upon immediate contingencies) that a man may impute to a
given act. Such considerations are preparatory to the kind of
over-all motive the author is preparing to advocate. But one
major difficulty must present itself to the reader here: At this
late stage an author would "normally" be merely advocating
a thesis with as much efficiency as he could possibly contrive,
having so set up the foregoing chapters that he would by now
be driving toward his conclusion with the pointedness of a
lawyer defending a case in court; in this instance, however,
the thesis continues to burden itself, even to the extent of
casting doubt upon the motives of someone who thus culti-
vates the burdensome. Above all, the search is for arguments
(with their burdensome complications!) whereby* Purpose
*may be restored as a primary term of motivation. Such a project
is called a "Metabiology". The term is justified insofar as each
biological organism has "purposes" intrinsic to its nature (a
specific nature which aims at some kinds of "good" rather
than others). When applied to human beings, it transcends
biology in the strict sense of the term, in that men's* social
*motives are not mere "projections" of their nature as animal
organisms not typically given to the motives of the verbal, or
symbolic. Such concerns lead to the "solution": the view of
man as "poet", the approach to human motives in terms of*
action *(with poetic or dramatic terminologies being prized as
the paradigms of action, a term that leads happily into the
realms of both ethical and poetic piety, or into the scientific,
too, by reason of the fact that "symbolic" acts are grounded
in "necessitous" ones). In summing up this section, we should
particularly stress the term "recalcitrance", as an* essential corrective *of the "poetic metaphor".*

CHAPTER ONE

CAUSALITY AND COMMUNICATION

Major Shifts in Perspective

AN ORIENTATION is largely a self-perpetuating system, in which each part tends to corroborate the other parts. Even when one attempts to criticize the structure, one must leave some parts of it intact in order to have a point of reference for his criticism. However, for all the self-perpetuating qualities of an orientation, it contains the germs of its dissolution. As some people may not prosper by its own tests of prosperity, the orientation itself gives them grounds to question its validity. Thus, by stressing the importance of commodities as an aspect of the "good life," capitalism eventually brings itself into disrepute insofar as it prevents the general distribution of these commodities. Or by stressing the value of private initiative, it finally creates conditions which hamper private initiative. One could multiply the instances *ad inf.* —and they are particularly troublesome because they attack the very roots of human motives. The ultimate result is the need of a reorientation, a direct attempt to *force* the critical structure by shifts of perspective.

We have considered in a general way the kinds of difficulty arising, especially during the Nineteenth Century (transitional, or romantic in the extreme), when attempts at reorientation were most intense and profuse. We tried to show how the orientation had broken into fragments, with nearly everyone tending to isolate a different feature of it as his point of reference. In the main, the Occidental world was approaching the *terminus ad quem* implicit in the individualistic movement formally inaugurated with the Renaissance.

It might be called Da Vinci's era—and one by one men fell into the rôle of "impiety" by questioning the central values of their group. A kind of persecution psychology came to the fore, as men condemned their fellows and were self-condemned by this very act of condemnation. Da Vinci saw faces in the façades of buildings; he confided his distrust of his pupils to the secrecies of his diary; his Mona Lisa bore a quizzical, schizoid smile; and in the perversity of his mirror-writing he even seems to have given us a symbolic act suggestive of the feeling that he was *thinking backwards*. In a sense he was thinking backwards, as judged by the orientation which he was bringing into question. For the Catholic schema had been fundamentally purposive or teleological—but by the scientific system of causality, as crystallized in the Cartesian formula of "organized doubt," even human motives were to be explained by the *vis a tergo*, the force from behind. In the new perspective, men were not *drawn as to a beacon*: they were *pushed* by the compulsion of prior circumstances.

A contrary trend is noticeable today, especially among the modern critics of scientific method who use science itself as the basis of their criticism. They love to illustrate their theories by quotation from the works of Lewis Carroll. Carroll lived in the two worlds of mathematics and nonsense—and though he was very humble about his gifts as a punster, his virtues as a forerunner of modern thought seem to have resided in his puns, the many gargoyles whose outrageousness was forever causing Alice bewilderment, and in the topsy-turvy perspectives that lie in the right-is-left, left-is-right world beyond the looking glass.

The Catholic point of view had considered the Creator as active and participant in His creation—but the scientific point of view considered the universe as a *fait accompli*. For the scientist, celestial legislation was over. One approached the Pythagorean book of nature in the passive rôle of audience.

CAUSALITY AND COMMUNICATION

Gradually men came to make a sharp distinction between the *ethical* and the *logical*—and though there is a great complexity of factors involved here, much of the cleavage seems to have started from the distinction between teleological and mechanistic notions of causality. Those who felt that human beings were somehow in partnership with a cosmic Purpose took the individual sense of purpose as fact No. 1—and those who believed in the immutable stability of natural law began with objective data.

The *logical* seemed distinct from the *ethical* insofar as the objective data offered no evidence of purpose—although, as Whitehead has made clear, there was an unconscious stacking of the cards here. For scientific method categorically makes the discovery of purpose impossible. The scientist was saying in effect: "Let's see what we can discover about experience by programmatically eliminating the concept of purpose, and even considering the phenomena of purpose in terms of mechanism." When considerations of purpose as purpose are reintroduced into such a frame, we may expect to see again some of the mirror reversals that took place when the frame itself was first being adopted as key perspective.

In any event, with the appearance of such romantic philosophers as Fichte and Schelling we see the priority of the ethical or teleological again coming to the fore. Hegel made the most ambitious attempt to dissolve the ethical-logical dichotomy by identifying the logic of history with the expression of a universal purpose. And we had the many Schopenhauerian philosophies of *will*, all more or less clearly implying a distrust of positivism since they emphasized the volitional factor in perception. Even while positive science was attaining its greatest conquests, there were forces at work tearing apart the orientation of the day. This tendency was accelerated as the century advanced, until the cult of paradox had brought into question the whole celestial mechanics which had been both implicit and explicit in the positivistic accounts of causality. New material for inclusion became bewilderingly complex, and men began to seek a fresh basis of simplification.

The Rock of Certainty

Thinkers "went nudist"—and it may be no accident that, in simpler souls today, we find the tendency bluntly symbolized by the literal doffing of clothes. The turn away from "Victorian hypocrisy" here reached its ultimate expression in symbolic behavior. And similarly it seems no accident that Carlyle, the author of *Sartor Resartus* (a book about the spiritual changing of clothes) should now be found to have fathered the philosophy of Black Shirts and Brown Shirts. Surely, at every point in history when an orientation has been radically brought into question, we may look for a nudist sect —and we may look for a parallel cult of nudism in the remoter areas of thought. Nudism represents an attempt to return to essentials, to get at the irreducible minimum of human certainty, to re-emphasize the *humanistic* as the sound basis above which any scheme of values must be constructed.

Such efforts at simplification led many thinkers to situate the essence of human relationships in the sphere of the brutal (a trend increasingly in evidence since the days of Hobbes with his *homo homini lupus* formula). Philosophies of *becoming* made life look like a perennial battlefield. Such an attitude fitted the ideals of positivistic science, in laying stress upon the notion that man must patch up the discordancie between himself and his environment by reshaping the environment. He must not *surrender* to the environment that oppresses him; he must *change* it.

This attitude amounted to a simple declaration of war economic and military conflict increased enormously; instead of reason as the guide of conduct we got intelligence, which was a mere implement of will; and the emphasis upon the permanent yielded to an emphasis upon the transitional. Seen from this angle, empire-building (of either the national or purely commercial sort), war, capitalism, positive science, historicism, voluntarism, innovation, the belief that the "good life" resides in the acquisition of commodities, the parliamentary battles of democracy, nationalism, individualism, liberalism, atheism, *laissez-faire*, and progress all seem to be of one piece, different words for the same process as named in different areas of our vocabulary. I do not mean to suggest that the whole must stand or fall as a unit. I mean simply that, in its given texture, this structure of manifestations was mutually reënforcing.

When a superstructure of certainties begins to topple, individual minds are correspondingly affected, since the mind is a social product, and our very concepts of character depend upon the verbalizations of our group. In its origins, language is an implement of action, a device which takes its shape by the coöperative patterns of the group that uses it. Our chapter on perspective by incongruity should serve to indicate how radical the impairment of the communicative and the mental could become if the coöperative process were frustrated for long—while the symbols of disintegration with which recent authors have so often ended their books should suggest that the more barometric minds already appreciate the increasing state of disorder.

At such a time, people naturally begin to look for some immovable "rock" upon which a new structure of certainties can be erected. The accepted terms of authority having fallen into disrepute, they seek in the cosmos or in the catacombs some undeniable body of criteria. They try to salvage whatever values, still intact, may serve as the basis of new exhortations and judgments.

Unclear both as to what they are against and what they a
for, they become confused as to their selection of means. Ar
the tragic proportions of their predicament often lead the
by sympathy to seek a tragic solution. The Nietzschean er
phasis upon the blond beast is the most picturesque exampl
Darwin himself had specifically recognized that the strugg
for life gives rise to coöperative attitudes, that tendernes
charity, good humor are as truly factors in the survival of
man as was any primitive ability to track and slay animals
the jungle. But this aspect of his doctrine was generally i
nored—and the struggle for life was usually interpreted in
bluntly militaristic sense. As a result, the world seemed to l
composed simply of harsh antitheses, impossible choices, lil
the choice between *conquest* and *surrender*. Happiness b
came associated with the search for prey, or with the feelir
of triumph which an eagle must feel in swooping dow
upon a lamb. Or if one chose to deny such an ideal, l
opened himself to the suspicion of being a weakling, unfit f
the rigors of life's glorious combat. In the face of such bra
antitheses, the realm of humane satisfactions was almo
wholly ignored. A concern with sentiments became "sen
mental."

This attitude was intensified by the growing intensity
economic conflict itself. Such humane sentiments as goodw
were becoming forbiddingly expensive for millions of t
population: If they ceased to be fierce or designing, they we
threatened with extinction. It was only those with assur
incomes who could afford to exude much love of their fello
man. Many luxuries had become necessities—but converse
the most basic necessity, the necessity of kindness, hones
tolerance, had too often become a luxury.

The economic compulsion also refined itself in the real
of art and abstract speculation. Since extreme statements we
more likely to attract an audience than better balanced on

thinkers unconsciously adjusted their whole machinery of communication to this competitive demand. Everyone attempted to make his thesis as salient as possible. To be "noticeable," he had to distract the attention of his audience from other works which were equally striving to be noticeable. A premium came to be placed upon the most drastic kind of perspectives. Thoroughness no longer meant the search for proportions: it meant the intensification of one's particular gift—one became thorough by being a freak. Barnum's sideshows found their exact replica in art. In an age of specialization, everyone became a specialist: mechanic, stamp collector, sex pervert, what you will. The short story of the Poe sort had definitely introduced the test of efficiency as central to the artist's purposes; nothing was so valuable to a writer as the possession of some mental colored-spectacles by which, when looking upon the world, he could find everywhere evidence of this one color.

The search for a rebeginning was further stimulated by the feeling that we had radically broken with the past. In contrast with modern enlightenment, all previous schemes of adjustment looked like mere superstition. Modern mankind was detached: as regards its relationship with the continent of previous thought, it was insular. This attitude, which Russell calls "parochial," may be questioned, but it nonetheless prevailed. The race distrusted its parentage, and children distrusted their parents. In this respect the era was one long record of symbolic parricide: no wonder many came to consider the "Œdipus complex" as the basis of human motivation.

Two Aspects of Speech

We might distinguish two functions in the communicativeness of speech. Speech is communicative in the sense that it provides a common basis of feeling—or it is communicative in the sense that it serves as the common implement of action. In primitive societies these two functions are nearly identical: the emotional overtones of the tribal idiom stimulate the kinds of behavior by which the tribe works and survives. The word for the tribal enemies will contain the overtones of evil that reënforce the organization for combating the enemy. Or the words for the tribal purposes will contain favorable overtones which perpetuate these same purposes. By such an identity between the *communion* and *action* aspects of speech, the vocabulary of doing, thinking, and feeling is made an integer.

But the great variety of new matter and new relationships which science and commerce had brought into the modern world had broken this integral relationship between thought and feeling in the communicative medium. Hence a paradox: Scientists attempted to make a *neutral* vocabulary in the interests of more effective *action*. They learned that by "suspending judgment," by inventing a non-moral vocabulary for the study of cosmic and human processes, they could get a much clearer idea as to how these processes work, and could establish a more efficient system of control over them.

In a strictly moral approach, where one's attitude toward the object is formed in advance, the range and quality of one's observations are restricted by the attitude. If one studied criminals, for instance, on the moral assumption that they are wilfully bad, one might automatically vow himself to purely vindictive kinds of treatment; but if one studied them by *suspended judgment*, simply as *social phenomena*, one might learn important new facts about the genesis of crime, and from these facts a whole new program for the treatment and prevention of crime might follow. In such ways, it was held, *neutrality* of approach might eventually further the ends of *action*.

But speech in its essence is not neutral. Far from aiming at suspended judgment, the spontaneous speech of a people is loaded with judgments. It is intensely moral—its names for objects contain the emotional overtones which give us the cues as to how we should act toward these objects. Even a word like "automobile" will usually contain a concealed choice (it designates not merely an *object*, but a *desirable object*). Spontaneous speech is not a naming at all, but a system of attitudes, of implicit exhortations. To call a man a friend or an enemy is *per se* to suggest a program of action with regard to him. An important ingredient in the meaning of such words is precisely the attitudes and acts which go with them. Regardless of whether we should call the implicit program of action *adequate* (as when speech aids a primitive tribe to organize a successful fishing expedition) or *inadequate* (as when speech confuses the handling of non-racial issues by stimulating racial persecution) these emotional or moral weightings inherent in spontaneous speech tend to reenforce the act itself, hence making the communicative and active aspects of speech identical.

Such speech is profoundly *partisan*. And it was precisely this partisan quality in speech which Bentham, who specifically formulated the project for a neutral vocabulary, would eliminate. He rightly discerned in it the "poetry" of speech, and resented its "magical" powers in promoting unreasoned action.

Naturally, with such an information-giving ideal as the basis of scientific effort, and with science enjoying prestige as the basic ideal of modern effort, the poet often felt his trade in jeopardy, a misgiving which he sometimes symbolized by despair, and sometimes by effrontery. In any event he knew—without telling himself in so many words—that this was not *his* kind of communication. It was not his business to give information about objects; he communicated when he established a moral identity with his group by using the same moral weightings as they used (for instance, a war poem in wartime). Add now the fact that this communalty of moral weightings was itself impaired, and you see the magnitude of his problems.

The proletarian morality advocated by Marx is an attempt to found such communalty of attitude upon a class basis instead of considering society as a homogeneous whole. It seeks to found a new system of partisanship—and in this sense, although it is considered scientific by its adherents, it tends to replace the strictly scientific hopes for a neutral vocabulary by a new weighted vocabulary, which would be moral, or poetic. Probably the entire project for a neutral attitude toward the matter of experience is but transitional, resulting from the fact that so much new matter had come forward for inclusion in our scheme of judgments.[1]

[1] There is another important condition necessary for a prevalence of skepticism. Skepticism requires a considerable amount of security before it can be developed in any systematic form. Those who doubt for a living must in some way or another be paid for their doubts. In the case of a skeptical privileged class, the order tends to be reversed: Instead of being paid for their doubts, they receive the pay first (in the form of unearned increment) and then doubt afterwards. At such a period many "proletarians of thought" earn their living by purveying the material of doubt to this skeptical class. Nothing makes doubt *safer* than an adequate productive and distributive system which is decaying but has not yet decayed. Hence, skeptics were happier in the Nineteenth Century, when the capitalist system was fairly serviceable despite its obvious inadequacies, than they can be in the Twentieth Century, particularly in those highly industrialized countries where capitalism is approaching its limits of expansion. Skeptics, at such a time, become subtly unemployed. The time has passed when one can be content to question old certainties—one must align himself with new certainties.

CHAPTER TWO

PERMANENCE AND CHANGE

Modern Parallels to Ancient Thought

EVEN IF one ascribes the rise of an orientation to its useful-ness, one cannot conclude that it necessarily serves the ends of use. It may survive from conditions for which it was fit into conditions for which it is unfit (*cultural lag*). And its fossilized existence may be prolonged, after it has become dangerous to the social body as a whole, if some group which profits by it controls the educative, legislative, and constabu-lary resources of the state (*class morality*). The members of a group specifically charged with upholding a given orienta-tion may be said to perform a *priesthood function*. If we de-fine a priesthood in this technical sense, we find that in the priesthood of today the clergy take a minor part: The func-tion is mainly performed by our college professors, journal-ists, public relations counselors, sales promoters, writers of advertising copy, many of whom will usually fume at the hypocrisy of the medieval Church while excusing their own position on the grounds of necessity. The decay of a priest-hood (when they more or less definitely resent the work that is asked of them) leads to a division between *priests* and *prophets*. The priests devote their efforts to maintaining the vestigial structure; the prophets seek new perspectives where-by this vestigial structure may be criticized and a new one established in its place. In this sense, Marx could be said to have performed a prophecy-function, as distinct from a priesthood-function.

William Loftus Hare, in his *Mysticism of East and West*, has noted a similar division in the writings of the Jews dur-ing the two centuries preceding the founding of Christianity.

He also says: "In the earlier prophetic writings there are occasional instances where the seers enjoy symbolic visions from some lofty eminence, and in Ezekiel (written in Babylon during the captivity) we have the frequent and significant phrase describing how the prophet 'was lifted up by the hair of his head and placed upon a high mountain whence he was able to discern the historical landscape of the immediate future'." In discussing the nature of the apocalypse in general, he writes: "Not only is the seer removed from the *place* he normally occupies on earth, but in the order of *time* also—and this is its special feature—he is removed backwards to a period so remote that he is able thence to look forward over the whole expanse of history, past, present, and to come. In doing this he gains an understanding of the events in a perspective which makes known to him their relation to the past and the future."

We have shown that the business of "symbolic visions" is as rife today as in those two hundred years preceding the Jewish-Hellenic-pagan mergers. The desire to recharacterize events necessarily requires a new reading of the signs—and though men have ever "looked backwards," the backward-looking of the "prophets" is coupled with a new principle of interpretation, a new perspective or point of view, whereby the picture of "things as they *really* are" is reorganized. We found our critical systems upon prophetic reference to the past; and we also attempt to retrace time "geographically" by examining "savage" societies still intact today. Even though our contemporary prophets seldom arrogate to themselves a "lofty eminence" from which to survey the entire course of events, is there not something like a modernization of loftiness in the scientific cult of the *impersonal* attitude? The basic device of modern secular prophesying is *abstraction*, which etymologically signifies a "drawing away from."

If the eighteenth and nineteenth centuries have been increasingly given to the search for new perspectives by which the matter of experience will be "seen in a different light," where does the Twentieth Century align itself in this trend? Can one, writing today and reviewing this accrued individualism of prophetic insight, feel that there is anything to be done but find his own point of view and add it to the general medley? Or may he ask himself whether the theories of "truth" really are as manifold as such a picture of our modern Babel would lead him to suspect? And instead of noting the great variety of religious, metaphysical, ethical, and psychological lore, might we try rather to detect the strains which run through it all? Might we take the variations not as essential, but as contingent?

Indeed, what could *discovery* be but *rediscovery*? A man makes a new invention. Yet it is simply the external embodiment of *prior* mental patterns. This invention produces a change in environment, as a result of which, *new* habits must be formed and *old* ones abandoned. But what would prompt people to feel the need of reorganizing their habits if not some constitutional character possessed already? Let us say, for instance, that man invents a new food. The new concoction appeals in some way to some established predilection of the palate. Let us suppose that it also happens to be "unbalanced." It is thus not wholly suited to all the "orthodoxies" of his bodily needs, physiological characters that existed prior to the invention of the new food. Eventually someone else makes a "discovery." He finds in what way the food is inadequate, what element must be restored or taken away before a balanced diet is restored. His newness is of value insofar as it hearkens unto a primeval oldness, a standard constitutional demand.

Such is the case with those elaborate regimens of social diet which we build up by a slowly selective process until certain ills gain prominence and authority enough to grow self-sustaining or creative. These ills become powers in themselves, leading us on to still further interests, all farther and farther afield from our original patterns of humane gratification. Endless "discoveries" are made, by "prophets," artists, humorists, caricaturists, manipulators of the grotesque, criminals, theorists, scientists, critics, what not. They are all, however bunglingly, "answering a call." In one way or another they are symbolizing *refusal*. They "experimentally grope" for something—and this something is simply the device of living and thinking by which the faulty emphases of their day may be rectified. Their innovations upon the established structure are in part analyzable as mere projections of the historic trends—but we must also discern here the age-old tests of contentment which have been outraged by the orientation's complexity. Thus, every turn toward resimplification, at every point in history, may be expected to show marked similarities with the basic or "nudist" attitudes of corresponding earlier periods.

We may say that an entire cultural movement is like a sentence. Let one say a sentence about something, and suppose that one uses a sea-metaphor to convey his meaning. If his auditors happen to be farmers, they may not follow the sea-metaphor in all its cogency—so one might try to express his meaning another way, this time using a metaphor that had to do with crops. Now, there is much in human discussion throughout the ages which is like this mere shifting of a metaphor, as men have ever approached ultimate concerns from out the given vocabularies of their day, such vocabularies being not words alone, but the social textures, the local psychoses, the institutional structures, the purposes and practices that lie behind these words. Piaget, in studying the language of children, noted that frequently the meaning of their sentences was entirely lost unless his investigators recorded along with the sentences the circumstances under which they vere said. In a more complex way, the terms by which we ommunicate are always thus *circumstantially* founded. Might ve not suspect, then, that even if one were talking about needs nd purposes universal to all mankind, one would necessarily tate his position differently in different social textures?

Piaget has shown that the child becomes socialized insofar s he acquires the use of the particular rationalizations by vhich the logic of human motives is verbalized in his partic-lar society. Similarly, in his *Towards an Understanding of Karl Marx*, Sidney Hook explains away some of the "incon-stencies" in Marxian doctrine by showing that Marx often ephrased his arguments to profit by the particular convic-ons of the particular group he happened to be addressing. ince the convictions of these groups varied, Marx's strategy or socializing his position varied accordingly—and it is not ard to see how his statements, when lifted bodily from their tuations and baldly compared, might seem inconsistent or ontradictory. Morris R. Cohen has noted a broader manifes-ation of the same process. Some Marxians, he says, are fatalists vho hold that the dictatorship of the proletariat is economic-lly inevitable; others, like Lenin, stress the need of intellec-ualistic effort in bringing about the success of their policies. ohen holds that the fatalistic emphasis stems from the dis-ouragements following the failure of the revolutionary move-ient in 1848, when men could console themselves only by he assurance that the triumph of their cause was historically reordained; while the emphasis upon the value of the edu-tional or intellectualistic came to the fore during the later rowth of the Socialist Party in Germany. We cannot com-re mere verbalizations—we must also correlate the situa-ons behind them.

Might the great plethora of symbolizations lead, through e science of symbolism itself, back to a concern with "the ay," the old notion of Tao, the conviction that there is one fundamental course of human satisfaction, forever being glimpsed and lost again, and forever being restated in th changing terms of reference that correspond with the change of historic texture? All that earlier thinkers said of the *uni verse* might at least be taken as applying to the nature o *man*. One may doubt that such places as heaven, hell, an purgatory await us after death—but one may well suspect tha the psychological patterns which they symbolize lie at th roots of our conduct here and now.

Indeed, one could find many disembodied purgatoria moods (times of indeterminacy, preparation, and waiting throughout some of the best art in the recent century. Fo though it is customary to deplore the *materialism* of moder. life, in some respects one may rightly complain that ou ways are not materialistic enough. The entire modern metho of production and distribution is based upon an elaborat superstructure of abstractions.[1]

Veblen has convincingly pointed out the tendency in tech nology to violate the more strictly "anthropomorphic" pat terns of behavior—as in the distinction between the mental o physical operations that went with the hand-shaped tools o earlier times and those that go with the machine method

[1] Note added for this edition: To be sure, many of the incentive towards abstraction derive from indirectnesses in a society's way o living, indirectnesses due to social and technical resources for the del gating of work to others. But the longer we have puzzled over th problem (noting, for instance, how spontaneously children often tak to the abstractions of card games), the more convinced we are that th impulse to abstraction is a driving force in itself. There seems to be i man an unremitting tendency to make himself over, in the image o his distinctive trait, language. It is as though one aimed to becom like the pure spirit of sheer words, words so essential that they woul not need to be spoken, but would be like the soundless Shelleyan musi vibrating in the memory after the song is finished. (Cf. Eliot's *Quartets*.

Thus it seems that, while the percentage of abstraction is increase

today. Consider the austere efficiency of the modern fac-
ry, with its exacting morality of production, as contrasted
ith the movements involved in the primitive making of
ottery. And a modern state requires a whole army of brain-
orkers whose activities hardly engage their physical genius
all. Veblen noted the extremely *spiritual* nature of account-
acy, which he considered basic to machine technique. In his
stinct of Workmanship he calls attention to the "impersonal
d dispassionate" quality in the "logic and concepts" of ac-
untancy. He sees in bookkeeping, with its emphasis upon
ins, losses, income, and outgo, the factors which inevitably
courage a "statistical habit of mind." Our office workers
al exclusively with the *symbols* of production, distribution,
d consumption. And in proportion as we learn to approach
ir problems in this "objective and statistical fashion," we
en impart such prestige to our method that anything not
en to similar treatment falls into disrepute. Any other point
view "may even come to be discounted as being of a lower
der of reality, or may even be denied factual value" (an
servation which might suggest how the "spirituality" of
countancy might discredit the "spirituality" of the senti-
ents). And having noted the integral relationship between

---

the increase of institutions and inventions that make for much in-
ectness in our ways of living, the very tendency of human societies
ain and again to develop towards abstraction (as with the Upward
ay towards the "divine" in the Platonic dialectic) is due to a prop-
y ingrained in language itself. Even our terms for the closest of
nily relationships have an abstract ingredient that makes them
dily serviceable for naming social relations not strictly familial at all
with the adapting of such terms to the ecclesiastical order). And
ugh poets who specialize in terms for sensation usually think that
y are thereby avoiding abstraction, such usage is sometimes a
nantic excess (like the step from "nature" to "tourism"); and some-
es it is but the choice of a concrete-*looking* word that stands for a
on or confusion of ideas, as with Yeats's rose.

accountancy and the price system, he deduces a corresponding integral relationship between the price system and the rise of machine technology (an observation which might suggest why the price system has been retained in Russia, as a set of abstractions necessary to exchange under any form of industrialism). He concludes that the abstractions of accountancy have "probably been the most powerful factor acting positively in early times to divest mechanical facts of that imputed workmanlike bent given them by habits of thought induced by the handicrafts."

Does he not here picture the Protestant God, Providence, converted through the medium of Investment into a vague Actuarial deity functioning as Business?[2] Is not Business but the secularization of futurism, inherent in our turn from *status* to *contract* as the basis of our productive order? Indeed, Veblen's greatest contribution to our thinking is to be found in his *Theory of Business Enterprise*, for it is here that he discloses the naïve metaphysical principles underlying the

---

[2] Though Veblen centers his attention upon the price system, one might extend the range of such observations to include the abstractions of *justice* and *law* out of which concepts of price may in turn be said to have developed. Thus, we might note in the West a development from custom, through law, to traffic regulation. In "magical" stage (during the hegemony of custom) the productive order is mainly regulated by unquestioned tests of propriety. If there is a slave function in such a culture, the class that so functions does not know itself a such. A true slave morality is implicitly obeyed—and while such morality is intact, the slave does not consider his obedience as slavery any more than a child normally considers obedience to its parent slavery. Before such obedience can be explicitly considered a state of slavery, a perspective by incongruity must arise.

At first, law is hardly more than the codification of custom. But it formulation probably occurs because the customs are ceasing to possess unquestioned authority among the group as a whole, whereas a fraction of the group would greatly profit by the continuance of the old habits. Law is thus an educative, or manipulative device. It begins a

entire so-called realistic attempt to establish values by the price system. And does not the actuarial approach, as defined in the above quotations, clearly indicate an aloofness equivalent to the "lofty eminence" by which earlier thinkers symbolized their position?

---

theological law, still close to its "magical" orgins—but as it develops and proliferates, a new situation arises: though it was originally a mere codification of custom, it now becomes an implement for the molding of custom. The popular resentment at lawyers, as symbolized in the play by Molière, may derive in part from the fact that their prestidigitation is fundamentally impious, manipulating the abstractions of legal *fiat* until the commands of law have diverged farther and farther from the commands of custom, and eventually threaten to throw custom into confusion. Law becomes incongruous, except insofar as people can alter their customs to fit the liquid, constantly shifting alterations of law.

Theological law is a kind of halfway stage, in part being a mere codification of customary judgments, in part being a direct attempt to remold custom by educative edict. If the first aspect may be called "magical," the second might be called "rational." It makes for a totally secular attitude towards the formulation of law—and law then becomes traffic regulation. We find it in Roosevelt's so-called program of experiment—which amounts to an assumption that the basic habits, purposes, judgments, and values of the people can be changed from day to day by Congressional stipulation, to meet the contingencies of the moment.

Seen from this point of view, an experimental state would be a fundamentally immoral one. For by introducing liquidity into the composition of the state itself, one permits the individual absolutely no point of reference at all by which to give himself definition as a character. In learning to shift seasonally into new schemes of ought and ought-not, the citizen suffers the disintegration of his entire moral framework. Traffic regulation, so well adapted to a batch of automobiles, may be suited to human beings only insofar as they are drivers of automobiles.

CHAPTER THREE

SECULAR MYSTICISM IN BENTHAM

Bentham's "Table of the Springs of Action"

IT WAS in England that the Industrial Revolution first flow-
ered—and it was here that the doctrines of Utilitarianism
had their clearest formulation. We have already noted that
the secular principle of the greatest good for the greatest
number comes close to the religious doctrine of the golden
rule, as regards the cultural function of both. Indeed, it so
happens that the principle of utility was first recommended
to the British public in theological guise, as witness the following letter to Bentham from his friend George Wilson,
cited in Charles Warren Everett's *The Education of Jeremy
Bentham*:

"Other people here are invading your province of a reformer. There is a Mr. Paley, a parson and arch-deacon of
Carlisle, who has written a book called *Principles of Moral
and Political Philosophy*, in quarto, and it has gone through
two editions, with prodigious applause. It is founded entirely
upon utility, or, as he chooses to call it, the will of God, as
declared by expediency, to which he adds, as a supplement,
the revealed will of God. . . . I could almost suspect, if it were
possible, that he had read your introduction; and I very
much fear that, if you ever do publish on these subjects, you
may be charged with stealing from him what you have hon-
estly invented with the sweat of your brow." [1]

---

[1] An earlier terminological bridge between supernaturalism and
naturalism may be noted in Spinoza's formula, *deus sive natura*. God
or nature. His *sive* really performs the same function as the hyphen in
our contemporary compound, mind-body.

SECULAR MYSTICISM IN BENTHAM

We have previously referred to Bentham's theories of language. We might now consider some aspects of them in greater detail. In his *Table of the Springs of Action* Bentham works out a triple vocabulary which brings him very close to the mystic's skepticism as regards the nature of speech. In charting the pleasures and pains by which people are motivated, he uses two kinds of terms, "neutral" and "censorial," the latter in turn being divided into "eulogistic" and "dyslogistic." It is *neutral,* for instance, to speak of thirst, hunger, the need for food, the desire for food, etc. It is *eulogistic* to employ such terms as the love of the pleasure of the social board, or the love of good cheer. It is *dyslogistic* to designate the same interest as gluttony, voracity, gormandizing, sottishness, etc.

Or again: The "motives" which we apply to the "Interest of the Spying-Glass" range from the neutral *curiosity,* through the eulogistic *love of knowledge, literature, science,* to the dyslogistic *impertinence, meddlesomeness, prying,* and the like. Or, for the "Interests of the Altar," we may "motivate" a man's concerns as religiousness (neutral), devotion, holiness, sanctity (eulogistic), and superstition, bigotry, fanaticism, sanctimoniousness, hypocrisy (dyslogistic). It is not necessary here to describe the fourteen categories of "interests," with their corresponding triplicate vocabulary of "motives," which Bentham offers for classifying the "springs" of human action. His purpose in thus dividing our vocabulary is to reveal the great amount of exhortation which is really based upon nothing else than the avoidance of the neutral word for a given motive, with the selection of a eulogistic or dyslogistic one instead, according to the bias of the speaker or writer. Any such censorial word, he says, is *question-begging;* since it always smuggles in an emotional weighting, it makes moral assumptions without revealing to uncritical listeners the fact that it does so. In Bentham's peculiarly legalistic phrasing:

"Having, without the *form*, the *force* of an assumption,—and having for its object, and but too commonly for its effect, a like assumption on the part of the reader,—the sort of allegation in question, how ill-grounded soever, is, when thus masked, apt to be more persuasive than when expressed simply and in its own proper form: especially where, to the character of a *censorial* adding the quality and tendency of an *impassioned allegation*, it tends to propagate, as it were by contagion, the passion by which it was suggested. On this occasion, it seeks and finds support in that *general* opinion, of the existence of which the eulogistic or dyslogistic sense, which thus, as it were by adhesion, has connected itself with the import of the appellative, operates as proof."

Perhaps his point is more clearly made when he says: "Applied to the several *springs of action*, and in particular to *pleasures* and to *motives*, these censorial and impassioned appellatives form no inconsiderable part of the *ammunition* employed in the *war of words*. Under the direction of *sinister interest* and *interest-begotten prejudice*, they have been employed in the character of *fallacies*, or instruments of deception, by polemics of all classes:—by politicians, lawyers, writers of controversial divinity, satirists, and literary censors."

And later he says: "In political contention, no line of conduct can be pursued by either of two parties, but what, by persons of the *same* party, is ascribed to *good* motives; by persons of the *opposite* party, to *bad* motives:—and so in every case of *competition*, which (as most such cases have) has anything in it of enmity."

Bentham seems to have been admonishing against the very manifestation of human thinking which Marx was later to advocate: he wanted to eliminate hidden moral judgments when discussing questions of expediency. Instead of hoping for a new *morality* that would arise by contradiction to offset the morality currently misused, he attempted to found a technique which would prevent as far as possible all moral coloration from seeping into issues which should be seen in terms of simple serviceability. He held that even were a counter-morality to prevail, it would be but "cheating the people for their good." For, since it failed to inform them about the fundamental fallacies of their thinking, it would leave them as exposed as ever to the blandishments of a demagogue who might manipulate censorial terms to the people's disadvantage while cloaking his intentions behind moralistic, question-begging terms.

Bentham's *Book of Fallacies* is a patient labor of hate. It is an exhaustive study of the Parliamentary devices whereby questions of expediency were obscured behind the ethical wrappings which the orators applied when they would recommend or condemn purely practical measures involving the material advantage of specific groups. Bentham hoped that by analyzing the nature of verbalization, he could militate against the tendency to elevate matters of public expediency to the impassioned and deceptive plane of heroism and indignation, where one's judgments are formed in advance. (It might be worthy of parenthetical note that Bentham's *form* was later employed for equally deceptive ends by our statistical jugglers who "would not stoop to rhetoric," but gave us instead a "calm presentation of the facts," and thereby simply moved their trickeries one step farther along by "calmly and dispassionately" giving us their *own selective version* of "the facts.")

Bentham is usually considered a mere reformer, owing to his influence in the liberal codification of law. His analysis of speech, however, is extremely radical, as radical as the "organized bad taste" of the quasi-mythical method proposed by Bergson. Bentham detected a kind of organic flaw in the nature of speech, at least as regards the linguistic ideals which we now ask our vocabularies to embody. Speech takes its shape from the fact that it is used by people acting together. It is an adjunct of action—and thus naturally contains the elements of exhortation and threat which guide and stimulate action. It thus tends naturally toward the use of implicit moral weightings, as the names for things and operations smuggle in connotations of *good* and *bad*, a noun tending to carry with it a kind of invisible adjective, and a verb an invisible adverb. Our attempts at impersonality, as Bentham noted, are generally made by the use of question-begging words, which are impersonal only insofar as speaker and auditor share the same interests.

Morals, shaped by the forms and needs of action, become man's most natural implement when exhorting to action. As implicit in censorial words, they are the linguistic projection of our bodily tools and weapons. Morals are fists. An issue, raised to a plane of moral indignation, is wholly combative in its choice of means. From this point of view, the moral elements in our vocabulary are symbolic warfare. To the handling of complex cultural issues we bring the equipment of the jungle. With the "censorial appellatives" of righteousness, one pardons or smites. No wonder we find the jungle still with us, in the very midst of our "enlightenment," when the law of the jungle is preserved in something so integral to our ways as speech. And since the combative quality is ingrained in speech, and since speech is basic to social relationships, we may realize how essentially *radical* Bentham's philological proposals were.

It need not concern us now that Bentham was asking a great deal of human nature. It may well be that Marx's appeal to a flat counter-morality, whereby one group squarely pits its structure of moral weightings against an opposing structure of moral weightings, is much more likely to continue as the only way in which people are equipped to act, even though they do thereby lay themselves open to the likelihood of being alternately cheated for their good and cheated for their harm. We are here interested mainly in the fact that Bentham's skeptical analysis of speech brought him into a realm of conceptual relativity which is usually the property of mystics. So cautious and canny are his methods, it is hard to say whether he is leading us into this mystical realm or trying to save us from it.

In any event, the subject matter is essentially that of mysticism. For despite its secular trappings, it is concerned *au fond* with the "problem of evil," the bewildering ways in which good and evil are intertwined, and it proposes a basic reorganization of our linguistic genius in ways that, if followed through, would strike at the roots of character. Bentham has analyzed speech to the extent of showing that in the most "righteous" aspect of our vocabulary, the moral or censorial, there lurks the stimulus to make action combative or competitive. And he sought to perfect a methodology which, by greatly increasing and documenting our linguistic skepticism, might give us better control at the "narrows" of human relationship, the communicative medium itself. Though his ideal is far beyond absolute attainment, it is perhaps *relatively* possible—at least to the extent that we may evolve a conscious dialectic discipline for playing moral weightings against one another and neutralizing them at any point where such neutralization seems imperative.

Another aspect of Bentham's critique was his concern with the part that metaphor plays in our thinking. Noting the metaphorical quality of all speech, Bentham, developed a formula which might lead thinkers to reveal the metaphors lurking in their own concepts. Bentham held that by such awareness we are equipped to guard against the tendency to follow out the implications of our metaphor too literally. For instance, the statement that an "obligation" is "incumbent upon a man" may lead us to frame our thoughts on this subject quite as though we were considering a real "burden" which actually does *weigh upon* the man, or a cord which really *binds* him; we might then devote ourselves to finding ways whereby the man can *lift* or *untie* his obligation. The suggestiveness of the metaphor inherent in our statement might thus induce us to overlook the processes by which an obligation becomes imposed. We forget that it arises as the result of certain legal measures, expedients adopted for specific ends, or for the advantage of specific groups. But if we programmatically guard against the false cues which the metaphor gives us, we force ourselves to discuss the obligation in terms of behavior, purpose, social context, etc.

The possibility suggests itself, however, that even while guarding against the misguidance of metaphor on one level, we are simply forcing the covert operation of metaphorical thought to a deeper level. For instance, Bentham's own entire philosophy of *values* seems to have been framed within the metaphor of *price*. He wanted to perfect a "moral arithmetic." (Hence that violent manipulator of the censorial, Carlyle, called Bentham's utilitarianism a "pigsty philosophy," though we must in fairness recognize that no self-respecting pig would greatly concern himself with anything so tasteless as bookkeeping.) It is precisely through metaphor that our perspectives, or analogical extensions, are made—a world without metaphor would be a world without purpose.

Bentham seems to have been more thorough than any other philosopher in finding the ultimate psychological speculations that go with a mechanistic theory of the universe—and perhaps it was this very thoroughness which brings him to the borders of a wholly different region, suggesting in his almost anarchistic indifference to traditional linguistic categories the kinds of confusion in which the mystic appears to be at home.

CHAPTER FOUR

THE ETHICAL CONFUSION

Recommending by Tragedy

WE MAY, like Kant and the theologians, locate ethics in a transcendental source. Or we may, like the Utilitarians, consider ethical weightings as hardly more than an epiphenomenon of buying and selling. But whether we discuss the moral as an outgrowth of the economic, or the economic as merely a low order of transcendental moral insight, the same ethical relationship between the individual and his group can be disclosed.

At the roots of the ethical there is tragedy. Tragedy is a complex kind of trial by jury in which the author symbolically charges himself or his characters with transgressions not necessarily considered transgressions in law, and metes out condemnation and penance by tests far deeper than any that could be codified in law. Since tragedy is essentially concerned with the processes of guilt and justification, every full religious expression touches upon tragedy (as witness the purgation ceremonies of primitive peoples, the slaying of the god in fertility rites, the religious function of tragedy in Greece, the integral relationship between the Crucifixion and Christianity, or the cult of self-sacrifice among revolutionaries despite the "rationalism" of their doctrines). Tragedy reveals most clearly the workings of the criminal and expiatory processes implicit in human relationships. And it particularly concerns the complexities of ethics and psychology because of the close connection between *tragedy* and *purpose*. We might almost lay it down as a rule of thumb: Where someone is straining to do something, look for evidence of the tragic mechanism.

Even if we assumed the most utilitarian basis imaginable as explanation for the rise of moral judgments, holding that when the ethically ennobled say *virtue* they mean *promise of profit* and when they say *wickedness* they mean *threat of a loss*, the conflicts of the tragic mechanism remain. For the tragic symbol is the device *par excellence* for *recommending* a cause. How could one better picture an issue in an appealing light than by showing that people were willing to be destroyed in behalf of it? Thus, though I felt that a certain measure or attitude was valuable in only the "grossest" sense, in that it would enable men properly to administer to their most rudimentary needs and appetites, how could I better convey this belief, within the strategy of communication, than by telling of the great difficulties involved in the appreciation of it, or of the dangers that one would incur in trying to convince men of its usefulness? Thus, *sacrifice* is the thing that properly goes with *value*, even though the value originally arose from the most utilitarian conception of benefit.

Even a policy advocated for the ends of *service* may lead by the tragic mechanism to a symbolism of *disservice*. To show that a good is worth having, one shows that it is worth a sacrifice. Thus, even while the rationalist agitator seeks to commend his cause by picturing the advantages it would bring to its adherents, his poetic allies carry on the same propaganda *tragically* by the picture of heroic sufferings, sacrifice, and death. And similar psychological patterns will manifest themselves in the practical agitator's relation to his cause.

I think that this fundamental discrepancy is at the roots of Miguel de Unamuno's confusing emphasis upon the "tragic sense of life." He is forever talking of plans for human benefit, while seeming to prize nothing so greatly as the thought of human wretchedness. His pages seem at times to present a kind of glorified bullfight, a gory spirituality concerned with the *need* to incur risk and inflict misery, coexistent with a profound, almost morbidly intense yearning to see mankind brought to a very pigeonry of ease. In his *Essays and Soliloquies*, he speaks of a groaning, heard at night from an adjoining room: "It produced upon me the illusion of coming out of the night itself, as if it were the silence of the night that lamented, and there was even a moment when I dreamt that that gentle lament rose to the surface from the depths of my own soul." Here is the connoisseur speaking. In the social sphere, he sees Don Quixote as the tragic symbol manifested in the channel of ridicule—for ridicule most cruelly puts us apart from others; hence by risking ridicule in the commending of one's cause, one is involved in tragedy.

We may also note a highly domesticated, but genuine aspect of the tragic device in the *ars poetica* of Flaubert who, in an age when the prestige of business was swiftly mounting, glorified his craft by constant grumbling about the colossal labors of the search for the *mot juste*.

The Peace-War Conflict

It is possible that this pattern of ideological conflict can be traced back to a prior biologic contradiction of which it is a mere spiritual projection. Sherrington has pointed out that, whatever consciousness may be, it occurs mainly in processes required for the *hunting* and *grasping* of nourishment. Awareness during the hunt and the eating is intense; but once the nourishment is swallowed, the organism's consciousness becomes blunted. Unless some disorder of digestion occurs, the organism slips into a vague state of wellbeing, relaxation, stupor, and sleep.

This inconsistency of human purpose seems to have plagued Nietzsche unceasingly. We might say that whereas the organism has developed an equipment for attaining the benign sluggishness of satiety, the very equipment for bringing about such a world Nirvana is in itself the essence of turbulence and struggle. We perceive here a contradiction at the very basis of behavior. For if the organism attained its state of quiescence permanently, the military equipment of nervous agility, of bodily and mental muscle, would fall into decay. On the other hand, to prevent such decay, one must exert himself in "warfare," abiding by the competitive genius of mind and body, thereby denying himself precisely that state of conscious death which he might derive from the booty acquired by his prowess.

Nietzsche accordingly held that a morality of combat is no despicable thing, however much it may plague us. He saw that we could not confine the sphere of combat to such activities as war and commercial invasion. By his way of thinking, we could not stop at noting the greed of a Wall Street speculator or the predatory grasp of a credit monopolist. There is the same fanaticism, tenacity, and even pugnacity, observable in the efforts of the scientist, artist, explorer, inventor, teacher, or reformer. These militaristic patterns may sometimes have bad results, sometimes good, but all cultural activity as we know it is erected upon them.[1]

[1] Various remarks which we have already made should serve to provide the necessary qualifications for approaching the Nietzschean formula with safety. But in the interests of clarity, we shall repeat them here. By showing the underlying element of combat in all action, we do not thereby obligate ourselves to glorify a philosophy of combat. Action can be something *qualitatively* very different from combat; and it is perhaps only in moments of great stress, as in extreme personal anguish or under the present disorders of our economic system, that the purely combative emphasis must come to the fore.

In his *Pleasure and Instinct* A. H. Burlton Allen points out a most momentous oversight made by the whole school of Schopenhauerian pessimists, whose emphasis upon the will obliged them either to glory in thoughts of eternal conquest or to attempt some melancholy scheme

THE ETHICAL CONFUSION

Critique of Veblen's Solution

One might have expected Veblen's institutionalism (with ts corollary that any institution will show the defects of its qualities) to involve him in the same point of view. His statement that a capacity can be an incapacity would seem identical with Unamuno's formula: "Vices and virtues proceed from the same stock, and a single passion may be turned to good or evil." But in the interests of a purely rational exhortaion Veblen tries to avoid this confusion by ascribing the predatory and the industrious to different "instincts." He distinguishes between an instinct of self-aggrandizement and an instinct of workmanship." From the first, come war, destrucion, competition, envy. The primitive rudiments of the second are to be seen in nest-building. By thus planting two divergent instincts at the roots of behavior, he could seem to have a doctrine of origins which could divide the sheep from the goats. In this way he could avoid the ethical paradox

---

f renunciation. For the exclusively volitional emphasis overlooks the ealth of gratification which man may enjoy in the normal course of is activities. The muscles, and the mental and nervous equipment ehind them, may have been evolved to equip us in the business of ursuit and slaughter; there is thus a psychological, or instinctive deiand that we use this equipment; yet the demand may be satisfactory met by forms of action undertaken without any militaristic purposes r results. Similarly, the volitional over-emphasis completely ignores ie realm of the sentiments, and the enormous wealth of contentment pen to one who would enjoy pleasant human relationships. Volitional emands may at times arise to impair or endanger such relationships, ut may likewise operate in cementing them. It is only from the standoint of Utopia that pessimism is justified. Pessimism is Utopianism one sour. Schopenhauer can make us feel that when we sit down in omfort, the compressed cells in our buttocks must be crying out in iguish.

which characterizes the tragic approach of Nietzsche an Unamuno.

The difficulty with this solution is that the typical acts o man in society usually contain such an intermingling o "competitive" and "nest-building" features (invidiousness an industry) that we confront the same ethical anomaly all ove again, merely restated as the confluence of a predatory in stinct and an instinct of workmanship. The carpenter wh builds a house for the goods his wages will bring him, is bot a workman and an aggrandizer of the self. The scientis equipping himself by study, perfects those combative re sources of logic, clarity, and documentation by which he ca best make his thesis *cogent* (that is: coercive or compelling In a crustacean, which happens to "build its nest" in organ connection with its body, we see that Veblen's entire conce of a nest is naïvely anthropocentric. A nest is a shelter; shelter is a tool; a tool is a weapon for use in the struggle fo survival. The nest itself is built with the help of the compet tive equipment. Or when the desert plant stores up ext water in its leaves to prepare for drought, is the act predator or constructive? It is as much an act of individual appropri tion as the ruse of any robber baron. It is the naked biologic parallel of "investment for profit." And when life eats lif the predatory and the industrious are one.

If there were a special "nest-building organ," we mig have more grounds for postulating a separate nest-buildi instinct. But as things stand, Veblen would seem as justifie formally had he postulated a special "instinct for doing goo and cited nest-building as an example of its expression.[2]

---

[2] A distinction which might be more clearly referable to biolog analogies would be a distinction between "larval feeding" and t hunt. For in the history of all higher organisms that live by locom tion there are two stages—and in the first of these there is usually need of ambition or enterprise as a way of earning a livelihood. T

THE ETHICAL CONFUSION

Egoistic-Altruistic Merger

Veblen's distinction between the predatory and the workmanlike may bring us to another way of considering the ethical confusion: the indeterminate relationship between egoism and altruism. Piaget has noted that the socialization of children's thinking occurs concomitantly with the growth of their tendency to feel themselves *distinct* from their group. The *individuality* of the child's desires and intentions acts as a *socializing* factor by inducing him to perfect *logical* modes of thought as distinct from "autistic." The purely mimetic, tonal devices of threat or pleading are found to be inadequate —and the socializing ways of reason and proof take their

---

foetus in the womb receives nourishment as the children of Israel received manna from heaven. The food simply descends benignly upon it, and the organism has but to open itself and receive the bounty. There is no competition here. The organism, we might say, thrives by pure receptivity. It is truly at one with its environment. The "Luciferian rebellion," the separation of the part from the whole, has not yet taken place. But once the "trauma of birth" has occurred, the situation is different. Henceforth the organism must learn to make its way as a huntsman. It must become "invidious." Its larval receptivity is no longer sufficient for survival. It acquires a technique of supression, or control.

If the ear is primarily receptive and the eye primarily acceptive, we might see in this distinction between larval feeding and predatory feeding an analogy to Nietzsche's distinction between "eye-men" and "ear-men." In any case, the entire scientific attitude, which has flourished concomitantly with the growth of a predatory society, tends to think of understanding as *ocular*, a matter of *seeing*. It has developed a style of expression which poorly recommends itself to the ear. The stylistic quality of Chinese thought seems to have been largely receptive, tending toward a maximum of stability. But Western thought has tended toward the abruptnesses that go with feeding by conquest. Might one also distinguish even in our poets between larval and predatory styles, the long flowing sentence of a De Quincey being larval,

place. Piaget estimates that this change from assertion to argument is definitely established around the age of eight.

Of course, this process of socialization can continue throughout one's life, extending further and further the circle of one's interests—and conversely, one may find in any man important aspects of thought which remain almost wholly unsocialized, not substantiated by reason, but upheld by the pure assertiveness of childhood. In fact, the verbalizations that would socialize a certain area of interests may be absent from an entire group, awaiting some individualist who will illuminate things with a new perspective which he will invent by an analogical extension of the socialized equipment already there.

If we take egoism to designate simply the self-centered or self-regarding principle, and apply the word altruism in the opposite sense of an extra-regarding principle (Bentham's terms), we can readily see how, in a complex universe, even a simple reference to the self involves the organism in a deep

---

and the harsh telegraphic manner of today being distinctly predatory?

In analyzing the Duke's speech at the opening of *Twelfth Night*, I noted that he first talks of music as though it were a gentle melancholy sifting down upon him like fine rain, filling his wholly receptive soul with pleasant thoughts of Olivia. This I should call larval. Then comes a change: The Duke shifts his trope, saying that music is like the scent of violets. But the sense of smell is predatory—it assists in the location of game. And sure enough, the tenor of the page is immediately altered. We find the Duke announcing that he will pursue his woman as the huntsman pursues the stag. This change from receptivity to aggression occurred after the Duke's melancholy had gone beyond the agreeable stage, and become unpleasant, a hunger. And precisely at this same point he falls into a piece of diagnostic statement, quite like the reasoned observations of a "disinterested scientist." Are not the delicate fluctuations of this passage a whole history of society in miniature, written by a man whose attunement to the patterns of human response was miraculously accurate?

concern for things outside the self. When the ape "protects" his harem, or the gentle gardener ministers to his vegetables, or the beeman provides for his bees, the egoistic and the altruistic become functionally merged. In fact, one is being altruistic in the technical sense when looking for dry wood to make his fire: he is considering externalities foreign to himself, he is as extra-regarding as a scientist who seeks to isolate some hitherto unfound bacillus.

Conversely, we may discuss the altruism of a general who, to win his battle, carefully takes all the circumstances of the case into account, patiently noting the disposition of forces, the relative strength of the opposing armies, the possibilities of flank attack, etc., his extra-regarding tendency thus being manifested to the fullest, if only in the interests of ambitions purely personal. Here again, however, we should note that even *personal* ambitions are largely shaped by extra-regarding factors, since the general's *desire to excel* was doubtless a *desire to excel by the criteria of his group.*

Even our monsters of greed and ambition are moved by springs of conduct imbedded in notions of approval, distinction, accomplishment, that arise from one aspect or another of the group psychosis. Thought and action are too social in their very essence for even a despot to act without reference to the approbation of his fellows. Despite our great mass of documentation as to the relativity of values, we still tend to think of evil as a specific isolable entity, unchangingly itself, rather than as the neutral or the good seen from a different point of view. A given event can be at once good, evil, and neutral, depending upon the frame of reference by which we "place" it. And insofar as we may (and frequently *must*) consider several frames of reference simultaneously, the event itself tends to become morally nondescript. (At this point the "muddle-headedness" of liberals verges upon the "irrationality" of mystics.)

We tend to rate the "motives" of an act proportionately to the act's consequences; yet there may be much genuine ferocity in an amusingly futile rejoinder, while the hand that releases a deadly explosive may be moved by obedience alone. The period of muckraking in American journalism was largely wasted because the writers so often assumed that certain "wicked" people were doing the damage to our society, and that if only "good" people were put in their stead, all would be well. But the trouble did not arise so much from abnormal greed, as from defects in our social and political organization whereby the effects of normal greed are so amplified that they have the effects of abnormal greed. There is probably no more cunning and fanaticism in one man's corralling of a fabulous fortune than in another man's scheming to elbow himself out of his twelve-dollar-a-week job into the fourteen-dollar-a-week job held by the clerk at the desk next to him. And the equipment which they employ is not essentially different from that of the artist or the scientist, who is as "opportunistic" as he can be in his willingness to revise his methods to attain his ends.

Ethicizing of the Means of Support

Perhaps the easiest way to observe the transition from the egoistic to the altruistic is in the ethicizing of work. Or we might extend the concept of work to include the *means of support* in any sense. Is the miser's devotion to his gold an egoistic or altruistic tendency? He will deny himself many comforts in behalf of it—and if self-sacrifice is any test of altruism, we could consider him as an instance of the extra-regarding principle carried to the suicidal extreme. Adjoining this, but more often placed by our canons of good taste in the *unselfish* category (particularly in obituary notices) is the instance of a man's "self-sacrificing devotion to his business"

-and it is undeniable that, though his business procures him many goods, he really does *ethicize* it into an absolute good-in-itself. He does not consider it merely as an *instrumental* good; in fact, he may so alter his ways of living in its behalf that he actually ruins his health, making many of life's firmest gratifications permanently impossible—and so he dies a victim of his long devotion, quite as the obituary says he did, for all that the journalist who wrote the obituary snorts between beers and exclaims: "Like hell he did—the crook!"

Ethicizing, as so considered, is no rarity—it is a ubiquity. As some of our most enterprising investigators have discovered after enormous research, even the infant will tend to ethicize its nurse or its bottle, turning these instrumentalities of support or service into absolute external goods-in-themselves, and bestowing upon them the smile of sanction which *projects the subjectively loved into the objectively lovable*. Did not Lindbergh show a similar tendency when he spoke of "We," feeling that the plane which bore him across the Atlantic was a *loyal* fellow, a *buddy?* And similarly Mattern, describing his forced descent in Siberia, says that in deliberately wrecking his plane he felt as though he had shot down a faithful horse for no good reason. At a time when the attention was focused upon fire as the chief source of social benefit, such institutions as the Vestal Virgins were established, the ethical quality of their function being revealed in the special rites and vows that were piously felt to go with it. The most basic support of all, the *Earth*, is perhaps the deepest source of reëstablishment for bewildered sophisticates who, having lost all sense of a moral fountainhead, would restore themselves by contact with the "telluric." Does not the very word suggest some massive, unwieldy kind of solace, which might explain why so many moral systems still retain their agrarian roots, and might throw a more sympathetic light upon the deep resentment felt by the medieval world when Copernicus and his school proposed to imperil such stability?

Or we may see a similar ethicizing in the attitude of the naïve card player, who loves to hold his trumps to the last even though they might bring in more tricks if played sooner. He is responding to the *absolute* quality of the cards' trump-hood, instead of considering their value as purely *functional* or *instrumental*. He holds them as long as possible, with a vague sense that he possesses "goods." Likewise we find the doctrine of "Art for Art's Sake" flourishing among those for whom art was a fundamental factor in "support"—for in the complexities of civilization, the concepts of support range far. We may be supported by honors that net us little. And one man may be "undermined" by the removal of spiritual props which another would barely suspect the need of (as Bertrand Russell tells us that doubts about the existence of God never greatly troubled him, but a questioning of mathematical ax-oms once threatened to unsettle the foundations of his mind). As regards "Business for Business' Sake," the ethicizing of commercial methods has become so profoundly ingrained in our people that, even during the worst calamities of our na-tional history, we try to distinguish between "good" men and "bad" men in business, rather than questioning business en-terprise itself.

And if a man lived alone in the woods, dependent for his livelihood upon the game which he shot for himself by his gun, I believe we should see a phenomenon that looked very much like a cult of "Gun for Gun's Sake." He would keep his gun in a favored spot, would probably clean it more often than necessary; on Sunday he might sit outside his cabin door and shoot at tincans—and if an accident happened to endanger its welfare, he might even risk his life in trying to save it, as were he to snatch at it when it was falling over a cliff.

THE ETHICAL CONFUSION

Though it is customary to deny that in our enlightened era
e have ethicized machinery, I might cite two kinds of evi-
ence to the contrary: (1) We have tended to consider ma-
hinery an absolute good, as witness the frequent identification
etween mechanization and progress; (2) We have been so
npressed by the prestige of machinery that we attempt to
rry the machine metaphor into other areas of investigation,
suming its *absolute* or *universal* interpretative value, as
hen we employ it to "explain" kinds of biologic behavior
tally different from mechanistic behavior.

Variants of the Ethicizing Tendency

A more complex way of ethicizing the means of support, a
ind of inverse deification, is to be seen in Edwin Seaver's
eeply felt collection of "white-collar" idylls, *The Company*,
articularly in his chapter "The Boss," where this forbidding
gure is characterized wholly with reference to the *employee
titude*. The chapter is a pious preoccupation with a despic-
le source of goodness. It thus shows deep resentment at the
ms and powers of this boss-function (he is vindictively de-
ied the properties of a man):

"The boss only smiles when he is having his picture taken.
he boss likes to have his picture taken and so he has it done
ts of times. Sometimes it is as the director of a great Safety
rive and the newspapers tell how he has helped to save
ousands of lives. Sometimes it is as chairman say of the
4th Street Centennial Celebration and the newspapers tell
ow the boss is working for a bigger and finer 34th Street.
nd sometimes it is just as one of the country's great big
usiness men. But always it is the same old boss with the
ftly smiling face, the satisfied quiet lips and the eyes that
ok right past you."

Thus, even the humaneness of a smile is confined to the

needs of business. The boss is pudgy; he is over-dressed;
"feeds his face"; he is not liked by his underlings; he is
climber who "gets there by using others as a stepladder";
is a hypocrite; for all his power over his subordinates, he
physically negligible; he takes credit for the authorship
articles written by others; he holds office conferences, not
improve the business but "because it makes him feel impo
tant to have us grouped around him like the host at the fe
of God"; those who agree with him are merely "yes men
having no genuine sympathy but merely looking for wh
they can get out of him; his jokes fall flat; he always "speal
of the Company as if it were some immaculate conception
which we both owe equal devotion"; his life after hours is a
emptiness ("After dinner . . . the boss pats the bang of th
grey hair on his forehead. He does not like to think of afte
It makes him feel morbid when he thinks of after"); whi
dictating letters he gloats over the memory of sharp practic
and burns ineffectually with lust for his stenographer;
winces at the thought that his chauffeur nearly ran down a
old woman, not because he is kindly but because he "trembl
when he thinks of the unfavorable publicity it would mear
if he had hit her; and as for the low vision of his satisfaction
note him as he is being driven homeward: "His hands care
the leather seat and his eyes rest satisfied upon the uph
stered interior of the car. Underneath, strong steel. The c
rocks gently as a cradle on its springs as it crosses troll
tracks. Everything is so sure, so real, like those steel fram
upon which the workers will shortly dress the new sk
scrapers. Prosperity in every rivet." Here indeed is the dubio
altar of one's livelihood, to which the deeply pious auth
brings all the appropriate offerings of his hate.

Still on this subject, we turn to Bentham's *Theory of Fi
tions*, edited by C. K. Ogden, and we read on page cxvi
under the heading "The Personification of Fictions":

THE ETHICAL CONFUSION

"Personification is usually regarded as a harmless literary device by which Ceres, for example, comes to the aid of the writer of Latin verse by deputizing for *corn*. Bentham, however, insists on its subtler uses:

'Amongst all the instruments of delusion employed for reconciling the people to the dominion of the one and the few, is the device of employing for the designations of persons, and classes of persons, instead of the ordinary and appropriate denominations, the names of so many abstract fictitious entities, contrived for the purpose. Take the following examples:

'Instead of Kings, or the King—the *Crown* and the *Throne*.

'Instead of a Churchman—the *Church*, and sometimes the *Altar*.

'Instead of Lawyers—the *Law*.

'Instead of Judges, or a Judge—the *Court*.

'Instead of Rich men, or the Rich—*Property*.

'Of this device, the object and effect is, that any unpleasant idea that in the mind of the hearer or reader might happen to stand associated with the idea of the person or the class, is disengaged from it: and in the stead of the more or less obnoxious individual or individuals, the object presented is a creature of the fancy, by the idea of which, as in poetry, the imagination is tickled—a phantom which, by means of the power with which the individual or class is clothed, is constituted an object of respect and veneration.

'In the first four cases just mentioned, the nature of the device is comparatively obvious.

'In the last case, it seems scarcely to have been observed. But perceived, or not perceived, such, by the speakers in question, has been the motive and efficient cause of the prodigious importance attached by so many to the term *property*: as if the value of it were intrinsic, and nothing else had any

value: as if man were made for property, not property fo[
man. Many, indeed, have gravely asserted, that the mainte[
nance of property was the only end of government."

Do we not see, in what Bentham is discussing, quite th[
same ethicizing procedure as Seaver uses, except that Seave[
had proceeded by the *antithetical* morality, and instead o[
deducing the intrinsic goodness of the individual boss fron[
the goodness of his function (as when one accorded [
Churchman the honors due "the Church," or an individua[
Judge the honors of "the Court") he works within the "clas[
morality" of the employee and deduces the intrinsic evil o[
the individual boss from the evil of his function? Our obser[
vations are made purely as illustrative of the ethical process
and are not in any way intended as an adverse criticism o[
Seaver, whose book is an admirably written piece of partisan[
ship, fully exemplifying the free working of the poetic pro[
cess. And it is no less pious through being a dyslogistic, rathe[
than a eulogistic, brand of piety.

Perhaps the most complicated case of such "ethicizing[
was the American Humanists' concern with the "inner check[
Classical philosophers, discovering that a very serviceabl[
principle for promoting human welfare was moderation, ad[
vocated moderation so strenuously and so long that it became
not a *means of procuring advantages* but an *end to be sough[
even at the risk of disadvantage*. But once it had become a[
end rather than a means, a new means was required to pro[
mote its attainment. This was supplied by the invention o[
the "inner check," which prompts us to feel the sanction o[
moderation. As this too quickly moves from an instrumen[
into an end, a good-in-itself, we find *education* being advo[
cated as the instrument for sharpening our sensitiveness t[
the inner check. Education also, as might be expected, tend[
to become a good-in-itself by the extension of the same pro[

cess—hence we verge upon the tragic confusion, as suffering, sorrow, and error become goods-in-themselves in that they in turn bring us to appreciate the need of education.

Our purpose in going into this matter at such length is not to convey any cynical notion that altruism is "mere egoism." Their interrelation could as justly be stated the other way round. In saying that altruism and egoism form a continuous series, we do not at all obligate ourselves to conclude that "altruism arises out of egoism." This was the usual application to which the notion of continuity was put during the heyday of nineteenth-century materialism—but such interpretations were made by preference, not by logical necessity. Since the Church had overstressed the tendency to interpret many "evil" manifestations from the "good" side, the Church's materialist opponents often tended by simple inversion to interpret all "good" manifestations from the "evil" side. Thus, the Church might interpret the desire to make money as merely a low form of desire to improve oneself; and the Anti-Church would counter by interpreting morals as a mere epiphenomenon of the desire to prosper in the materialistic sense.

I do not see how the establishment of a continuity between one extreme and the other forces us to select either as primary. *Some other judgment* must enter before we can make this choice. The supernaturalism of the Church threw the weight upon the upper register as the primary quality, or essence, of the series; the materialist's naturalism threw the weight toward the lower register as the essence of the series. But in the series itself there is no such weighting, either one way or the other. The concept of an egoistic-altruistic merger would simply indicate that egoism cannot exist without altruism. Or, otherwise stated: Egoism cannot operate unless it so transcends itself that it becomes *qualitatively* different.

Yet the materialists' observations are valuable, and should

not be neglected by a simple return to their counter-statement. The saying *Ubi bene, ibi patria* has been called the "sad confession of an ideal-less, brutal materialism." As a matter of fact, if our patriotism were clearly based upon such a sensible test, and if we were quick to despise our flag in times of adversity, as naïve Italians are said to trample the image of their patron saints whenever things turn out badly, the "ideal-less, brutal materialism" of our thinking would go far toward interfering with the perpetuation of brutal conditions under which so large a portion of our population now "ideally" suffers.

There is a fundamental relationship between *wealth* and *virtue* which no "spiritual" scheme must be allowed to deny by fiat. *Property* and *propriety* are not etymologically so close by mere accident (and "clean" hands would in French be called *propres*). Morals and property are integrally related. They are obverse and reverse of the same coin. They both equip us for living. There is an integral relationship between these two kinds of weapons, tools, or capital.

Following Bentham's cue to the effect that the word *industriousness* may be simply the "eulogistic covering" of *desire for gain*, we looked among the books of quotations in various languages, selecting such words in good repute as virtue, industry, loyalty, truthfulness, fatherland, home, friendship, and we are struck by the clear connection which could often be drawn, in this lore, between virtue and service, despite the fact that the quotations themselves definitely ignored such relationships. When we learn that "industriousness has three graces for daughters—virtue, science, and wealth" (*die Tätigkeit hat drei Grazien zu Töchtern: Tugend, Wissenschaft und Reichtum*), why plague ourselves further? Industry, virtue, science, and wealth are all clearly the instruments of good living. In a wider sense, they are all but the primitive need of *food* and *shelter*, culturally projected—and the sooner we unite them, the sooner we may prevent the ethicizing tendency from *perpetuating evils* while supposedly *idealizing goods*.

We may also cite the testimony of an ardent patriot who, presumably after extensive comparisons and consultations with men of many different opinions, assures us that "there is no country like that in which my cradle stood." As we dare assume that in his cradle he fared *bene*, we can understand why the region of such prosperity should be ethicized as his *patria*. Give us a large dose of Bentham's "pigsty philosophy" —for by such tests any country would be branded *gross* until its last slums were removed and its paupers were given not merely sustenance, but the cultural equivalents of sustenance —activity, virtue, science, and wealth.

The "Pathetic Fallacy"

Perhaps we should discuss one other way in which the ethical involves an internal-external merger, through the intricate workings of the "pathetic fallacy," for which we have many names. We call it animism, when objects are endowed with the purposes and characters of people—and as such it is now not generally prevalent among us, though poets use it, not quite so metaphorically as they and we sometimes think. And in his book *Eidetic Imagery* E. R. Jaensch discusses a "co-variation phenomenon" whereby subjective changes are interpreted as objective events. "A line will very easily alter its apparent length if the subject is pulled by the arms while he is observing. . . . This phenomenon is particularly striking if eidetic images are made of drawings of the Müller-Lyer illusion. Pulling at the arms may lengthen the image by as much as two yards." He describes many such experiments, whereby different types of children have been demonstrated to "see" correspondingly different kinds of "images" which arise from the nature of the subject and his interests rather than from the nature of the object alone.

Jaensch also relates that his studies brought him into contact with an investigator from a Spanish university who had collected hundreds of statements "to the effect that certain pictures of saints perform miracles, step out of their panels, carry out actions, etc." This material was "based in particular on sworn statements by scientifically educated persons, like engineers, doctors, etc., who are accustomed to sober thinking." Jaensch remarks: "We demonstrated the peculiarities of perceptive processes in eidetic subjects to our Spanish colleague. What he saw strengthened his supposition that these peculiarities were the key to the phenomena in Spain."

In characterizing the normal eidetic phenomena of childhood, whereby such transformations in objective perceptions take place, Jaensch borrows the words of Franz Werfel, "Love is nothing more than the capacity for passionately developing the picture of a human being in our inner dark-room." Werfel's words, applied to less extreme cases, would amount to little more than the statement that our interests shape our "perceptions" of objects. This brings us close to the "pathetic fallacy" in its purity: the tendency to find our own moods in the things outside us. And the equivalent for this, in the intellectual plane, would be the tendency to find our own patterns of thought in the *texture of events* outside us. The pathetic fallacy is obviously creative, or ethical. Jaensch writes:

"Productive logical thinking, even in the most exact sciences, is far more closely related to the type of mind of the artist and the child than the ideal of the logician would lead us to suppose. That is shown in the loving attention to the matter in hand, in that close union of object and subject in children and artists, of which eidetic phenomena are merely a particularly evident expression. It is shown in the fusion of the person with the object, so that every lifeless system of signs ranged in between is felt to be a hindrance. The grammatical structures of language are just a system of signs, unless concrete imagination infuses life into them. Only psychological research can discover how the thinking process takes place. Logic represents to us thoughts arranged in their inner order and deduces one from the other; but if we examine the autobiographies of successful scientists, we find that productive thinking must have a close relation to artistic production. Read, for instance, H. Poincaré's own description of his work," etc.

Perhaps this is but saying, in an elaborate way, that all is yellow to the jaundiced eye, and that there are many unsuspected and unnamed kinds of normal mental jaundice whereby the internal finds its external counterpart. We may designate the process variously: as hallucination, sympathy, empathy, discovery, metaphor, perspective, interest, bias, pathetic fallacy, personification, synecdoche, predisposition, psychosis. We might call it a mere analogical extension, as one invents external equivalents for his mental and emotional patterns. But in any case it is *assertive*, it is *productive* or *creative*—hence it is concerned with *action*, which is to say that it is profoundly *ethical*. The "pathetic fallacy" is not confined to a few half-genuine conceits on the part of ancient poets and modern poetasters. It is forever at work molding the qualities of our experience, as it sometimes induces us to single out those aspects of events which immediately reflect our interests, and at other times it trains our attention upon the selection of such means as will make events reflect our interests. In this sense, all action is poetic. Rockefeller's economic empire is as truly a symbolic replica of his personal character as Milton's epic was a symbolic replica of Milton. In both cases, the men "socialized" their specific patterns of interest by the manipulation of objective materials in a way whereby the internal and the external were indeterminately fused.

CHAPTER FIVE

THE SEARCH FOR MOTIVES

Magical and Scientific Interpretation

IN THE rationalizations of magic, the poetic nature of thought and action was not explicitly stated, but it was implicitly acknowledged at every point. The rituals of "homeopathic magic" whereby the savage attempts to coerce the processes of the universe are precisely those of the "pathetic fallacy." In the magical rationalization, the verbal and mimetic devices whereby men induce one another to respond in sympathy were transferred to the field of inanimate operations—and in keeping with the logic of this attitude, the operations themselves were taken to be animately motivated (just as we tend to reverse the process and apply the *inanimate* metaphor in our attempt to coerce biologic operations).

In the field of psychology, homeopathic magic is effective and necessary. A persuasive work of art is nothing else. We may recall again the story of the missionary who, because he wore a raincoat when it rained, was requested by the tribal doctors to don his coat during a period of drought. Since the wearing of this coat had become associated with rain, and the missionary had become associated with notions of authority, it was felt that he could bring rain by wearing the coat. An *accidental* correlation was interpreted as a *causal* correlation whereby the wearing of the coat might be expected to act therapeutically upon the state of the weather itself. Such simple reversibility is precisely the foundation of poetic effectiveness. It is Proustian piety. For if certain images have become associated with certain moods, the poet can and does induce in us these moods by presenting the corresponding images.

The religious rationalization likewise retained much of this poetic structure. The universe was considered to be in control of an arbitrary power who was besought for favors, quite as subjects beseech their king. The favors might or might not be granted. This imaginative pattern was wholly analogous to the relationships among men. The universe was still essentially *anthropomorphic*, having a psychological pattern. As Veblen has observed, about the time that the independent workers' guilds were arising, a shift began to take place in the nature of this rationalization. Instead of "What hath God ordained?" we began to get the question "What hath God wrought?" Veblen interprets this shift as a change in emphasis from God as monarch to God as artisan, paralleling the rise of the independent artisan class at the breakdown of medieval serfdom.

But another feature may be noted: In the question "What hath God wrought?" we have implicit the notion of a *completed* universe. It contains in germ the naturalistic trend away from a concern with the *Creator* toward a concern with the *Creation*. In the former schema, God is still involved in the tides of human history. His ordaining is not complete; it is still in progress. Not until Calvinism (which is a kind of halfway stage between Catholicism and science) do we replace "ordained" in our formula by "foreordained." In the materialistic causal theories of nineteenth-century positivism, the emphasis upon the *foreordained* is complete. God is through, as in the enlightened philosophies of late Rome.

Or, in completely secular terminology: However the universe may have originated, it is now to be considered as a set of celestial wheels which were fashioned long ago and were set going in a routine fashion, and we have but to discover the unchanging laws that underlie its operation. Here is an attempt to move definitely out of the poetic or creative field.

Instead of considering the universe as *being created*, the student of scientific causality considers it solely as *having been created*. He may adapt its course to his wishes by learning exactly what the original legislation was; but the act of legislation itself is finished. We could now retain the poetic metaphor only by considering ourselves as *audience*, or perhaps more accurately, *critics*. We attend the play, we comment upon its methods, but we do not write it. If Æschylus was magical, and Sophocles religious, Aristotle classifying their procedures in his Poetics was scientific.

Statistical Motives

Of course, the analogy is not wholly complete. Aristotle's criticism was itself a creative act. And even if the universe is completed, our lives and our histories are constantly in the making. Though the materials of experience are established, we are poetic in our rearrangement of them. But the distinction may explain how a kind of conflict may seem to arise at times between logical and ethical approach. For the *logical* rationalization has tended to shape its accounts of the universal process without regard for the most characteristic patterns of individual human experience: the sense of *acting upon something* rather than of *being acted upon by something*. The spontaneous words for human motivation all imply the element of *choice*; but the scientific words imply *compulsion*. All causal schemes for explaining our actions begin by eliminating the very quality which most strongly characterizes our own feelings with regard to our actions. Only in cases of acute distress, as with a "compulsion neurosis," do we feel ourselves driven. We go up the street or down the street, as we "choose," though we may speculatively add that we did whatever we did "by necessity."

The explanations which a scientist would give for some

vast migration, after statistically observing the behavior of millions, would be wholly different from the "reasons" which each individual would have assigned for his part in the migratory movement. One man will tell you that he went west to avoid his creditors, another that he had always intended to do so ever since reading certain adventure stories in his youth, another that he migrated because Aunt Mary died, etc. The "statistical motive" will contain a generalization foreign to all these particular motives. It may disclose some economic factor common to all cases. Or it may disclose that a certain "psychological type" of person moved on while a certain other "type" remained behind. Or it may offer some Spenglerian formula concerning the lure of the setting sun. But in one way or another, the new causal interpretation obtained statistically will have the *incongruous* qualities of a perspective, since it offers a *generic* motive distinct from the motives experienced by the members of the migration *as individuals*.

We may subsequently attempt, with varying degrees of success, *to incorporate the statistical term into our consciousness*, as when a man today actually *feels* himself writing in a certain way because he is a "bourgeois" or a "proletarian" (whereas Dickens wrote "bourgeois" novels without any thought of a specifically "bourgeois" motive). In sum: We might say that the statistical interpreter has offered his system of motives from a point of view and for a purpose other than the point of view and purposes which were uppermost in the minds of the doers prior to acquaintance with the formula. One is "statistically" a bourgeois, a hyperthyroid, a Nordic, an extravert, what you will. But until he is specifically indoctrinated with such a concept, it does not figure as a motive in his acts, so far as he personally is concerned. Hence the resentment of a staunch Catholic when told by Freudian or Marxian that his religious system is motivated by interests wholly different from those which it specifically verbalizes.[1]

Where Scientists and Mystics Meet

In our section "On Interpretation" we attempted to show that man's words for motives are merely shorthand descriptions of *situations*. One tends to think of a duality here, to assume some kind of breach between a situation and a response. Yet the two are identical. When we wish to influence a man's response, for instance, we emphasize factors which he had understressed or neglected, and minimize factors which he had laid great weight upon. This amounts to nothing other than an attempt to *redefine the situation itself.* In this respect, our whole vocabulary of motivation is tautological. It is *not* tautological if we consider it as merely an elliptical way of defining the situation. It *is* tautological if we consider it as something distinct from the situation, as though there were *both* situations *and* motives. The situation was our

[1] We have previously discussed the censorial quality which tends to surround terms of motivation, once they have come into general use. Even such apparently neutral terms as introvert and extravert, invented for purely descriptive purposes, can take on strongly emotional weighting. And it is not hard to imagine a future society in which, since all material necessities had been conquered, men stoutly devoted themselves to a vast doctrinal battle as to which of these types our educational and hygienic facilities should be shaped to encourage and which should be eliminated. Glandular patients show a preference for diagnoses which attribute their ills to some *excess* of endocrine functioning rather than to an *insufficiency* (a situation which can probably be met satisfactorily by any obliging diagnostician—for the endocrines are so interdependent upon one another, being hardly more than the individual peaks in a single mountain range, that an insufficiency at one point can be stated as an excess at some other point). It is probable that no neutral term could come into general use as a description of human motives or interests without slipping into the categories of "eulogy" and "dyslogy."

motive, and our word for the motive characterizes the situation.

As the bluntest possible example in support of our thesis that motives and situations are one, let us make up a motive, even a very tangible one. Let us use an alarm clock as a motive. A man, let us say, must arise at a certain hour each morning. This need of arising (based upon such contingencies as office hours, distance of his home from his place of business, time required to dress and have breakfast) is a *situation*. He sets an alarm clock to arouse him at the desired time. The ringing of the clock thus becomes the *motive* of his rising. Yet when it rings, its sound is but a shorthand term for the situation which we have just described. The man acts as he does because the clock has said, in brief translation: "This is the time for you to arise since you live at such-and such distance from your office, the trip requires so-and-so many minutes". . . etc.

Such considerations seem important as a way of indicating the issues that confront us when we attempt to disclose the "ultimate motives" behind human conduct. For if there is *one underlying motive or set of motives that activates all men* there must be *one underlying situation common to all men*. It seems obvious that before we could establish the existence of a common situation or motive for all men, we should have *to define the cosmic situation and man's place in it*. In the last analysis, psychology is but a subdivision of metaphysics—and when the psychologist does not explicitly state a metaphysics, he assumes one. In Freud's distinction between a pleasure principle and a reality principle there is an assumed metaphysic; Marx's vocabulary of motives explicitly traces the connection between his theories of action and dialectical materialism. It is worthy of note that Freudianism could "explain" Marxists psychologically and that Marxism could "explain" Freudians sociologically.

Mysticism may cover a variety of manifestations. But in the

main it seems to be an attempt to define the ultimate motivation of human conduct by seeing around the corner of our accepted verbalizations. For this reason mystical movements usually arise on a large scale at periods in history when orientations are in confusion—for at such times the certainties we live by are most easily and inevitably brought into question. The mystic seeks a sounder basis of certainty than those provided by the flux of history. He seeks the ultimate motive behind our acts; that is, he seeks an ultimate situation common to all men. The Church mystics usually state this ultimate situation as an immediate relationship between man and God. In China, the same interest seems to have been verbalized as a concern with the ultimate relationship between man and the universe. The contemporary secular mystic, D. H. Lawrence, apparently began by taking life itself as the fundamental motive. He would stress in the biologic pattern the productive or creative element, and would have all else flow from it. If life is the *ultimate*, the universe becomes teleologically involved as an instrument for the sustaining and expression of life; hence Lawrence's simple reversal of the scientist's *vis a tergo* causal system, his blunt affirmation that growing crops make the sun shine.

The identity between motives and situations should suggest why the modern sciences of statistics tend to turn up conclusions of a strongly mystical cast. By examining a multitude of situations, individually distinct, the scientist attempts statistically to extract a generalization common to all. The mystic makes somewhat the same attempt by looking within and naming as the ultimate motive a quality of experience common to all. Frequently he has selected time, since the sense of duration seems to pervade all consciousness, despite the great variety of particulars we may be conscious of.

It is *practical* (as distinct from *mystical*) to shape our concepts of duty and purpose purely in accordance with the demands that reach us each day over the telephone or through the mails, or by any other contingencies that may affect us. But we move toward the skeptical realms of mysticism and statistical symbolism as soon as we attempt to derive our imperatives of action by seeing behind these contingencies. Obviously, the symbolic or mystical approach to the conception of duty will more readily come to the fore in eras when the contingent criteria of action are frustrated or have in some other way been brought into disrepute. Mysticism, being the farthest reach of the search for new perspectives, may be expected to flourish at periods when traditional ways of seeing and doing (with their accompanying verbalizations) have begun to lose their authority.

We are perhaps most comfortable when we can derive our concepts of duty from contingencies alone, as when we open a window because the air is stuffy, or write a letter because it requires an answer. Doubtless for this reason people seem most contented in simple social structures where the demands are regular and few, and wherein one assists the general prosperity by wholeheartedly meeting those demands. But at times like ours, where the entire commercial ethic shaping our contingent demands has brought us to extremities, and where so many patterns of living require us to slight or repress the most rudimentary needs, a "hand to mouth" conception of duty is not enough.

One must go in search of authoritative tests that lie deeper. One must seek definitions of human purpose whereby the whole ailing world of contingent demands can be appraised. Otherwise, one is trapped in a circle of self-perpetuating judgments, quite as with the practical politician of the Roosevelt type, who must do something for the banks to help the insurance companies, and something for the railroads to help the banks, and something for the insurance companies to help the policy holders, and so on, *ad inf.* and *ad nauseam,* "experimentalism" being the eulogistic word that serves to conceal the fundamental pointlessness of the legislative and administrative whole. *Experimentalism* is here synonymous with *lack of perspective*. Obviously, it can serve the ends of the "good life" only if the pattern of the contingencies themselves happens to make for the good life, as it shows few signs of doing.

The Basis of Reference

The Marxian perspective presents a point of view outside the accepted circle of contingencies. Or more accurately stated: the Marxian perspective is *partially* outside this circle. It is outside as regards the basic tenets of capitalistic enterprise. It is inside as regards the belief in the ultimate values of industrialism. From Lawrence's perspective, capitalist and Marxist would merge, since both factions accept industrial values which Lawrence would contemn. Not content to adopt a point of view which would allow the genius of industry to shape the patterns of the state, Lawrence would emphasize biologic factors by which the genius of industry might in turn be tested. He would seek a stratum of motives that lies deeper than the motives (or situations) supplied by mechanization: he would seek an ultimate biologic situation of which the entire mechanical era would be merely one historic aspect.

There is evidence that Marx himself verged upon this Laurentian territory. For Marx's talk of *liberty* would seem to imply that the desire for liberty is a primary impulse, and instigates the very scientific explorations which, while captured by liberal capitalists, make freedom for the masses impossible. But though the primacy of the desire for liberty may be implicit in Marx, it is not explicit. For his system specifically starts from material, or non-biological factors, as the determinants of human conduct. This "dialectical materialism" has nowhere, to my knowledge, been more succinctly stated than in the following passage from John Strachey's *The Coming Struggle for Power*:

"The causal chain which we have attempted to trace has not been exclusively composed of material links (using the word material in its narrowest sense). It has involved the view that certain economic and material conditions determine certain mental and psychological points of view; and these mental and psychological points of view, in their turn, determine by reaction further material developments. In the causal chain, each economic link has been followed by a mental and psychological one; it has been a chain of action and reaction between the economic basis and the ideal structure, which has been built on that basis. To instance a few successive links, the growth of large-scale production caused certain consequences in the minds of entrepreneurs which made them strive toward the formation of monopolies. The formation of monopolies in turn caused . . . certain changes in the minds of statesmen which caused them to undertake imperialist adventures. The existence of empires causes certain further tendencies in the minds of the governing class which must sooner or later involve them in war. And no one denies that wars, in their turn, cause marked economic changes."

It should be noted that Mr. Strachey, whose book has been accepted as a reliable statement of Marxian theory, began this circular series with "the growth of large-scale production." Yet it would seem obvious that any material point selected in an endless chain of "dialectically" interacting material and spiritual factors must have been immediately preceded by a spiritual one. For instance, we may ask: What lay behind the "growth of large-scale production" itself? There must at least have been certain purely psychological factors, judgments concerning the ends and means of living, interest in mechanical speculations, which prompted men to pour so much effort and ambition into the development of machinery at all. Materials may determine the *forms* our enterprise takes, but they can hardly explain the *origin* of enterprise.

Mr. Strachey begins his book arrestingly by asserting that all the slogans of emancipation which have fired Europe since the Middle Ages were grounded in the fight for free markets, for the unimpeded right to buy and sell—yet the behaviorist John B. Watson confined the arms of a newborn infant, and showed by its anger and struggles that the human organism manifests a thriving "cult of liberty" long before it comes into contact with the stimulus of the "struggle for free markets." The cult of liberty evidently comes to the fore whenever our ways of interpretation suggest to us that we are being confined. In an infant such meanings are rudimentary, involving a response to purely physical stimuli. But in the complexities of adult interpretation, the meanings are more "spiritual." The same act can be free or necessitous, according to our concepts of freedom. A room is a prison if we *know* that we are compelled to stay there.

Suppose that we took Watson's experiment as a starting point. We should then have to begin our cycle of dialectically interacting material and psychological factors with a *psychological* one. We should have to describe "the desire for freedom of movement" as a fundamental disposition of men (as might be expected of an organism that lives by locomotion). Hence we should find that a certain organic genius exists *prior* to any particular historic texture. And we might even interpret the historic texture as an embodiment, in external forms, of this organic genius. We might note the cult of freedom revealing itself from time to time transiently in human expression, before it ever attained the organized character of a world movement as it did in Western thought. We might find it definitely externalized in such anti-authoritarian inestigations as those of Galileo. We might say that such methods, proving fertile, were by analogical extension applied to other fields of thought and action, until eventually the entire environmental texture had been altered by them, as the fruits of similar efforts multiplied and accumulated.

As the external embodiments of this point of view proliferated, the cultural movement was no longer confined to a few transient glimpses in the minds of poets, philosophers, or inventors: it was put forward in solid, feelable things—hence, people of a less speculative cast could begin to sense its significance and to take an active part in its development. They saw ways of putting the insight to "profit." Science has thus been put to profit in our days, as religion was in earlier times, or even a people's *state of mind* is in itself an implement which can be employed for private ends, quite like a hoe or a tractor. The investigative mind was also applied to *business*, in this category manifesting itself as a "struggle for free markets."

Such ways of "profiting" by the entire complex of liberalism (in both its material embodiments and spiritual proclivities) also create demands of their own, quite as the accumulation of correspondence in an office creates the need of a filing system. At the same time, the vast material embodiment of the originally frail and transient glimpse gives a substantiality that instigates still further effort along the same lines. Eventually the demands arising out of this great interacting historic body have become so exacting that a new trend is found necessary. At this point, we feel the need of a fresh perspective, or schema of interpretation. We require a new basis of reference.

Now: Watson also noted that a newborn infant fears loss of support. Hence, if a world has got itself into a deplorable state through too much liberalism, going so far that our entire need of support is frustrated, we might expect doctrines of conformity to emerge again. These might "motivate" a fresh line of thought, making for a new version of economic architecture somewhat akin to that which existed in the Middle Ages, when men valued support more than liberty, and had not yet given impetus to a cult of liberty by agreeing with Copernicus that they would kick the very props of the world from beneath them. Or perhaps, since Watson's child also cried when an iron bar was struck violently, we might move toward such doctrines of "harmony" as seemed to motivate old China in her happiest eras.

Such possibilities are offered only tentatively, and primarily as illustration of our thesis that no given *historical* texture need be accepted as the underlying basis of a universal causal series. We might further note that the entire question of dialectic interaction derives a new form from such researches as Sherrington's, which seem to indicate that the brain is hardly more than a "motor ganglion." In other words, thought and action are integrally related to begin with—and Sherrington cites the instance of an organism which spends one period of its life in motion and another period clinging to other objects, its brain almost wholly atrophying during the stationary period. Such an observation would seem to justify the present mode of interpretation in accordance with which all of man's historic institutions would be considered the externalization of biologic, or non-historic factors. It would suggest that the materials of invention (of either the speculative or applied varieties) are but the objective projection of subjective patterns grounded in our organic equipment.

To be sure, the externalizing of these biologic patterns will bring forth by-products that raise important demands in themselves. And these by-products may eventually attain such proportions that a new set of interpretations must be invented to handle them, because the accumulation in its advanced stage either frustrates the same biologic need as is satisfied at an earlier stage, or frustrates other biologic need equally important. But the new patterns of interpretation will also take their shape from biologic, or non-historic factors. Historic textures can be said to "cause" our frameworks of interpretation in the sense that they present varying kinds of materials for us to synthesize—but the synthesis is necessarily made with reference to non-historic demands, the genius of the human body as projected into its ideological counterparts.

By the biologic point of reference, disputes between materialists and idealists would seem to be dialectically dissolved. Marx himself implicitly acknowledges this fact when saying that he had simply turned Hegel upside down. Whether you call the fundamental substance matter or idea seems of no great moment when you talk of mind and body with a hyphen, as mind-body. Once the implications of this hyphen are carried through the entire texture of one's thoughts, Strachey's starting point in an interacting cycle is seen to be justified only as a convenience of discourse. And the recent electronic theories of the physicists, who reduce all cosmic activity to phenomena of radiation, and whose conception of the electric field is quite in keeping with the biologic metaphor, have similarly destroyed the basis of the earlier quarrel. Is electricity *matter* or *soul*? You may take your choice, without altering your pragmatic methods.

In this respect, materialism, idealism, and dialectical materialism merge into a kind of "dialectical biologism," framed in keeping with the hyphenated usage, mind-body. And we point toward a somewhat Spinozistic conception of substance as possessing two integrally interlocking modes. Such a rephrasing of the interactive principle (known in the language of the Marxists as dialectical materialism) is designed to take into account shifts which have taken place in the language of science itself. But materialism, idealism, dialectical materialism, and "dialectical biologism" may all be alike in this one notable respect: All four systems of verbalization may stress, in accord with science, *the need of manipulating objective material factors as an essential ingredient to spiritual welfare.* In a world where food and shelter are the obvious prerequisites of adequate biologic functioning, a philosophy of "dialectical biologism" would emphasize, quite as dialectical materialism does, that food and shelter in both their primitive forms and their cultural projections are *necessities* of the "good life."

The Part and the Whole

Another important tendency which all four schools may share is the programmatic attempt to discuss any single event in terms of a larger context, to seek the *whole* of which the event is a *part*. The business of philosophy automatically commits one to this search for the wholes from which parts derive their meaning. To think through a matter is to trace an ever-widening circle of interrelationships.

This search for interrelationships tends to involve us in an important methodological dilemma. For it leads us to select some portion of the whole and call it the "cause" of the rest. The procedure would be somewhat like that of a man who, noting that lungs, heart, kidneys, liver, and stomach all function together, attempted to decide which of these organs is the *cause* of all the others. When Lawrence bluntly and stubbornly reversed the scientific version of causality by insisting that growing crops make the sun shine, he was doubtless admitting a certain degree of poetic license into his statement— but if we discount the picturesque element of his stratagem, what we have left is an insistence that a purposive or teleological factor must be reaffirmed in our attempts to understand man's relation to his environment. The *vis a tergo* concept of causality (the notion that all human acts are prompted by a "kick in the rear") too patently ignores the operations of biologic growth.

Again, in the simplest kinds of action or esthetic production, we see initial steps being shaped by ultimate intentions—and our awareness of such processes is as truly a "fact of experience" as any meter reading, hence requires inclusion in our metaphysics. To say that a man's intentions were in turn shaped by prior factors is simply to open oneself to an infinite regress, which the orthodox scheme of scientific causality avoids solely by truncating its speculations. It stops at a convenient point, and interprets this convenience as a cosmic reality.

On considering the progress of an electric current from cathode to anode, would one think of trying to isolate either of these arbitrarily selected points as the *cause* of the event? Would one not rather consider them as logical conveniences, purely conventional notations for describing two organically interdependent points in a continuous series? Lawrence's zeal as a poet goaded him to a certain effrontery of expression, driving him to propose a cosmic schema which, as I. A. Richards has shown, is wholly like the poetic world-view of primitive magic. His assertions are thus strategically ineffective, when measured by the conventions of pragmatic discourse. For one thing, they do not contain the "perhaps" and "maybe" in which we now customarily cloak our dogmas. But if we attempt to translate his remarks in the ways which Richards himself has recommended for dissolving verbal disputes, we may find that Lawrence was merely contriving to say, in a picturesque and arresting fashion, that the positivist's doctrines of causality are insufficient.

The positivist, looking upon the universe as *created*, says that the last chapter flows inexorably from the conditions laid down in the first chapter. Lawrence would look upon the universe as *being created*. He would restore the poetic point of view. Behind the effrontery of his assertions, he seems to be saying simply that the last chapter is not *caused* by the first, but that all the chapters are merely different aspects of a single process.

Outlines of a "Metabiology"

The keystone of *vis a tergo* causality, when applied to the biological, anthropological, and sociological spheres, was an evolutionary relationship between organism and environment. In true individualistic fashion, the organism was considered as a separate unit more or less at odds with its environmental context—and to this context it sought with varying degrees of success to adapt itself. By this schema, the environment was causally prior.

Yet it is obvious that any living genus possesses an authority of its own, since different genera manifest totally different "laws" of growth and action. As M. H. Woodger observes in his *Biological Principles*, whereas the doctrine of evolution is based upon a theory of continuity, assuming the uniform and constant operation of natural law, its own theory of "mutations" directly violates this belief in the constancy of natural law. For when a new race of organism arises, a new set of "laws" arises. Let a certain new kind of grasshopper come into being, for instance, and you have a new set of "principles" which move certain bits of the universe about in certain ways. Conversely, were this family of grasshopper completely destroyed, certain "laws" of movement would have passed out of the universe. By the doctrine of evolution, which went with the *vis a tergo* notion of causality, the continuity of natural law was based upon reasoning which denied such continuity.

In fact, as Richard Rothschild has noted in his *Illusion and Reality*, the entire attempt to distinguish between organism and environment is suspect. An environment gets its quality nature, or meaning from the demands which a particular organism makes of it. Grass is not the same environment for a lion as it is for a horse. And lions are part of the horse's environment (if they threaten him) while horses are part of the lion's environment (if he feeds on them). Is oxygen environmental or internal? Are the microscopic creatures in our blood stream separate from us or a part of us? They are members of a "civic corporation" which we call *the* organism. Who knows?—perhaps they were originally invaders which the body, in learning to tolerate, eventually naturalized as an integral part of its economy. [We were merely "improvising" when we wrote these sentences. But we could now cite the biologists' statement that a termite digests wood by the aid of certain micro-organisms which enter its body from without. 1953.]

All told, it seems hard to understand how we can select the environmental as the distinctly prior factor. The evidence of interaction which Strachey recognizes cannot be arbitrarily begun from one point in a series which he himself takes to be continuous, unless that point be the first crack of Creation itself. What we do find is a universal texture of some sort—and in it there are some events manifesting sufficient individuality from our point of view to be classed as separate organisms. But as our range of investigation has increased, this same point of view obliges us to apply the organic metaphor even to such events as electric fields. And a point of view also must be considered as belonging to the universal texture, as *actually existing*. A grasshopper's appetites, and the perspective or system of values that goes with them, are as *real* as any chemical.

Another aspect of the positivist's causal scheme is that it assumes complete rationality at the basis of biologic phenomena. Causality is conceived in a wholly mechanistic sense (machines being the perfect embodiment of the rational ideal). Behavior is interpreted quite as if it were as rational as a stone which, upon being pushed over a hill, obediently rolls toward the valley. But might we not avoid the whole question as to whether man is a rational or an irrational being by saying simply that man is *methodical*? Man is methodical, even methodological. To sprawl under a tree at noontime, besotted with food, wine, and relaxation after labor, as with the harvesters in Breughel's painting—should we call this rational, irrational, or simply method? As we say of philanderers, man "has a way with him."

Metabolism is a method. Our ways or methods vary in their details, and in the criteria by which we test them. In earlier thinking the Way was capitalized, but it was a literal translation of the Greek word, *hodos*. In modern thought we have disguised it by calling it *met-hodos*, which means the "way after." In any case, we are and always have been methodical. Mr. Paul Radin wrote a book, *Primitive Man as Philosopher*, to prove that savages are as advanced in their thinking as we are; and Messrs. Ogden and Richards wrote a book, *The Meaning of Meaning*, to prove that we are as backward in our thinking as savages—and I have begun to wonder whether we must choose between them.

Might we, noting the suspiciously close connection between the *hodical* and the *methodical*, be once more encouraged to look for a unitary technique, called in religious verbalizations the *way* and in scientific verbalizations the *way after*? Might we assume a constancy of message throughout history precisely to the extent that the biologic purposes of the human genus have remained a constant—and might we, attempting the sort of translation which Ogden and Richards advocate, suspect that our label of doctrines is much less varied in its essence than it appears on the surface, where it manifests only the shifting symbolizations of history and status?

Such a project would obviously involve us in attempting to state what the underlying purpose of the human genus is. Shall we say with the Nietzscheans, for instance, that man is in essence a fighter, and that he has merely made himself miserable and bewildered by his attempts to erect rational structures which restrict his militaristic equipment? Or shall we say that man is essentially a *participant*, and that his military propensities are merely one aspect of his active and communicative needs? What would be man's *vocation*, his ultimate motive or situation, if we were to define it "statistically," by observing the generalization that seemed to characterize *all* his acts?

Since war and action are both parts of a graded series, having cruelty and vengeance at one end and the highest manifestations of thought and sympathy at the other, I see no logical necessity for selecting the dyslogistic choice of the Nietzscheans as descriptive of the series' essence. Dyslogy itself can be considered as but the deterioration of eulogy, a kind of regrettable by-product (for in the inverted alchemy of this "imperfect world" much gold is eventually transformed into base metal). Man lives by purpose—and purpose is basically *preference*. Hence, where we have an even choice between conversion downwards and conversion upwards, who would feel logically obliged to select the direction which implied the destruction of human society? In choosing the Nietzschean interpretation, we should not be sufficiently *methodical*.

Every system of exhortation hinges about some definite act of faith, a deliberate selection of alternatives. When this crucial act is not specifically stated, it merely lies hidden beneath the ramifications of the system. I have sought to hunt out this crucial point in my own statements, and I suspect that I have found it in my admission that, when considering war and participation, or war and action, as the two ends of a graded series, I have chosen *action* or *participation* as the word that shall designate the *essence* of this series. Or we might choose such words as *coöperation* and *communication*, and note that even in war the coöperative or communicative element is largely present.

Here, in all its nudity, is the Jamesian "will to believe." It amounts in the end to the assumption that good, rather than evil, lies at the roots of human purpose. And as for those who would suggest that this is merely a verbal solution, I would answer that by no other fiction can men truly coöperate in historic processes, hence the fiction itself is universally grounded.

If one says that activity is merely a neutral quality rather than a good, I should answer that inactivity is categorically an evil, since it is not possible to the biologic process. To acquiesce in the methods that preserve humanity is *per se* to concede that life is a good, however perversely one may choose to verbalize such implications. Life, activity, coöperation, communication—they are identical; and even the Schopenhauerian philosopher inevitably proclaims their goodness by the zeal with which he frames his message.[1]

---

[1] To specifically link up the matter of coöperation with the ethicizing of the means of support: We may glimpse something of the relationship between individual minds and collective enterprise by noting the part which such unifying concepts as totem, godhead, nation, class, or group play in mental integration. The individual's deepest means of support in the civic texture resides in such a communicative or coöperative bond. By it he is "transcendentally" fortified. His personal solidity depends upon his allegiance to it.

Thus, the founders of a new line do really "die that we may live," for by their poignant renunciation of an old shelter they prepare the foundation of a new shelter. The morbid persecutional aspects of the messianic (insofar as the messianic marks a new beginning) may derive in part from the transitional loss of support involved in the radical attempt at a redirection of purpose. Though naturalists may explain Eucharistic symbolism as a mere survival of pagan fertility rites, one might with equal justice consider these rites themselves to have arisen in obedience to such patterns.

CHAPTER SIX

OCCUPATION AND PREOCCUPATION

Extending the Concept of Occupation

WHAT ARE our occupations? Is their number confined to the trades and professions listed in a business directory? Are people solely occupied as plumbers, bakers, bank clerks, doctors, writers, and the like? Or is it not also an occupation to be a hunchback, or to have read the Bible oftener than the Pope, or to experience a "run of hard luck"? Eliot has said: "The author of *Biographia Literaria* was already a ruined man. Sometimes, however, to be a 'ruined man' is itself a vocation." Indeed, one of the most remarkable features of the religious rationalization was its ability to socialize a man's ruin by making it the foundation of his recovery.

Such men as Jung and Jaensch have investigated the possibility of distinct mental types. Kretschmer has sought to chart correlations between physique and character. Recent speculations (somewhat in the stage of alchemy or astrology) have attempted to describe distinct patterns of endocrine balance. Are not all such inquiries deeply concerned with the *fundamental occupations* of the persons studied? For several weeks after the shoe salesman Mr. Van Q. had rescued a little girl from drowning, his true occupation was not that of *selling shoes*, but that of *having rescued a little girl from drowning*. As Baudelaire and Dostoievsky knew (from having, in their way, experienced the drought of the cloister), *obsession, possession*, and *vision* are also callings. They are more than occupational, they are preoccupational. In our sense, hobbies are occupations: They are symbolic labor, undertaken as compensation when our patterns of necessitous labor happen for one reason or another to be at odds with our profoundest needs.

Occupation and morality are integrally intermingled. This is obvious when occupation reaches the stage of preoccupation. For we are preoccupied with something which we value: a woman, a business, a book. We ethicize something when we act toward it as though it were an intrinsic good. And since the tests of goodness ultimately involve our welfare in some form or another, spiritual or material, present or future, we can be said to ethicize the serviceable. As has been pointed out, such notions of service can even lead to sacrifice.

We may also note a kind of transference, or peripheral charging, in this wise: If the particular good in our hypothetical case were Mr. *A*'s copresence with Miss *B*, an entire set of neutral factors would promptly take on goodness or badness insofar as they furthered or obstructed the attainment of this good. A conveyance, detested for its noise and stench on other occasions, might become a positive boon as it carried *A* to his destination. It is such peripheral charging that makes the many annoyances of our cities tolerable, since they are instruments in the attaining of goods. If food, comfort, and pleasant intercourse are desirable, and if money procures them, and if some dismal, unmuscular, unimaginative, and unbalanced kind of drudgery will procure the money, one may actually see a person's eyes light up with hope when told that the drudgery is to be permitted him. He "got the job." Eventually, he rounds out his values in keeping with such contingencies: He develops the emphases, standards, desires, kinds of observation, expression, and repression, that will equip him for his task. This is his occupational psychosis, a moral network, complex beyond all possibilities of charting. It is probably carried into the most casual bit of slang.

OCCUPATION AND PREOCCUPATION

Such ethical structures tend to become self-perpetuating. It is *ethical* for the child raised on city streets to feel loneliness and emptiness when in the country—and such Proustian pieties must be expected to persist even in cases where the situation to which one had adapted himself was highly unpleasant. For even if one had abandoned a given context of experience, he would retain much of the traumatic pattern to which it had given rise. And as evidence that the factor of peripheral charging can even induce us to convert the unpleasant into the pleasurable, we may recall that if animals are subjected to painful shocks before feeding, they will become so conditioned that pain leads to salivation. However, theorists who would take this experiment to indicate that people will learn to convert even the most intolerable means of shelter and livelihood into *goods* should be reminded that when the pains are increased beyond a certain intensity, the response of the experimenter's rats is radically altered. Far from ethicizing the pain (salivating), they become distracted, and conduct themselves in ways which, when applied to humans, we generally describe as "running riot."

Perhaps the old novel is a perfect illustration of the ways in which goods are transferred from purpose to means, the process which we have called peripheral charging. Witness the novel's pedestrian beginning, its patient and circumstantial concern with prosaic details. Such introductory material is in itself low-powered—it derives its charge mainly from the reader's awareness that it lies at the edge of a central plot which will gradually be unfolded. The descriptive and informative passages, the somewhat rambling conversations which never attain the sharpness of the lines in great poetic drama, all this was acquiesced in, even enjoyed, possibly because the lives of the readers were integrated in precisely the same way, since they might go to town, not because of some intense event that might await them there, but to buy a pair of shoes which they could wear when going to work to earn money to buy shoes. And if such an esthetic manifestation could be taken as evidence of a psychosis (a certain way of thinking that went with a certain way of living), might we see the break down of this same psychosis revealed in the demand for book that begin with the spitting of a revolver, that are racy, pun gent, scandalous, or violent from the very first line, requiring that all incidental matter be "hopped up" accordingly?

Work both reflects our interests and forms them. One may study medicine through an interest in medicine—but when one has steeped himself in his discipline it will become cre ative, supplying him with new incentives for seeing all life "from the doctor's point of view." Or our relation with ma chinery may become so intimate that we attempt to discuss even non-mechanistic aspects of experience in mechanistic terms. Or to take more transitory instances of occupation (as suggested by the technique of perspective): Upon accident ally burning oneself, one will be for the time occupied with this situation alone. One may even adopt measures of expres sion so exclusively attuned to this single situation that he will greatly outrage persons who, though present, are living in a totally different situation.

In the case of geniuses, we readily note the preoccupationa factor, as a man's exceptional aptitude in one category of action places him permanently in a different situation from that of ordinary men (or, otherwise stated: His special gif provides him with special motives). Indeed, one's special gift must largely determine what kinds of experience can have a traumatic effect upon one. Perhaps no contingency is categor ically or absolutely traumatic. An encounter with a dog may leave a lasting impression upon one mind, while it contrib utes only a minor meaning to another; which is to say that one man was more gifted for being affected by the dog and the other was more gifted for not being affected.

OCCUPATION AND PREOCCUPATION

Ambivalence of Weakness and Prowess

We should also note a paradoxical relationship between "superiority" and "inferiority." Adler sees the genesis of man's motivations in some "organ inferiority." This inferiority is supposed to endow one with an "inferiority complex" so firmly imbedded that one's life is henceforth devoted to an ambitious compensatory struggle for domination. But one's *inferiority* depends largely upon the kind of *attainment* by which one rates himself. As regards the ability to breathe underground, we are sadly inferior to the coelentera, though few are kept awake by a sense of organ inferiority in this respect. And when talking of the part which inferiority plays in the genesis of dementia præcox and paranoia, Rivers habitually qualifies by saying "inferiority, real or supposed," "inferiority, real or imaginary." In other words, the inferiority is a matter of interpretation: It must be felt as inferiority before it can be a determining factor in the mental state.

Mr. Ogden cites the instance of the musical prodigy, Erwin Nyiregyházi, who at the age of seven could analyze chords of extreme complexity the first time they were played to him. Where should we look for the "inferiority" of such a person if not in music? His musical gifts, that is, could be expected to make him inferior to great musicians, whereas a young tough's genial "wallop" would make him inferior to the world's champion heavyweight.[2]

[2] Similarly with McDougall's discussion of "split personality." For McDougall has said that we are all characterized by dissociative mental structures. We are all, in our compartmentalized responses, like the man who is a tyrant in his office and a weakling among his family, or like the musician who is assertive in his art and self-effacing in his personal relationships. Such dissociation becomes a difficulty when we attempt to unite these compartments (as, were the man who is a tyrant in his office and a weakling at home suddenly to employ his wife or

As a vocational emphasis is finally pieced together, abilities of a certain sort lead to the selection of certain "interests" as uppermost, these interests lead to the partial upbuilding of their equivalents in the external scene, and the externalities in turn reënforce the interests themselves. All this is involved in the statement that one learns to use his gifts. Because one learns to use his gifts, Goethe wrote *Faust*, Herostratus burned down the temple, and Mr. X committed suicide (suicide presumably being his particular aptitude).

In a world where one has at his disposal a million ways in which to be inferior, one must necessarily be selective—and one's gifts guide the selection. The trouble seems to arise from the fact that certain superiorities do not reward us or prosper us, so that in the very act of succeeding we may fail. Our abilities may prove obstructive, forcing us either to renounce our best capacities and to concentrate upon more serviceable ones, or to persevere in our ways at the risk of disaster. Usually, in the normal social texture the vocational is marked by a balance of favorable and unfavorable factors. A Beethoven somehow managed to live by the same habits of mind that on occasion gravely endangered him.

The difficulty generally arises from the fact that one tries to solve too much by the devices of his gift. In the business of means-selecting, instead of choosing the means with respect to the nature of the problem to be solved, one tends to *state*

---

children, he would find his dissociative devices inadequate, and might become bewildered or tormented).

Even the dissociative, therefore, does not become a *problem* unless new *interests* require that contradictory compartments of response be merged. Such interests may be supplied by changes in the external situation. Or they may arise from "gifts," as when a man feels some intense desire to make all parts of himself consistent with all other parts. Such sensitiveness may be aggravated by leisure, unemployment, or drudgery, since all three give rise to frustration as regards contingent duties.

the problem in such a way that his particular aptitude becomes the "solution" for it. Thus, the young pugilist will so ethicize his fists that he tends to simplify a great diversity of human relationships by considering them capable of treatment in terms of an actual or threatened rap on the chin. And an earnest musician might spontaneously turn to his violin as a cure for disorders which might better be solved by political expedients. Conversely, radical agitators become so engrossed in their political preoccupations that they begin to look upon any other mode of action as evasive.

The psychotic or vocational, in our extended use of the term, was viewed from another angle by Freud in his concept of the "Œdipus complex." In his *Sex and Repression in Savage Society*, Bronislaw Malinowski analyzes the myths of the Trobriand Islanders as a test case for Freud's concept of the Œdipus complex, and his findings both corroborate and rectify Freud's formula. Malinowski shows that among these people, whose society is basically matriarchal, in contrast with the patriarchally organized society with which Freud was dealing, a corresponding complex arises: but there the myths, dreams, obscenities, and mental disorders of the tribe are built about a different core. They are altered to take into account the different conceptions of authority, incest, etc., which prevail under a matriarchal system.

If Malinowski is right, the vocational factor here arises from the fact that insofar as a given social pattern applies in a general way to all the individuals in a group, we may expect a rough correspondence of psychosis throughout the group. Malinowski's statement stands halfway between the pure sexual psychoanalysis of the Freudians and the pure economic psychoanalysis of the Marxians.

Another direction is revealed in the researches of men like Ernst Kretschmer, whose work, *Physique and Character*, is concerned with the description and measurement of bodily types, and of the mental patterns correlated with these. Kret-schmer would note different classifications of mind-body structure. Such differences of structure would amount in the end to differences in occupation, as each man tended toward forms of thought and action in keeping with his type or class. Rivers had observed that among his military patients, "hysteria tends to occur especially in the private soldier, and re-pression-neurosis in the officer." He ascribes this difference to distinctions in training, as the emphasis upon obedience en-hanced the hysteric factor of *suggestibility* in the private soldier whereas the stressing of initiative and authoritativeness in the officers led them to intensify the *repression* of their fears. But with Kretschmer, the *economic correspondences* between status and thought are of a more fundamental sort, as they vary, say, between the "occupation of being a short and stocky man" and the "occupation of being a tall, thin one."

Such a line of thought can readily lead into speculations as to the part which "disease" sometimes plays in shaping occu-pational or preoccupational patterns—and in his *Psychology of Men of Genius* Kretschmer notes important correlations between the nature of a man's disorders and the nature of his attainments. Reversing the emphasis of Max Nordau's famous blast on *Degeneracy*, in which Nordau discredited the products of geniuses by showing their relationship to dis-ease, Kretschmer tends rather to show the ways in which gen-iuses converted their liabilities into assets. (In this we find the clinician tending to rediscover the Church's attitude, the con-ception of man's "burden" as the basis of his "redemption.")

Particularly in eras of great uncertainty, we might expect disease to appear significantly as an occupation—for though one be in doubt about all else, he finds an unquestioned authority in the reality of his own discomfitures. We might say that hypochondriasis is merely the restricted manifesta-tion of the tragic mechanism, the man's physical and mental burden being in itself the monastery walls that hold him to his vow. The altar of his concerns, the central factor of his *livelihood* or *support*, is his illness—and since this illness is both painful and creative (the unifying jaundice of the eye) it contains the serviceable-disserviceable duality.

It is surely for such reasons that a writer so social-minded and deeply tragic as Thomas Mann gives recognition to the hypochondriac incentive in his art, knowing as he does that the hypochondriac's preoccupation need not by any means be confined to his own personal symptoms, but may merely serve to *force* integrity of outlook upon a man, thus providing him, by the very nature of the case, with an authoritative form into which the fluids of experience are poured. Such an incentive will transcend its beginnings in that the thinker attempts to socialize his position, and in doing so must include areas of symbolization not at all local to himself.

To be sure, the cult of "temperament" has brought such an attitude toward the "usefulness" of disease into disrepute today. Communists and Fascists alike, for varying reasons, have decreed a "sanitation" of art which would put disease out of fashion. There is a growing insistence that a writer's integration be drawn from some principle in the State, and not from a "prophetic" burden arising within. It is not our point here to argue the justice of this position. We have already pointed out that, whatever the source of a writer's preoccupations, he can communicate only by manipulating the symbols common to his group; hence there is much justice underlying the new schools of "health," at any rate if we mean by individual health a conformity with the psychosis of one's group. The particular value of disease in insight, however, may arise precisely from the fact that the diseased man's burden sharpens him to some corresponding issue involving society at large. And our prophets of health must also remember that revolution itself is a social morbidity; it necessarily involves many neurotic factors as one attempts to reorganize the national or racial pieties by conversion to new ways of classification that are incongruous with ways of classification previously formed and still educationally perpetuated. Indeed, revolutionaries might understand themselves better, and be better equipped to handle the problem of schism, if they recognized the morbidities of their rôle and the ways in which the tragic mechanism may lead to a deliberate courting of martyrdom, while their occupational psychosis as professional revolutionaries may complicate their relations with those they would proselytize.

All such considerations may remind us that, whatever the future of art may be, in the past a man's "sin" often proved basic to his work. The possession of social stigmata, such as homosexuality, bellicosity, tactlessness, pathological "bashfulness," "eccentric" interests, does not merely act as stimulus in the sense of providing an authoritative basis of integration. It also drives a man into great piety of style—and for two reasons. First, the graveness of his concern—his "altar"—will lead him to seek similarly solemn things with which to surround it. Second, since style in literature as in social behavior is used for the purposes of ingratiation, the sense of guilt can quicken the sense of style by intensifying a retributive attitude. We have elsewhere noted the integral relationship between conflict, consciousness, conscientiousness, and conscience. And we may also note the socially constructive character of guilt, since piety is a system-builder, impelling one to go farther and farther in search of appropriate materials that will go with his concerns, while the attempt to socialize this material for purposes of communication leads one far beyond the character of the initial stimulus.

Variations of the stigmatic situation as a vocational incentive can be imagined *ad lib*. Mann, Gide, Proust, and Joyce seem outstanding examples in the cultural movement now coming to a close.

CHAPTER SEVEN

THE POETRY OF ACTION

The Mystic's Sterilization of Combat

WE HAVE previously considered that troublous graded series whereby action emerges purely and simply as combat. The mystic, it seems, has often attempted to find disciplines whereby the combative aspect of action may be completely sterilized, so that the practitioner may enjoy the gratifications of attainment without the by-product, conquest. In the West, for instance, with its great respect for "climbing," the first stage of initiation into the state of mystic unity is usually reached through the postures of prayer, with its deliberate mimetics of humiliation. In a society stressing advancement, the mystic begins his rites by a symbolic self-abasement. In the East, the corresponding initiatory stage seems to have been generally contrived by assuming the out-ward postures of complete calm, with particular emphasis upon regularity of breathing. By reason of the deep corres-pondence between mind and body, these external conditions become the organic imagery that may be expected to call forth its psychic counterparts.

Descriptions of the mystic state, as attained by these delib-erate techniques, suggest that the ultimate result is a kind of "pure action." It is usually referred to as "complete passivity," but the intensities of mystical experience would seem to make this description inadequate. Sherrington's account of the nerv-ous system gives some clues as to the possible status of the body while the mystic trance is on. For he has noted that our movements are integrated by an elaborate system of controls, or repressions. The frog swims, for instance, by subjecting the "extensor thrust" to a set of commands in some way issuing from centers of the brain. If these centers are excised, a stimulus applied by the experimenter reveals the workings of the extensor thrust in its simplicity. The brain is thus considered by Sherrington a kind of absolute monarch or coördinator who insists that his subjects (the various bodily reflexes) restrict their activities in accordance with his own criteria of purpose. If this monarch would walk, he cannot permit the reflex involved in the frog's extensor thrust to assert its complete individuality. He *represses* it in part by legislation (which he enforces by the authority of contrary nervous impulses). Thus, according to this metaphor, our nervous integration is essentially repressive.

This notion would suggest that the mystic's state of passivity may be a kind of "assertion *in vacuo*," as were all the conflicting nervous impulses to be called into play at once. For instance, since a muscle is moved by the stimulation of a nerve, any *directed* movement (such as a practical act) would involve the repression of some other nervous impulse. But if the nerves could be stimulated without the accompaniment of muscular movement, even conflicting nervous impulses could proclaim themselves simultaneously.

It is at least a possibility that the pronounced sense of unity to which mystics habitually testify involves some such neurological condition of "pure action," wherein a kind of dissociation between impulse and movement is established, and all the conflicting kinds of nervous impulse may "glow" at once since they do not lead to overt muscular response. Such a possibility would explain why we could choose either the words *pure action* or *total passivity* to describe the state. And it would explain why the sense of attainment that goes with it would be both complete and noncombative, suggesting a oneness with the universal texture as thorough as that which the organism must have experienced during its period of "larval feeding" in the womb.

Such mystic "revelation" does not necessarily make for a permanent state of inaction, however. History bears evidence that some mystics were only too active, as they went forth to carve up whole countrysides of heretics and schismatics in their attempts to establish in the practical realm the "ideal city" which they had experienced in their trance. But the normal religious rationalization based upon this mystic sense of unity had one notable cultural advantage, in that it provided a man with *categorical* dignity. His sense of partnership with God or the Universe was in itself an "attainment" of a major order, hence could often serve to sterilize competitive ambitions.

But this virtue of religion was consciously or unconsciously manipulated for all it was worth as a device for making man contented with his lot, and thus for gradually worsening his lot until it became physically unbearable. Such conversion of a good device into a bad device has its parallel in modern finance: The highly complex methods of production and distribution required by an industrial society led to such simplifying abstractions as price and credit—and the rise of these abstractions came to be written into the entire texture of our social and economic organization. But financiers learned how to manipulate these fundamental abstractions to their private advantage, with the result that some would uproot the entire commercial structure to eradicate the special privileges.

In any event, action of an external sort must eventually lead to combat in one form or another. Such action is no longer harmony; it lacks the symphonic quality whereby the notes of coexistent melodies can at the same time both proclaim their individual identity and function as parts in a whole. Action in the realm of normal experience involves patterns of striving, competition, and conquest which reach their ultimate conclusion in war. We have cited Bentham's observations that this warlike element is fully as present in the censorial quality of speech as in the patterns of overt combat. A "dyslogistic" adjective is the equivalent of a blow —and enough of them can lead to one. We have also cited Bentham's speculations upon the relationship between the censorial and poetry.

In Qualified Defense of Lawrence

All our foregoing discussion should serve to pull a great many words together by showing their engagement in one another. Action is fundamentally ethical, since it involves preferences. Poetry is ethical. Occupation and preoccupation are ethical. The ethical shapes our selection of means. It shapes our structures of orientation, while these in turn shape the perceptions of the individuals born within the orientation. Hence it radically affects our coöperative processes. The ethical is thus linked with the communicative (particularly when we consider communication in its broadest sense, not merely as the purveying of information, but also as the sharing of sympathies and purposes, the doing of acts in common, as with the leveling process of communicating vessels). Thus, I cannot see the justice of Mr. Richards' remark when he *accuses* Lawrence of "ethical universe-building." For the charge implies that there is some other kind of universe-building which is not ethical. But it would seem that all universe-building is ethical, since it is occupationally and pre-occupationally based.

When discussing the *Fantasia of the Unconscious*, Richards charts Lawrence's method with great acumen. He writes:

"First, undergo an intense emotion, located with unusual definiteness in the body, which can be described as 'a feeling *as though* the solar plexus were connected by a current of dark passional energy with another person.' Those whose emotions tend to be localized will be familiar with such feelings. The second step is to say 'I must trust my feelings.' The third is to call the feeling an intuition. The last is to say 'I *know* that my solar plexus is, etc.' By this means we arrive at indubitable knowledge that the sun's energy is recruited from the life on earth and that astronomers are wrong in what they say about the moon, and so on.'"

As so stated, the case looks black for Lawrence—and I do not wish it for one moment to appear that I am subscribing to Lawrence's ways of verbalizing his attitude. For one thing, Lawrence's assertions are too often distorted by precisely the order of knowledge which he is condemning. The "facts" which he tells us about the moon, in bald opposition to the astronomer's facts, are simply bad astronomy. The kind of "facts" which might eventually be found out about the moon, were all society to begin thinking along Lawrence's lines, subjecting his statements to all the revision required in the course of such a vast coöperative enterprise, would doubtless be of a quite different order. Instead of being bad astronomy, they would probably not be astronomy at all, as the term is now understood. Were a whole Laurentian movement to develop, not a singe assertion in Lawrence's *Fantasia* would be left unaltered. After the general attitude had been fully exposed to the revisionary processes of group treatment, its "facts" would be changed in ways which Lawrence could not possibly have foreseen.

Since Richards likes Lawrence's poetry as much as he dislikes his "science," he proposes to save the day by making a fundamental distinction between "statements" and "pseudo-statements." He believes that Lawrence's remarks may be acceptable, and even useful, if considered purely as poetic metaphors, but that such ethical universe-building must be rigidly confined to the category of pseudo-statement. Such pseudo-statements, he holds, may serve to give us courage, and thus to carry us through trying times by providing a haven of make-believe in which we can recoup our strength after the rigors of doubt and bewilderment. He writes: "In many quarters there is a tendency to suppose that the series of attacks upon received ideas which began, shall we say, with Galileo and rose to a climax with Darwinism, has overreached itself with Einstein and Eddington, and that the battle is now due to die down. This view seems to be too optimistic. The most dangerous of the sciences is only now beginning to come into action. I am thinking less of Psychoanalysis or of Behaviorism than of the whole subject which includes them. It is very probable that the Hindenburg Line to which the defence of our traditions retired as a result of the onslaughts of the last century will be blown up in the near future. If this should happen a mental chaos such as man has never experienced may be expected."

And elsewhere he says: "Our attitudes and impulses are being compelled to become self-supporting; they are being driven back upon their biological justification, made once again sufficient to themselves. And the only impulses which seem strong enough to continue unflagging are commonly so crude that, to more finely developed individuals, they hardly seem worth having. Such people cannot live by warmth, food, fighting, drink, and sex alone."

As a way of meeting this problem, of facing the possible chaos with composure, he proposes that we become adept in accepting the many pseudo-statements of poetry and using them purely for their value as mental prophylactics: "We shall be thrown back, as Matthew Arnold foresaw, upon poetry. It is capable of saving us; it is a perfectly possible means of overcoming chaos. But whether man is capable of the reorientation required, whether he can loosen in time the entanglement with belief which now takes from poetry half its power and would then take all, is another question, and too large for the scope of this essay."

THE POETRY OF ACTION

But how can our pseudo-statements be confined to the pages of a book? Has not Richards himself, in his *Principles of Literary Criticism*, recognized an integral relationship between thought and action? He there tells us that an attitude is an incipient plan of action, and that the poet can modify our attitudes.[1] Furthermore, fictions are *implicit in our acts*. Not only is there the obvious symbolism of poetry on the page. We also recognize a symbolism of posture, gesture, and tonality, a purely mimetic symbolism, such as we find not only in formal modes of expression like the dance, but also in our spontaneous mind-body correlations between mood and appearance. It is to be seen, for instance, in the erectness that goes with defiance, anger, and confidence, or the skeletal droop that goes with dejection, or the great variety of symbolic acts which psychologists have noted in the conduct of both normal and abnormal persons. Nor dare we stop at this. Insofar as life itself is a creative or expressive process, even the most external manifestations of purpose must be symbolic of such purpose. A sense of order, for example, is as clearly symbolized in financial and military organizations as in a play by Shakespeare. And conversely, from this point of view, it would be just as truly a pseudo-statement to stroke a person's hair as it would be to write, "I stroke the head of Cleopatra."

[1] The possible "chaos" which Richards foresees seems to be something like an aggravation of the process which we described in our section on "Perspective by Incongruity." For with a pronounced heterogeneity of action-patterns, plus a speculative or statistical or philosophical or accountant group dealing almost exclusively in the problems of spiritual coördination that the many distinct moralities of production (interests) give rise to, we seem to have the perfect setting for a culture of gargoyles, grotesques, and caricatures unless some distinct master-purpose can both guide and restrict the speculative output. In other words, *freedom* must be defined by *purpose*. Otherwise we are simply "free" to continue flying apart from one another in the direction of mental "chaos."

We make a "pseudo-statement" each time we treat an acquaintance as friend or enemy—for in thus automatically asserting a moral position, we necessarily leave the laboratory method of scientific judgment far in arrears. Obviously, there is no such thing as an absolute friend or an absolute enemy, for our "enemies" may often do us greater services than our "friends," and another man's character is not integrated with reference to us alone. Hence, any assertion of a moral attitude toward a man contains an element of pseudo-statement. Life itself is a poem in the sense that, in the course of living, we gradually erect a structure of relationships about us in conformity with our interests. As Rothschild would say, all acts are "synthetic," each being a new way of putting things together, quite as each line of a drama is. The remarks we make in conversation (and the results they produce) are essentially "artful." Hence one may reasonably expect to find the same symbolic factors in practical production that one finds in the realm of the æsthetic. Even a class that passively lives on its dividends is *acting a pseudo-statement* by simply leaving things as they are. It is acting *as if* certain situations must be accepted.

Thus, it is hard to see why the encouragements of pseudo-statement either should or could be confined to formal art; they must also extend to those informal arts we usually call life, experience, or action. They must show in our likes and dislikes, and in the choices and means-selecting implicit in such attitudes. We may admit a much wider range of ethical relativity than is customary; by observing how ethical norms tend to cancel one another, we may get that *appearance* of non-moral neutrality which is sometimes called logic—but in the end, this deviousness of scope does not eliminate moral attitudes, it merely makes the documentation behind them more complex. In the mimesis of the practical the distinction between acting and play-acting, between real and make-believe, becomes obliterated. A man can extract courage from a poem by reading that he is captain of his soul; he can reënforce this same statement mimetically by walking down the street as vigorously as though he were the captain of his soul; or he can translate the mood into a more complex set of relationships by greeting an acquaintance as one captain-of-his-soul to another; and the two of them can embark upon such a project as two captains-of-their-souls might embark upon.

Recalcitrance

To be sure, when we attempt to extend our pseudo-statements into the full complexity of life, we meet with considerable recalcitrance. But so does the poet meet with considerable recalcitrance in arranging the materials of his poem. We must "altruistically" take into account the order of difficulty that goes with the order of our intentions. The factor of recalcitrance may force us to alter our original strategy of expression greatly. And in the end, our *pseudo-statements* may have been so altered by the revisions which the recalcitrance of the material has forced upon us that we can now more properly refer to them as *statements*.

It is a pseudo-statement to say "I am a bird." Our symbolism has been revised into a complete practical statement when we can say "I am an aviator." A mimetic stage half-way between the two might have been "I am a diver." But all three are purely and simply *statements* insofar as the man who makes any one of them must take certain orders of recalcitrance into account. A statement is a completed pseudo-statement—which is to say that *a statement is an attitude rephrased in accordance with the strategy of revision made necessary by the recalcitrance of the materials employed for embodying this attitude.* "I can safely jump from this high place" may be a pseudo-statement. "I can safely jump from this high place with the aid of a parachute" might be the statement as revised after one had taken the recalcitrance of his material adequately into account. But both might spring from the same attitude.

We make this distinction (or rather, we obliterate Richards' distinction) to justify our contention that all universe-building is ethical universe-building. The objection to Lawrence's statements is that they have not yet undergone the scope of revision required by the recalcitrance of the material which would be disclosed were we to extend them into all walks of investigation. They have not been *socialized*, as the coöperation of an entire historic movement might have caused them to be in the past or might again cause them to be in the future. But our interests (in the widest sense, our vocations) are essential in shaping the nature of our discoveries, tentatives, and revisions. And our interests are ethical. The grasshopper will find a universe that is different from ours because the vocation or ethics of a grasshopper is different. Man and grasshopper have different "work patterns," which will be reflected in different systems of values. Each approaches the universe from a different "point of view," and the difference in point of view will reveal a corresponding difference in the discovery of relevant "facts."

Such a position does not involve us in subjectivism, or solipsism. It does not imply that the universe is merely the product of our interpretations. For the interpretations themselves must be altered as the universe displays various orders of recalcitrance to them. We are emphasizing the fact that the ethical bent from which one approaches the universe is itself a part of the universe, and a very important part. Our calling has its roots in the biological, and our biological demands are clearly implicit in the universal texture. To live is to have a vocation, and to have a vocation is to have an ethics or scheme of values, and to have a scheme of values is to have a point of

THE POETRY OF ACTION

view, and to have a point of view is to have a prejudice or bias which will motivate and color our choice of means. In this respect, my thesis might be called subjective, or solipsistic.

But the "discoveries" which flow from the point of view are nothing other than revisions made necessary by the nature of the world itself. They thus have an objective validity. Our interests may tend to confine our thinking within certain channels, being prejudicial to the extent that they give us cues as to what we shall stress or discard. But interests need not deceive us in the sense that "the wish is father to the thought." For the point of view, in seeking its corroboration or externalization, also discloses many significant respects in which the material of externalization is recalcitrant. And our "opportunistic" shifts of strategy, as shaped to take this recalcitrance into account, are objective. The underlying process, however, is inescapably ethical—and what is usually termed *disinterestedness* is merely a different order of *interests*.

The universe "yields" to our point of view by disclosing the different orders of recalcitrance which arise when the universe is considered from this point of view.[2] Thus, suppose

[2] Determinism is a theory that the universe can make no mistakes. Not only is everything caused, but it is *accurately* caused. Alter the nature of the stimulus ever so little, and by the doctrine of determinism you get a corresponding alteration of the response. Shift the direction of the pressure against a stone even an infinitesimal amount, and the yield of the stone will shift accordingly. Such is determinism: the picture of a vast and complex structure, acting without a single error, and without a creative purpose, a machine permanently in order. Once you introduce a *point of view* into the universe, however (as it is introduced by biological vocation), a new factor enters. The point of view requires an *interpretation of events*, a reading of the recalcitrant factors favorable and unfavorable to the point of view. But an interpretation can be wrong. Hence, a point of view introduces the possibility of error. But where there is the possibility of a wrong interpretation, there is also the possibility of a right one. The *freedom to err* argues a *freedom to be right*.

that you begin by saying, "Oceans are clocks," or "Milton was an Eskimo." As you seek to complete these statements, to socialize them by corroborative data, the recalcitrance of your material discovered *en route* may eventually compel you to revise your first statement as "Oceans have periodic movements." And the second might become, "Milton was a Nordic."

Roughly, we might expect the point of view to express itself first in fancy, metaphor, hypothesis, "vision." New lines of cosmological speculation may be opened up. Relevant inventions may follow, until eventually the point of view finds embodiment in our institutions and our ways of living. It may be expected to reveal itself first in the visionary categories, since here recalcitrance is at a minimum. It is metaphorical, a "perhaps." But as one goes farther afield, attempting more thoroughly to communicate his vision, new aspects of recalcitrance arise. One strategically alters his statements, insofar as he is able, to shape them in conformity with the use and wont of his group. At this stage his message is taken up and variously reworked by many different kinds of men—and by the time they have fitted it to the recalcitrance of social relationships, political exigencies, economic procedures, etc., transferring it from the private architecture of a poem into the public architecture of a social order, those who dealt with it in its incipient or emergent stages could hardly recognize it as having stemmed from them. But by now, surely, it would be so firmly established in our habits of thought that we could everywhere find it corroborated in "hard fact," particularly since the instruments of precision and thought by which we made our examinations were themselves shaped by this same point of view.

But let us return to Lawrence. At bottom, he would seem to have started from the point of view provided by his own vocation. He would begin with the poetic man (which would explain why his world-scheme bears such close resemblance to the systems of homeopathic magic). His statements are un-compromisingly ethical in the subjective sense: they had not yet been objectively modified in accordance with the recalci-trance of "the facts." Basically, however, they aim to empha-size such observations of the universe and the historic process as definitely fit our poetic needs. Insofar as all men are poets, even in those kinds of action generally considered distinct from poetry, *he is selecting as his starting point our ultimate motive, the situation common to all, the creative, assertive, synthetic act.* He would stress or ignore, in accordance with the authority of our biologic genius as he conceives it to be.

Noting an organic relationship between growing crops and shining sun, Lawrence says that growing crops make the sun shine. The positivist would tend toward the reverse statement: The shining sun makes the crops grow. Either statement is at best a *partial* one. The positivist would himself admit that his own statement is abbreviated, a figure of synecdoche, as if we meant ten men and said ten noses. For a great confluence of agencies is required to make the crops grow. In America, mortgages sometimes seem to be a more critical factor even than sunlight. Live seed is necessary, rain, soil, climate, etc. The simplified statements of the case which we make for convenience are in a sense pseudo-statements, singling out one factor or another *as if* it were the central or informing factor.

It is generally supposed that a belief in cosmic determinism would invalidate the kind of reversal which Lawrence is guilty of. But a thorough-going deterministic doctrine, pur-sued to the end, would seem to make such paradoxes inevi-table. For if there is a total causal structure, we can as justly say that the past is determined by the future as that the future is determined by the past. Where a part is implicated in the whole, any given selection from the whole may be dis-cussible as either the cause or the result of the rest. For alter the part, and the rest would be altered—alter the rest and the part would be altered.

To state the issue in another way: Crops and sun alike may be considered as different manifestations of a larger event encompassing them both, just as one would not like to say that the beginning of a story causes its end or that the end causes the beginning. One would feel much happier in stating that there is a larger process involved, a comprehensive purpose of which both beginning and end are but partial manifestations. And when one considers the universe as a *Making* rather than as a *Made*, discussing it from the ethical, creative, poetic point of view, there arises a similar need to explain a partial event by reference to a total event.

Who, after all, decrees what we shall call a separate event? Why must I call crops one thing and sunlight something essentially different, particularly when I have so much evidence to indicate that one can *become* the other? Why could I not as well consider as one event the arising of certain rays, their journey from the sun, their inclusion in the plant's life through the functioning of chlorophyl, and their final subsidence in the autumn? The new realist considers experience by precisely such an altered way of dividing wholes when he says that we must not speak of green as an "illusion," a mere phenomenal restating of certain vibrations affecting nerve tissues. Instead, he says, we must consider the entire "arc" as the "real experience," accepting as one event the external vibrations, the nervous responses, and the resultant sense of green. By this method, the quality green becomes as "real" in our speculations as it is in our everyday experience. It is not an "illusion," but an actual part of the universe.

Such liquidity in the description of an event can make in the end for much the kind of integration which Lawrence seems to be driving at. Essentially, it involves the selection of a purposive or teleological metaphor (the metaphor of human action or poetry) as distinct from a mechanistic metaphor (the *vis a tergo* causality of machinery) for the shaping of our attitude toward the universe and history. And it bases this choice upon the most undeniable point of reference we could possibly have: the biological. It aims less at a *metaphysic* than at a *metabiology*. And a point of view biologically rooted seems to be as near to "rock bottom" as human thought could take us.

The preference for the poetic metaphor over the mechanistic one is admittedly a matter of choice, but so is the opposite preference a matter of choice. And the notion of life as a method would suggest that all the universe could likewise be designated as a method or aggregate of methods—in which case the selection of the biologic metaphor should not necessarily interrupt our rational investigations. For the methods of appeal in a poem can be analyzed, quite as we may analyze the methods of production in a machine. The exclusively mechanistic metaphor is objectionable not because it is directly counter to the poetic, but because it leaves too much out of account. It shows us merely those aspects of experience which can be phrased with its terms. It is truncated, as the poetic metaphor, *buttressed by the concept of recalcitrance*, is not.

PERMANENCE AND CHANGE

CONCLUSIONS

In the course of our three parts we have attempted to show an integral relationship existing among a great variety of cultural manifestations which are often considered in isolation. We have tried to handle conjunctly much that is usually considered disjunctly. We have tried to suggest in what way an orientation, or *Weltanschauung*, tends to become a self-perpetuating structure, creating the measures by which it shall be measured. It moves to form a closed circle, though individual or class divergencies ever tend to break the regularity of this circle. Essentially, however, we aimed to show that the circle is basically *ethical*. In the simplest summary, let us say that *we have been attempting to consider the many ramifications implicit in the statement that "our thoughts and acts are affected by our interests."*

To this end we sought to trace the tie-up among many manifestations of the ethical or creative impulse, which we here list more or less at random: orientation, rationalization, motivation, interpretation, verbalization, socialization, communication, expectancy, meaning, "illusion," occupational psychosis, trained incapacity, means-selecting, attention, "escape," style, sense of what goes with what, piety, propriety, property (tools and "shelter"), custom, ingratiation, inducement, "hypocrisy," ritual, right, virtue, power, utility, analogical extension, "peripheral charging," abstraction, logic, "cause," purpose, will, metaphor, perspective, "conversion," method, "nudism," point of view, statistics, symbolism, situation, simplification, prejudice, censoriousness, vocation, sympathy, "egoistic-altruistic merger," ethicizing of the means of support, inferiority, "burden," obsession, "genius," guilt, doubt, symbolic and necessitous labor, "justification," education, evangelism, legislation, action, combat, participation, ultimate situation of motive, ethical universe-building, "opportunistic revision," and recalcitrance. Let us call the whole complex: civilization.

It is obvious that the lines connecting these concepts could be drawn at random. We can go from any point in the series to any other point in the series without ellipsis. We might arrange our steps: ethical universe-building, "illusion," recalcitrance, attention, means-selecting, etc. Or: metaphor, simplification, master purpose, evangelism, justification, piety, sense of what goes with what, interpretation, occupational psychosis, etc. Or: property (tools and "shelter"), expectancy, prejudice, legislation, sympathy, "egoistic-altruistic merger," ingratiation, right, abstraction, statistics, verbalization, etc. In some cases the connectives may be more obvious on their face —but they are no closer in reality, for the whole ethical texture is somewhat in design like the diagram of the relationship between a parent holding and its subsidiary corporations, with such a system of "interlocking directorates" that lines may be drawn from each to all.

Thus, though not agreeing with the specific results of Lawrence's "ethical universe-building," we contend that there is no other kind of orientation possible. We do recognize that the universe can manifest orders of recalcitrance corresponding to the orders of assertion—but we held that even this recalcitrance requires specific points of view before it can be disclosed, and alters its nature when the point of view is altered. We did not consider such ambiguity subjective, however, since the recalcitrance is real, and the purposes that reveal the recalcitrance are real.

The conclusion we should draw from our thesis is a belief that the ultimate metaphor for discussing the universe and man's relations to it must be the poetic or dramatic metaphor. Many metaphors are possible. Unamuno lists the political being of Aristotle, Rousseau's signer of the social contract, the economic man of the Manchester school, the *homo sapi-*

ens of Linnæus, "or, if you like, the vertical mammal." He votes for "the man of flesh and bone," as the romantic philosophers had stressed a concept of *volitional* man which reached its culmination in Nietzsche's metaphor, man as warrior. Many others, doubtless moved by the prestige of machinery, have proposed to build their perspective by considering man as mechanism. And though any of these simplifications can serve as a postulate from which important and useful considerations (usually called "proof") will follow, we suggest that the metaphor of the poetic or dramatic man can include them all and go beyond them all.

In adopting such metaphor as key, we have a vocabulary of motives already at hand, evolved through the whole history of human thought. Indeed, beginning with such a word as *composition* to designate the architectonic nature of either a poem, a social construct, or a method of practical action, we can take over the whole vocabulary of tropes (as formulated by the rhetoricians) to describe the specific patterns of human behavior. Since social life, like art, is a *problem of appeal*, the poetic metaphor would give us invaluable hints for describing modes of practical action which are too often measured by simple tests of utility and too seldom with reference to the communicative, sympathetic, *propitiatory* factors that are clearly present in the procedures of formal art and must be as truly present in those informal arts of living we do not happen to call arts.

Would we not be actually living an onomatopœia, for instance, if in a moment of anger we abruptly disarranged the furniture in our room or our relations with friends? Are no such clinical words as fetishism and transference discussing much the same phenomenon as was discussed in the old books of rhetoric under the name of synecdoche, or part for the whole? Does not the "egoistic-altruistic merger" involve in practical life that same intimate relationship which w

THE POETRY OF ACTION

observe in the identity of poet and material, of internal attitude and external embodiment? Is not the civic process everywhere marked by acts of ingratiation and justification[1] quite analogous to the motivations of art? Is not the relation between individual and group greatly illumined by reference to the corresponding relation between writer and audience? And as has often been pointed out, our very word for personality derives etymologically from a word signifying the part played by an actor. And lastly, the psychology of *translation* that is implicit in our concept of recalcitrance could lessen sectarian divisions by prompting a man to remember that his assertions are necessarily *socialized by revision*, an attitude which might make for greater patience.

We shall not pause here to examine just how well man's patterns of purpose and choice might be characterized by

[1] Theologians clearly recognized the importance of justification as a social motive in their formulæ, justification by works and justification by faith. The former seems to have advocated symbolic penance as the primary mechanism of retribution. This technique probably served to sterilize individual ambition, since it absolved one of "guilt" by purely ritualistic or esthetic procedures, hence freeing him of any further psychological incentive to "set himself right" by practical attainments. The Protestant justification by faith seems to have promoted individual initiative by questioning the basis of such purely ritualistic reclamation. In another sense it was really the formula that should have been called justification by works, since it led its adherents to seek retribution for their real or imagined offensiveness by going forth and "bringing home the bacon." It was clearly a step toward our secular-scientific-commercial code, sometimes avowed and sometimes merely implicit, justification by success.

With increasing forcefulness in recent years, we have seen a new emphasis arising. As the world tries painfully to retrench after its long debauch, we see, not without misgivings, the emergent outlines of a justification by conformity. If a race for conformity became the basis of a new competitiveness, it would be the critic's problem to present as many counter-influences as possible.

borrowings from the terminology of rhetoric, the "art of appeal." A completely systematized "poetic psychology" should form the subject of another work, though we have attempted to scatter throughout the present book many hints as to the ways in which it should be applied in our attempts to chart the civic process. What we wish to emphasize now is the fact that the poetic metaphor offers an invaluable perspective from which to judge the world of contingencies. It promptly suggests the possibility that far too many of our contingent duties are the poems of a poetaster. And since poetry is essentially ethical, the poetic metaphor clearly identifies the ethical with the æsthetic, in Hellenic fashion defining the "beautiful" life as the "good" life.

The metaphor also has the advantage of emphasizing the *participant* aspect of action rather than its *competitive* aspect, hence offering a prompt basis of objection when the contingencies of our economic structure force us to overstress competitive attitudes. And in a world which has lost its faith in transcendental revelation, the poetic metaphor enables us to start from a point of reference wherein the "revelation" is of a secular nature: the biologic assertion itself. Projecting the metaphor by analogical extension, we find that the entire universe again takes life, as a mighty drama still in progress. And even if we are led to fear that this drama is essentially tragic, the poetic metaphor reminds us that in a perfect tragedy there is "catharsis," hence we may be heartened to inquire what form this catharsis may take.

As we look back over the psychological schools of recent decades, we might note two main emphases. One school explained normal conduct with reference to the phenomena of *abnormal conduct*. The other, particularly the various experimenters with animals and children, explained normal conduct with reference to the phenomena of *learning*. The typical procedure of the first was to observe a man in the extremities of mental confusion, when characteristics are most strikingly apparent, and to infer the presence of similar processes in everyday life. The typical procedure of the second was to place animals in a maze, subjecting them to various pleasant and unpleasant stimuli, noting their ways of solving or failing to solve the problems which the experimenter arranged for them, and inferring the presence of similar processes in normal human life. A study of communication, which necessarily emphasizes the *social* nature of human adjustment, should combine these methods, considering men as *possessed*, and men as the *inventors of new solutions*—but these two frames would be subdivisions in a larger frame, *men as communicants*.

If there are radical changes to be made in the State, what metaphor can better guide us than the poetic one as to the direction in which these changes must point? Particularly at this time, when the circle of contingencies is badly broken, so that millions cannot respect their efforts, and many more millions cannot even expend their efforts, the poetic metaphor provides us with necessary admonitions. A critic as perceptive as T. S. Eliot, for instance, can be misled by his emphasis upon cultural *homogeneity* to conclude that we must attempt the suppression of racial minorities insofar as they impair such homogeneity. Yet he himself has accurately characterized the poetic act as an act of *fusion*. The thought would suggest that he has completely overlooked the part which *unity of purpose* always plays as a catalyzer of heterogeneous elements. Having found that the pursuit of poetry in isolation can lead one far afield, he would conclude that a "critical ideal" must look askance at poetry. He might as reasonably have concluded that the methods of poetry had been too rigorously restricted to the printed page. We suggest that the second of these conclusions is preferable, even as judged by Eliot's statements. For though he verbally warns against mere traditionalism, the remainder of his exhortations is purely traditionalistic in its implications. It is essentially traditionalistic to call for the preservation of a past homogeneity rather than for the establishment of a new one through the powers of fusion provided by a fresh unity of purpose. His position is essentially unpoetic, and entails the ideal denial of his own methods.

Once a coöperative way of life were firmly established in human institutions, I believe that the poetic metaphor would be the best guide (indeed the only conceivable guide) in shaping the new pieties of living. By laying great emphasis upon the cultural value of style, it can lead toward the construction of a world based primarily upon the devices of ingratiation and inducement, which are necessary to the free and satisfactory play of sentiments. Indeed, I should even venture the suggestion that our loss of style has greatly reënforced in the psychological plane the competitive emphasis that has plagued the Western world with increasing violence.

For style is an elaborate set of prescriptions and proscriptions for "doing the right thing"—and when an individual cannot "justify" himself by the spontaneous use of such "congregational" responses, he is driven all the more intensely to attain his justification through "segregational" acts and attitudes. Success becomes identical with conquest—but in an era greatly marked by style and rite, we "succeed" by acquiescing to its many non-competitive ways of being "right." At present, such modes of ingratiation are reduced to a minimum. And what remnants of style we have, are converted by class prerogatives into a purely *invidious* label, a way of suggesting superiority rather than of affirming solidarity.

In addition, the rigors of our economic system would, for many people, make the cultivation of style and all that it implies a mere equivalent to suicide. As a result, the symbolic acts and intiatory steps required for the full humane adjust-

ent to any specific line of discipline are necessarily ignored
and this lack, I suspect, goes far to explain the sense of
mptiness that accompanies so many forms of effort. (There
no philosophy and ritual of teaching, for instance, but
erely a technique. The annoyances of the profession are
t rationalized by a complete rounding out of symboliza-
on: they must simply be "put up with.")

Our responses to experience are truncated by too restricted
concept of utility involving rigors which even the most
imitive societies were spared. In the poetic or humane sense,
ility has a much broader range than is suggested by the
strictions which the industrial economist places upon the
rm. It contains elements of self-interference which the cult
dominance, as preserved and fostered by current institu-
ons, has no place for. It implies kinds of abnegation and
signation which our combative society would probably de-
ribe as mere cowardice. It is in the truest sense *active*, but
acts move toward the *participant*, rather than the *militant*,
d of the combat-action-coöperation spectrum.[2]

The ultimate goal of the poetic metaphor would be a soci-

[2] Style is a constant meeting of obligations, a state-of-being-without-
ense, a repeated doing of the "right" thing. It molds our actions by
ntingencies, but these contingencies go to the farthest reaches of the
mmunicative. For style (custom) is a complex schema of what-goes-
th-what, carried through all the subtleties of manner and attitudes.
ample practice in social relationships can take the place of competi-
e success because it *is* success. We tend to think of customary actions
compulsive—yet values exist today only insofar as custom survives.
is not humane to refrain from murder simply because there are laws
ainst murder—no gratifying social relationships could be constructed
on such a basis. Friendship does not enjoy the protection of the
rts—it is upheld by *styles* dictating the obligations which friends
l toward each other. To codify such obligations would be tantamount
repealing them. The normal tendency to refrain from the murder of
e's allies is "rational" only because it reflects an unquestioned taboo,
undeviating sense of what goes with what. And an obedience to

ety in which the participant aspect of action attained i‖
maximum expression. By its great stress upon the commun‖
cative, it would emphasize certain important *civic* qualitie
to which both naturalistic and supernaturalistic rationaliz‖

---

such customary values is not cowardice, but piety.

We have suggested many reasons why old systems of piety must ‖
partially abandoned: any important change in the material conditio‖
to which they were adapted is sufficient to throw them into disorde‖
Again, style can have its own form of deterioration. For in societi‖
greatly marked by class prerogatives, style itself tends to become ‖
competitive implement, as a privileged group may cultivate style ‖
advertise its privileges and perpetuate them. Style then ceases to be pr‖
pitiatory. It becomes boastful. It is no longer a mode of ingratiatio‖
but a device for instilling fear, like the emperor's insignia. (Such fe‖
is generally called respect.) As style assumes this invidious functio‖
there is a corresponding social movement from inducement towa‖
dominance. Its congregational qualities are lessened, its segregation‖
qualities are stressed. Thus such a feudalistic manifestation of style ‖
probably evidence, in the spiritual plane, of a maladjustment in t‖
material plane.

"Fads" express the *need* for conformity at a time when the oppc‖
tunities for conformity are of a low order. They are instinctively soun‖
since they are strongly communicative, but they are far too liquid a‖
superficial to perform fully the pious function. They are the cultur‖
result of the attempts to patch up the inadequacies of custom by pr‖
fuse and shifty legislation. Legislation is soundest when it is merely t‖
codification of custom. But when custom becomes inadequate (for o‖
reason or another) we attempt to reverse the process and mold custc‖
by legislative fiat. This reverse process would be particularly dangero‖
insofar as the legislative mechanism were in the control of any spec‖
group who manipulated both educative and parliamentary resourc‖
to maintain privileges for this special group alone, without regard ‖
the requirements of the community as a whole. At such times legis‖
tion becomes doubly ominous. For not only does it tend to "liquidat‖
customary sanctions, but it attempts to establish new sanctions inimi‖
to the demands of the group as a whole. It thus blocks the fusive p‖
pose by which style can be wholesomely resynthesized.

ons have given less attention than seems necessary to our
modern urbanized ways of living. Meanwhile, alas! we are
forced to live by economic patterns which reduce the coöper-
tive aspects of action to a minimum.

In closing, we might add a few remarks on the relation be-
ween the permanent and the historic. An ethics involves one
ultimately in a philosophy of *being*, as distinct from a philosophy of *becoming*, because it aims to consider the *generic*
equipment of man as a social and biologic organism. To this
extent, any schema of the "good life" tends to be anhistoric in
quite the same way that an account of digestion or metabol-
m would be.

But let us remind the reader that a philosophy of being, as
advocated in these pages, must not be taken as synonymous
with a philosophy of passivity, or acquiescence. There are
many forms of "resignation." One may also "resign" oneself
o struggle—and our treatment of the combat-action-coöpera-
on spectrum is framed with an activist concept of resigna-
on clearly in mind. Our anhistoric position does not in the
east imply surrender to historic textures through failure to
onsider their importance. On the contrary, we believe that
n many respects it is the *historical* point of view which leads
o such surrender on the grounds that one must adjust him-
elf to temporal conditions as he finds them (teaching him-
elf, for instance, to *accept* more and more mechanization
imply because the trend of history points in this direction).

In subscribing to a philosophy of being, as here conceived,
ne may hold that certain historically conditioned institutions
nterfere with the establishment of decent social or communi-
ative relationships, and thereby affront the permanent bio-
ogic norms. He may further hold that certain groups or
asses of persons are mainly responsible for the retention of
hese socially dangerous institutions. And since we insist that

a point of view requires, as its material counterpart, adequat
embodiment in the architecture of the State, a philosophy o
being may commit one to open conflict with any persons o
class of persons who would use their power to uphold inst
tutions serving an anti-social function.

In such conflict, one's natural mode of action will be tha
of education, propaganda, or suasion. And any instigation t
select one's means from the realm of violence must com
solely from the violence of those who attack him for h
peaceful work as a propounder of new meanings—a state o
affairs which he will strive to avoid as far as possible by cult
vating the arts of translation and inducement. He will accep
it that the pieties of others are no less real or deep throug
being different from his, and he will seek to recommend h
position by considering such orders of recalcitrance and r
vising his statements accordingly.

In these troublesome antics, we may even find it wise o
occasion to adopt incongruous perspectives for the dwarfin
of our impatience. We in cities rightly grow shrewd at ap
praising man-made institutions—but beyond these tiny con
centration points of rhetoric and traffic, there lies the eternal
unsolvable Enigma, the preposterous fact that both existenc
and nothingness are equally unthinkable. Our speculatior
may run the whole qualitative gamut, from play, throug
reverence, even to an occasional shiver of cold metaphysic
dread—for always the Eternal Enigma is there, right on th
edges of our metropolitan bickerings, stretching outward t
interstellar infinity and inward to the depths of the min
And in this staggering disproportion between man and n
man, there is no place for purely human boasts of grandeu
or for forgetting that men build their cultures by huddlir
together, nervously loquacious, at the edge of an abyss.

ON HUMAN BEHAVIOR
CONSIDERED "DRAMATISTICALLY"

Human conduct, being in the realm of action and end (as contrasted with the physicist's realm of motion and position) is most directly discussible in dramatistic terms. By "dramatistic" terms are meant those that begin in theories of *action* rather than in theories of *knowledge*. Terminologies grounded in the observing of sensory perception would be classed as theories of Knowledge. In the same classification would fall all theories of *conditioning* (which is the lowest form of learning). We do not mean to imply that "scientist" approaches (in terms of knowledge or learning), do not yield good results. On the contrary, such perspectives can contribute many important *modifiers* to the *essential nouns* of human relationship. Also, it often happens that "scientist" perspectives

[We might now describe *P & C* dialectics-wise as an individual's approach to motives in terms of the collectivity. Asking what new but related item we might append to the present edition by way of indicating later developments in this same direction, we append the somewhat reworked version of a paper that was originally presented in a symposium on "Organizational Behavior," held at Princeton University in 1951, under the auspices of the Ford Foundation. The conference concerned the problem of ideal "models" that might guide the social scientist in his attempts to discuss human conduct, as it is affected by specific organizations.

Several of the papers approached the problem in mathematical or technological ways (as with the theory of "stochastic processes," or with the "Cybernetics" approach to such problems). But the present paper was among those that favored the retaining of an ethical or psychological terminology. It is based on the assumption that, human behavior being in the realm of morals, the kind of certainty best obtainable here is "moral certainty." Abandoning hopes of "scientific prediction," it believes rather in the "scientifically documented admonition." That is, it looks upon historiography purely as a kind of parable or Æsop's fable, as a mere *warning* backed by data, as a reminder that "We should take such-and-such into account, or else..."

However, in contrast with a sheerly pluralistic emphasis that might look upon each situation as unique, the attempt here is to consider what should be the over-all terms for naming relationships and developments that, *mutatis mutandis*, are likely to figure in all human association. To this end, the stress is placed upon the motives of Guilt, Redemption, Hierarchy, and Victimage that supplement and modify men's purely natural or biological inclinations. Such social, linguistically grounded motives can be said to "perfect" nature, in a purely *technical* sense.]

end by adding coordinates which, while not strictly deducible from the basic experiment upon which they are presumably based, do contrive, by a kind of "leap," or *non-sequitur*, to use an experiment of narrower circumference as specious justification for an interpretation of wider circumference.

Man being specifically a symbol-using animal, we take it that a terminology for the discussion of his social behavior must stress symbolism as a motive, if maximum scope and relevancy is required of the terminology.

However, man being generically a biological organism, the ideal terminology must present his symbolic behavior as grounded in biological conditions. (This statement is *not* the same as saying that symbolism is *reducible* to biology. *On the contrary*.)

In this purely biological sense, property is a necessity. (The science of "ecology" has to do with the kinds of balance that prevail among biological organisms, considered as members of a sub-verbal, extra-verbal, or non-verbal community. The members of such a community are so interrelated that assimilation, or appropriation, is mutual, as with animals that fertilize the vegetation they feed on.)

Though man as a biological organism requires property in the sheerly biological sense, by reason of his nature as a characteristically symbol-using species he can conceptualize a symbolic analogue. We have particularly in mind his terms for "rights" and "obligations." Biologically, the rudimentary properties of living, such as food and shelter, are not "rights," but "necessities." *Symbolically*, there can be property to which one has, or claims, a "right," though the possessing of it may not be biologically necessary.

The notion of "rights" in nature is a quasi-naturalistic, metaphysical subterfuge for sanctioning in apparently biological terms a state of affairs that is properly discussed in terms specifically suited to the treatment of symbolism as motive. Jeremy Bentham's juristic critique of language was particularly sharp in helping us to realize that "rights" are not in "nature"; rather, like "obligations," they are a result of man-made laws, which depend upon the resources of language for their form.

The function of words is obvious, in the inventing, perfecting, and handing-on of instruments and methods. (Think of a factory or a laboratory planned and managed without the guidance of terms!) But the full rôle of symbols in shaping men's views of such property, or "capital," is not obvious. For once the division of labor and the handing-down of property (with its attendant "rights" and "obligations") have given rise to classes, there must be some "order" among these classes.[1]

Such "order" is not just "regularity." It also involves a distribution of *authority*. And such mutuality of rule and service, with its uncertain dividing-line between loyalty and servitude, takes roughly a pyramidal or hierarchal form (or, at least, it is like a ladder with "up" and "down").

Thus the purely *operational* motives binding a society become inspirited by a corresponding condition of *Mystery*. (Owing to their different modes of living and livelihood, classes of people become "mysteries" to one another.) This condition of Mystery is revealed most perfectly in primitive priestcraft, which serves in part to promote cohesion among disparate classes, and in part to perpetuate ways that, while favoring some at the expense of others, may at times thereby endanger the prosperity of the tribe as a whole.

But in a society so complicated as ours, the normal priestly function, of partly upholding and partly transcending the Mysteries of class, is distributed among many kinds of symbol-users (particularly educators, legislators, journalists, advertising men, and artists).

The priestly stress upon Mystery (which attains its grandest

---

[1] Though other animals may manifest the rudiments of language or of tool-using, man's distinctive genius is in his capacity for doing things at one remove, as when he uses words about words and makes tools for making tools.

expression in the vision of a celestial hierarchy loosely imagined after the analogy of a human social order) becomes secularized and distributed among these other rôles, each of which treats the social Mystery after its fashion. Thus, the educator has his testimonials of academic rank; the legislator has ways of identifying respect for himself with respect for the august body of which he is a member; the artist helps surround a system of social values with "glamor," as he finds tricks that transform the austere religious passion into a corresponding romantic, erotic passion; journalists and advertising men make a good team, since the one group keeps us abreast of the world's miseries, and the other keeps us agog with promises of extreme comfort, the two combining to provide a crude, secular analogue of the distinction between Christus Crucifixus and Christus Triumphans.

In part, the new modes of Mystery are needed because the many new instruments have given the world a strongly secular cast. In part they are needed because the traditionalists of religion come in time to rely upon images surviving from an earlier social order. And while these have their appeal precisely by reason of their remoteness, they must be supplemented by images more in tune with the times.

Though we would stress the element of Mystery arising from the social hierarchy, we must recognize that there are other mysteries, other orders. There are the mysteries of dream, of creation, of death, of life's stages, of thought (its arising, its remembering, its diseases). There are the mysteries of adventure and love. (As property is part natural, part doctrinal, so love is part natural, part courtesy.) We mention such other sources of mystery to guard against the assumption that we are reducing mystery in general to the social mystery in particular. On the contrary, we are saying: The social mystery gains in depth, persuasiveness, allusiveness and illusiveness precisely by reason of the fact that it becomes inextricably interwoven with mysteries of these other sorts, quite as these other mysteries must in part be perceived through the fog of the social mystery.[2]

II. *The Hierarchal Embarrassment*

As Mystery is the obverse expression of the disrelationship among classes, so the reverse expression is Guilt. (One can most readily realize this fact by considering an attitude midway between: Embarrassment. The specialist in one field is not "guilty" with regard to the specialist in another field; he is *embarrassed*. He doesn't know exactly how much to question, how much to take on authority, how much to be merely polite about. Indeed, nineteenth-century Russian fiction is evidence enough that, once the principle of disrelation among classes approaches the absolute, even people within a single class approach one another in terms of the embarrassment prevailing through the hierarchy as a whole.)

The most perfect reflection of hierarchal embarrassment is in the theological doctrine of Original Sin. "Original sin" is *categorical* Guilt, one's "guilt" not as the result of any personal transgression, but by reason of a tribal or dynastic inheritance. (It is the equivalent, in the Christian terminology, to the curse laid upon Orestes *before* the murder of his mother, since his sheer membership in the House of Atreus made him a fit tragic offering.) "Tribally," one inherits *status*. For though the concept of "original sin" may seem, in its formal mode of generalization, to fall outside the disrelations of social rank, the "context of situation" prevailing at the time when the idea was so vigorously developed should certainly be considered as an aspect of its meaning, at least in case one can show specifically why it should be.

[2] The attempt to treat *social* "rights" as though they were "natural rights" would be a case in point. The social rights were first *ascribed* to nature, and then "derived" from it. Such a mode of sanction could seem persuasive only because "nature" itself was being perceived through a terministic fog that took form by analogy with sociopolitical principles then current.

(Before we continue, perhaps we should pause to make one point clear, lest we take on unnecessary burdens. In thus equating "original sin" with a "hierarchal psychosis," we do not imply that a formal "socializing" of "private property" would resolve the difficulty. We take it for granted that the pyramidal magic is inevitable in social relations, whereby *individuals*, whether rightly or wrongly, become endowed with the attributes of their *office*. "Private property" may change its name and its nature; and surely it can be so modified that it becomes a better fit for a given social situation than it might be otherwise. But whatever name it may go by, even if its name be "no property," it must exist *in function* insofar as a certain cluster of expectancies, rights, material rewards, honors, and the like is normal to such-and-such a person, as distinct from all other persons, who carries out certain responsibilities or obligations duly recognized as such in his society. In this sense, the slogan of "no property" may be rhetorically persuasive in a given historical situation. But it will be made effective only insofar as backed by organizational means that allocate "properties" all along the line.)

For the next step, let us quote from Coleridge ("First Landing-Place, Essay IV," in *The Friend*) a passage where he is discussing the sheer *form* of his exposition:

"Among my earliest impressions I still distinctly remember that of my first entrance into the mansion of a neighboring baronet, awefully known to me by the name of the great house, its exterior having been long connected in my childish imagination with the feelings and fancies stirred up in me by the perusal of the Arabian Nights' Entertainments. Beyond all other objects, I was most struck with the magnificent staircase, relieved at well-proportioned intervals by spacious landing-places, this adorned with grand or showy plants, the next looking out on an extensive prospect through the stately window, with its side-panes of rich blues and saturated amber or orange tints; while from the last and highest the eye commanded the whole spiral ascent with the marble pavement of the great hall; from which it seemed to spring up as if it merely used the ground on which it rested. My readers will find no difficulty in translating these forms of the outward senses into their intellectual analogies, so as to understand the purport of The Friend's landing-places, and the objects I proposed to myself, in the small groups of essays interposed under this title between the main divisions of the work."

Coleridge is here discussing the series of stages in his exposition. He is idealizing the procedure somewhat, since his actual presentation is much more rambling at times than this version would suggest. But for our purposes, the important thing to note is how explicitly he equates his dialectical method with the image of a staircase which is itself clearly equated with the principle of social distinction. The thought gives us glimpses into the ways in which even purely formal devices, such as the Platonic dialectic so characteristic of Coleridge, can be socially infused, in the total action of the person using it, though technically or operationally such a spirit could be ignored, and even unnoticed.

We could trace further tie-ups. For instance, consider Coleridge's vigorous way of including the Arabian Nights in this same motivational cluster (an emphasis reënforced by a footnote describing the fascination that the book had for him as a child, and the "mixture of obscure dread and intense desire" the sight of it aroused in him, as he hesitated to touch it "till the morning sunshine had reached and nearly covered it"). Here we glimpse ways of showing how the strongly hierarchal magic of these stories, by similarly appealing to his childhood sense of wonder, secondarily added to the magic of the staircase. Since Coleridge himself, in *Table Talk*, talks of the Arabian Nights in connection with his most famous poem, *The Ancient Mariner*, we could proceed to strengthen inferences as to the social motives behind the imagery of the "supernatural" in this poem. But we shall be content, rather, to show by another citation how "celestial" motives can add their powers to the same motivational cluster. We refer to a passage from *Anima Poetæ* (selections from Coleridge's notebooks), a passage in connection with which the editor (Ernest Hartley Coleridge) quoted portions of the paragraph we have already cited:

"The progress of human intellect from earth to heaven is not a Jacob's ladder, but a geometrical staircase with five or more landing-places. That on which we stand enables us to see clearly and count all below us, while that or those above us are so transparent for our eyes that they appear the canopy of heaven. We do not see them, and believe ourselves on the highest."

III. Hierarchy, Bureaucracy, Order

It may be thought that, by the "hierarchal motive," we are merely offering a synonym for some such term as "prestige." In one sense, yes, since any term implying emulation can serve the purposes. But our concern is not so much with any one term, as with the question of *companion-terms*. Too often, the argument over some one term conceals the really important matter: the way in which (with the given terministic system) the one term is *modified* by *other terms*.

In an early work (*Attitudes Toward History*), when talking about man as a political animal, we featured the term, "bureaucracy." Or, more accurately, "bureaucratization." It was matched by an antithetical term, "the imaginative." That is, there were said to be plans or purposes, somewhat vaguely conceived in the imagination; and by the forming and use of organizational devices, these "imagined" ends were carried out, with varying degrees of success and varying degrees of public acquiescence.

The notion had a degree of relevance. It also had its metaphysics. We now see that the pattern was essentially idealistic. We have in mind Royce's formula for idealism, in its view of the world as the incarnating of a god, the bringing of a god down to earth. In sum: In the Idealist perspective, there is pure Spirit, Idea, Ideal, Purpose; this Idea attains its mediation, or materialization (incarnation, embodiment) in the temporal order (of "nature" and "history"). In this sense, historiography would be the vision of a god descended to earth, made manifest in the flesh. (We are paraphrasing Royce.) And seen from that point of view, our formula, "the bureaucratization of the imaginative," was a further seculari zation of idealistic metaphysics, which was itself a partia secularizing of a theological doctrine.

The idealism could in turn be modified in the direction of pragmatism by a secondary consideration. Thus, as *idealism* could be said to have universalized, cosmologized, the rela tion between an original purpose and its corresponding em bodiment in physical and human materials, so *pragmatism* would note how the particular choice of materials and meth ods in which to embody the ideal gives rise to condition somewhat at variance with the spirit of the ideal. (We calle such eventualities "unintended by-products.") And out o these unforeseen conditions, there arises the need for a redef nition of aim. Hence, where idealism stresses the mediator step from end to means, (from purpose to agency) pragma tism stresses rather the step from agency to purpose (as derives ends from the nature of the available means).

And since enterprises of either sort necessarily involve the acceptance or rejection of Authority, or some otherwis qualified relation to Authority, we constructed a terminolog with relation to Symbols of Authority.

Bureaucracy and Hierarchy obviously imply each othe Logically, you can't have a Hierarchy without, by the sam token, having a Bureaucracy (in the sense of "organization" But you might, conceivably, have a Bureaucracy without Hierarchy. That is: there does not seem to be any logica contradiction in the idea of *organized collaboration amon absolute equals*. But unless, in practice, authority is at lea delegated, organized behavior as we know it becomes im possible. Such authority may be in many ways modified. B its absolute elimination in any feasible enterprise of ar scope is beyond our knowledge and imagination.

The practical need of an authoritative ladder in offic

organization is matched (in art and in the scientific laboratory) by the notion of *steps*. Unless processes *proceed in a "proper" order*, their nature as efficacies is impaired. But whether the enterprise be authoritative in the social sense or successful in the natural sense, in either realm there is necessarily a mode of "order" that is not merely *regular* but *ordinal* (with canons of first, second, third, etc.—canons ranging from absolutes in pope and king, down to purely pragmatic conveniences in *some moments* of *localized* free enterprise).

IV. The "Two Great Moments"

In the three preceding sections, we observed: (1) Man's specific nature as a symbol-using animal transcends his generic nature as sheer animal, thereby giving rise to property, rights, and obligations of purely man-made sorts; (2) the necessary nature of property in a complex social order makes for the "embarrassments" of social mystery in men's relations to one another, thereby giving rise to attitudes that pervade areas of thought not strictly germane to it; (3) the terms 'Bureaucracy,' "Hierarchy," and "Order" all touch upon this realm of social mystery, because of their relation to Authority, and to canons of Propriety. We are now ready for the statement that we consider basic to our thesis. We cite Coleridge, *Aids to Reflection*:

"The two great moments of the Christian Religion are, Original Sin and Redemption; that the ground, this the superstructure of our faith."

This paper is based on the assumption that a purely social terminology of human relations (conceived in terms of the conditions that mark organized efforts, and of the typical responses to such conditions) can not do better than to hover about that accurate and succinct theological formula, *as we watch always for ways of locating its possible secular equivalents.*

Basically, the pattern proclaims a principle of *absolute*

"guilt," matched by a principle that is designed for the corresponding absolute cancellation of such guilt. And this cancellation is contrived by *victimage*, by the choice of a sacrificial offering that is correspondingly absolute in the perfection of its fitness. We assume that, insofar as the "guilt" were but "fragmentary," a victim correspondingly "fragmentary" would be adequate for the redeeming of such a debt, except insofar as "fragmentation" itself becomes an "absolute" condition.

In brief, given "original sin," (tribal, or "inherited" guilt), it follows, by the ultimate logic of symbols, that the compensatory sacrifice of a ritually perfect victim would be the corresponding "norm." Hence, insofar as the religious pattern (of "original sin" and sacrificial redeemer) is adequate to the "cathartic" needs of a human hierarchy (with the modes of mystery appropriate to such a hierarchy) it would follow that the promoting of social cohesion through victimage is "normal" and "natural."

We are here discussing the problem in its widest aspects. As regards particular cases, the particular choice of "fragmentary" scapegoats may be even fantastically and morbidly irrelevant. (Obvious drastic recent example: the Hitlerite promoting of social cohesion through the choice of the Jew, considered generically, as "perfect" ritual offering.) But we are suggesting that, if the great pyramidal social structure of medieval Europe found its ultimate expression in a system of moral purgation based on the two "moments" of "original sin" and "redemption," it would seem to follow that the "guilt" intrinsic to hierarchal order (the only kind of "organizational" order we have ever known) calls correspondingly for "redemption" through *victimage*.

We are *not* saying that such *should* be the case. We are simply saying that, as regards Coleridge's statement about the two essential "moments" of Christian doctrine, such *is* the case, in the great religious and theological doctrine that forms the incunabula of our culture (and so secondarily the incunabula of the scientific or technological views that are now so characteristic a part of it).

It so happens that the present writer felt the logic of this pattern with a new intensity when he was considering, not our society at all, but a purely literary problem with relation to Greek tragedy: the problem of "catharsis" (upon which Aristotle's *Poetics* laid stress in his definition of tragedy, though the pages in which he explained his ideas have been lost, except for a few references in the *Politics* where he says that his main treatment is in the *Poetics*).

We take it that Greek tragedy, being a typically civic ceremony, was designed for the ritual resolving of civic tensions (tensions that, in the last analysis, are always referrible to problems of property). And, noting that in tragedy (as also in Aristophanic comedy) the principle of victimage plays so essential a rôle, we began to ask ourselves whether human societies could possibly cohere without symbolic victims which the individual members of the group share in common.

We are offering the proposition that, as with Coleridge's two "moments," here is the very centre of man's social motivation. And any scheme that shifts the attention to other motivational areas is a costly error, *except insofar as its insights can be brought back into the area of this central quandary.*

Asking ourselves, then, how Greek tragedy produced "catharsis" (a stylistic cleansing of the audience) by the imitation of victimage designed to arouse such emotions as pity and terror, we began to see how "normal" the ways of victimage are. They may be used crudely. Hitlerism is an insultingly clear example of their crude usage. But considering *both* the rationale behind the doctrinal placement of the Crucifixion, *and* the pattern of Greek tragedy (nor should we forget the other great line from which the doctrines of our culture are derived, in this instance the lore of *Azazel*), we began to ask how profound the motive of victimage might be. That is: Insofar as all complex social order will necessarily be grounded in some kind of property structure, and insofar as all such order in its divisive aspects makes for the kind of social malaise which theologians would explain in terms of "original sin," is it possible that rituals of victimage are the "natural" means for affirming the principle of social cohesion above the principle of social division?

V. The "Perfecting" of Victimage

In one sense, we are here but rediscovering a platitude. For everyone recognizes as "natural" or "normal" the practical politicians' ways of temporarily shelving differences among themselves insofar as they can form alliances defined by the sharing of an enemy in common. Then are we, at this late date, but rediscovering some possible Machiavellian uses of the "scapegoat principle"!

The "scapegoat principle" (as used by priesthoods and rhetoricians, and as studied by anthropologists and theorists of political behavior) is certainly involved here. And it should obviously have a prominent place in *any* terminology of social motivations, even if we were but reviewing what is generally known about it. (The mere fact that it is a platitude should not rob it of its high place in a terminology of human and organizational behavior.) But we have a further step in mind here, thus:

Many people with a naturalist or positivist cast of mind look upon the ritual scapegoat as a mere "illusion." They recognize its use as "natural" in the sense that savages, children, political spell-binders, story-writers, and the like spontaneously use such devices, even without any need to be schooled in such usage. Indeed, the need is on the other side: For the spreading of a *naturalistic* lore that will immunize mankind to this *natural* weakness.

Such people usually seem to feel that the cultivating of the scientific mind in general protects against susceptibility to the attempt to solve practical problems by the use of ritualistic (symbolic) victims. But insofar as such a tendency does recur, they seem to assume that the problem is solved by fragmentation. In effect, they would keep the devil on the run by making him legion. That is, they say in effect: Let one fragment of the curative victim be in the villain of a Grade B motion picture, let another fragment be in a radio fool, another in the corpse of a murder mystery, another in the butchery of a prizefight, another in a hard-fought game, another in the momentary flare-up of a political campaign, another in a practical joke played on a rival at the office, another in weeding the garden or ferociously rubbing out a cigarette butt, etc., etc. Insofar as our civilization is marked by great diversity in both labor and leisure, it is fragmentary —and to this extent, there would seem to be something curative in a victimage correspondingly fragmentary.

But there is also a sense in which the condition of fragmentation itself might be felt to need an over-all cure. Fragmentation makes for triviality. And although there are curative elements in triviality, (elements fervently sought, as is evident in the current radio "gag-writer's" cult of the explosive "yak") they can add up to a kind of organized inanity that is socially morbid. The whole aggregate of petty fragmentary victimage may thus require a "total" victim, if it in turn is to be cured.

Now, if people were truly devout in the full religious sense of the term, there should be no difficulty here. For in the pious contemplation of a perfect sacrificial *universal* god, there might be the elements of wholeness needed to correct the morbidities of fragmentation. And the basic structure of such a myth has the classic purity of the ritual sacrifices in Greek tragedy (as contrasted with the loss of such simplicity in dramas where the catharsis of victimage is obscured by a tangle of intrigue).

However, we say as much, not by way of a plea for the religious myth as such, but rather to point up the great temptation confronting a social order which is in its very texture so obviously inclined to materialistic, operational, administrative, technological emphases (as attested by the range and proportion of topics even in its *Sunday* newspapers!). And as regards religion itself, we must consider how its pacific, evangelical aspects come to retreat behind its militant, organizational aspects.

But as we are not pleading for religion, neither are we attacking it. In referring to the curative totality of the perfect sacrifice, as modified by the predominantly secular nature of modern civilization, we would suggest that the kind of victimage most "natural" to such a situation would be some variant of the Hitlerite emphasis (which put the stress upon the idea of a total cathartic *enemy* rather than upon the idea of a total cathartic *friend*).

Here was an apparent absolute means of redemption: through the sacrifice of a speciously "perfect" victim, the material embodiment of an "idealized" foe.

But our stress upon "totality" of enmity as a cure for the malaise of fragmentation should not be allowed to conceal our major point: That "order" *as such* makes for a tangle of guilt, mystery, ambition ("adventure") and vindication that infuses even the most visible and tangible of material "things" with the spirit of the order through which they are perceived. In this sense, man as symbol-using animal must perceive even his most "animalistic" traits dimly through the symbolic fog arising from the social order of which he is a part. Thus, empiricist, naturalist, positivist, behaviorist, operationalist, and psychologistic views of man's organizational behavior must of necessity but add to the illusion, as regards man's ultimate motives in society, by giving a specious reality to the purely non-symbolic aspect of material property (in things and methods).

The laboratory or the office is as much inhabited by a spirit, a *genius loci*, as any temple (a spirit in turn related to a wider order and deriving authority from it). And unless such a motive is conceived essentially in terms of pyramidal structure (with its corresponding modes of guilt and redemption), it is hard to see how one can get a wholly relevant terminology for the charting of social behavior. Thus, as with theology, an ideal terminology should be dramatistic rather than operational. And while recognizing the tremendous motivational importance of all the new properties which modern technology has produced, and the importance of techniques for the management of these, the ideal terminology must be designed, first of all, to perceive how man's relation to his properties is *symbolically* constituted.

VI. Variants of Victimage

Here would be the sort of considerations that would seem to follow from our Dramatistic emphasis:

Along with a search for the modes of vindication by victimage, look for a variant, in possible secularized equivalents of "mortification." To quote from an article published elsewhere, "Thanatopsis for Critics: A Brief Thesaurus of Deaths and Dyings" (*Essays in Criticism*, October 1952):

"If there are social burdens to which one resigns oneself, if there are social barriers which one conscientiously seeks not to want to cross, such moralistic confinements placed upon ambition and trespass are 'sacrificial' in attitude. They reach their ultimate in ascetic disciplines aimed at the programmatic 'mortifying' of the senses. A gallant excess of self-control thus becomes organized into a strategy for living, that attains its grand rationale in a cult of the 'dying life'. Its antithesis is celebrated hugely in Rabelais' rules for the Abbey of Thelema, headed in the slogan, *fais ce que vouldras*....

"Mortification is a scrupulous and deliberate clamping of limitation upon the self. Certain requirements for the maintaining of a given social order attain their counterparts in the requirements of an individual conscience; and when the *principle* of such requirements is scrupulously carried to excess, you get 'mortification'. (For instance, if conditions of private property call forth corresponding ideals of mono-gamistic love, and if the carrying-out of such ideals, to be scrupulously complete, requires that one should not trespass upon the property of another's wife, then by the rules of 'mortification' one should voluntarily punish whatever 'senses' are thought to make such trespass seem desirable.)"

Such modes of thinking are institutionalized in vows of chastity willingly taken for reasons of piety. But it seems likely that psychogenic illnesses can often be disguised variants of the same motive, though without the conscious code of discipline; for they would be, as it were, the carrying-out of judgments pronounced, willy-nilly, against the self.

"Crime" would be a similar order of motives, but inclining to the "homicidal" rather than the "suicidal" slope. Consider the typical reversal of motives (often noted by criminologists) whereby the *attitude* of criminality precedes the *actual* committing of a crime, so that the crime is in effect the translating of a vague, unreal, and even mysterious sentiment into the conditions of something really here and now. (There is a sense in which crime can even be considered more "normal" and "healthy" than is the case when the sense of criminality eats like an acid into the conscience, producing instead a world of sheer fantasy.)

All told, we are suggesting that the relation is like that between "original sin" and "actual sin" ("original sin" corresponding to the uneasiness or categorical "guilts" implicit in the social order; and the temptation to "actual sin" being a kind of casuistry for the reduction of such generic motives to individual criminal impulses with regard to unlawful encroachment upon property and persons). We are suggesting that, under certain conditions, the *categorical* motive may serve as the matrix for a corresponding *personal* motive. That is: insofar as the notion of an absolute generic or "tribal" guilt is not adequately matched by a correspondingly absolute means of cancellation, crime becomes another partial "solution." Indeed, it even provides a kind of "unity," in that, for the hunted or undetected criminal, danger is "everywhere." (Consider the "mystery" of crime in Dostoevsky.)

Similarly warfare, in its nature as "imagery" (a nature reënforced by the pronouncedly pyramidal design of military hierarchy) can readily be so much more "cathartic" in its promises than in its deliveries. The dialectic of antithesis contributes spontaneously to the imagining of an enemy so "perfectly" suited to his ritual rôle that by his sacrifice all evils would be redeemed. And the false promises arising from his imputed cathartic rôle explain why, although such motives can add to the intensity with which a war is pursued (by making it "holy"), they are a costly encumbrance not only to peaceful international relations but even to the intelligent planning for military defence.

Most in need of study, but hardest of all to study, or even to discern, are the ways whereby the very existence of a hierarchy encourages undue acquiescence among persons otherwise most competent to be its useful critics. This condition probably results much less from over-caution or obsequiousness than from the network of "proprieties" that spontaneously accumulate about a given order. This explicit and methodical study of the "hierarchal psychosis" is needed, if those in authority would guard against the natural tendency to protect their special interests in ways that ultimately impair those interests by bringing the society as a whole into disarray.

A variant of this difficulty is to be seen in the tendency to encourage the teaching of humanistic studies wastefully. A mere glance at a typical list of doctoral theses is enough to make clear the kind of elegant irrelevancies (with question mark after the "elegant") that are still being encouraged. This adds up to a vast subsidizing of inaccuracy such as might have been welcomed in less exacting times, but is almost insupportable now. The purpose seems to be to teach the acquiring of insignia so full of false promises that they are questionable even as insignia.

VII.   *"Perfection" as a Motive*

When considering such a notion as the "redemption of guilt," one might note what Bentham would call the "archetypal image" here: the satisfying of a debtor by the paying of a ransom. Next, in line with such thinking generally, one might note how a society's material means of livelihood provide analogies for the building of purely "spiritual" concepts and ideas. And in this respect, one might deem it enough to show how the conception of guilt and redemption reflected certain present or past habits of the society with regard to the exchange of material property.

While not denying the fertility of such speculations, and their relevance for certain purposes, we would remind the reader that the present "Dramatistic" treatment requires the addition of an important intermediate step between the "material" field from which the image is borrowed and the "spiritual" field to which it is applied as a "fiction." This intermediate step involves a kind of "perfecting" or "absolutizing" of the notion or relation from which the analogy is borrowed.

"Implicit" in the notion of a ransomed debt there is a kind of "logical conclusion" or "ultimate reduction." That is: in the idea of an act of trade as such, there lurks as it were the question: "What would be the *most perfect act* of trade, the 'tradiest' trade, or 'trade of trades'?" As soon as some act is brought within the realm of symbols, there is such an end-of-the-line speculation vibrant within the terms for it. The logic of symbolic resources drives towards its fullness in a universal definition. (And this purely technical impulse of symbolism, manifested logically in the demand for definition, is manifested morally and politically in the mind's spontaneous concern with the problems of "justice.")

Then, individual acts ("fragmentary" acts) can be conceived, not just "after the analogy of such-and-such," but *in terms of a corresponding perfection.* The theological notion of God as the *ens perfectissimum* is perhaps the ultimate formulation of the "logic of ultimates" implicit in symbolism.

So, when we encounter "fragmentary" terms got by translating the visible and tangible into their corresponding "fictions," we should not seek for their persuasiveness merely in the seeming "naturalness" of the analogy (as with the anthropomorphic notion that God, like Shakespeare's Shylock, wants vindictive satisfaction for default in a bargain). Rather, we should watch to disclose ways whereby "ultimate" motivations come to be implicit even in the world of contingencies.

Thus, when searching "socio-anagogically" for the "spirit" in *things*, we may begin with simple correspondences. We may note that regulated grass on a college campus, besides its nature as sheer grass, has a social rôle as insignia, standing for a certain order of promises and distinctions connected with the discharging of certain moral and academic obligations. But all such direct correspondences add up to a *principle* of hierarchal order that, by reason of its nature as a principle, is "perfect," an "ultimate" (hence, *technically* equatable with "God," whereat social distinction can become subtly interwoven with divinity, perhaps to the disadvantage of our ideas about divinity, but certainly to the advantage of our ideas about social distinction).

The "perfection" of a secular enemy is the clearest observable instance of ways whereby the intermediate absolutizing step is involved. Given the vast complexities of the modern world, it would be hard to find a "perfect" material victim for any of our ills. But because the *principle* of a "perfect" victim is so implicit in the very concept of victimage, and because men have so "natural" or spontaneous a desire for a "perfect" view of their discomforts, they are eager to tell themselves of victims so thoroughgoing that the sacrifice of such offerings would bring about a correspondingly thoroughgoing cure. The "fragmentary" nature of the enemy thus comes to take on the attributes of an absolute.

The hierarchal psychosis (interweaving the social order

with the motives of guilt, wonder, adventure, catharsis, and victimage) arises so spontaneously from the social order, it would seem that a free society should emphasize in its secular educational methods the kinds of observation that make the building of hierarchal magic most difficult. The "efficient" coordinating of such magic seems to go best with dictatorship. Yet as evidence of the way in which hierarchy arises even in the questioning of it: Note that, on principle, science is against such kinds of "mystery"; yet also note that, necessarily, there is the same categorical value placed upon rank and office in scientific and technological hierarchies as elsewhere.

Indeed, the proper educational approach to the motives of hierarchy should not, as now, vacillate between "mystification" and "unmasking," between the journalistic "build up" and the compensatory "character assassination," but should aim at the kinds of contemplation and sufferance that are best adapted to the recognition and acceptance of a social form inevitable to social order.

In the short run, "mystification" may seem to be the best way of promoting social cohesion. But it has been so often misused in history by the defenders of special sinister interests, we clearly see its limitations, as regards the long run. Similarly, in a world wholly "unmasked," no social cohesion would be possible. (However, there is usually an element of deception here. While leading you to watch his act of destruction at one point, the "unmasker" is always furtively building at another point, and by his prestidigitation he can forestall accurate observation of his own moves.)

Fluctuation between one extreme and the other seems to be the usual way in which society considers individual persons enacting rôles in the social order (and, at times of radical upset, certain of the categorical rôles themselves undergo such fluctuation). But might it not be possible that, were an educational system designed to that end, this very fluctuancy could be intelligently stabilized, through the interposing of method?

The Library of Liberal Arts